PUNISHMENT

Punishment

THE SUPPOSED JUSTIFICATIONS

TED HONDERICH

Polity Press

Copyright © Ted Honderich, 1971, 1976, 1984, 1989

First published by Hutchinson 1969
Published in Pelican Books 1971
Revised edition reissued in Peregrine Books 1976
Reissued in Pelican Books with a new Postscript 1984
This edition first published 1989 by Polity Press
in association with Basil Blackwell

Editorial office:
Polity Press, 65 Bridge Street, Cambridge CB2 1UR

Marketing and production:
Basil Blackwell Ltd
108 Cowley Road, Oxford OX4 1JF, UK

Basil Blackwell Inc.
3 Cambridge Center
Cambridge, MA 02142, USA

ISBN 0 7456 0775 6 (pbk)

British Library Cataloguing in Publication Data
A CIP catalogue record for this book is available from
the British Library.

Printed in Great Britain by
Billings and Sons Ltd, Worcester.

For Pauline, Kiaran, John Ruan

CONTENTS

PREFACE TO THE NEW EDITION

It would be alarming for me, and no reassurance to the reader, if the seven chapters of this book written fifteen years ago seemed to me as right now as they did then. Fortunately for its peace, my mind has changed about some things. In the fifteen years, as well, despite my initial and momentary certitude that I had got hold of the truth about punishment, and that was that, others have gone on announcing the truth as they see it. We do not entirely agree.

It is a pleasure, then, to be able to include a long postscript, 'The New Retributivism and Political Philosophy', in this new edition. It records my changes of mind, above all about the Principle of Equality and what is finally to be said of the justification of punishment in our societies. It takes account of doctrines about punishment that have been born, or more likely revived or resurrected, since this book was first published. The postscript comes from a lecture to the Royal Institute of Philosophy. I am most grateful to it, and to Professor A. Phillips Griffiths, for permission to reprint from the annual volume of the Institute's proceedings, *Philosophy and Practice*, under his editorship.

The book is given over to the analysis and assessment of arguments. It is its somewhat grand intention to consider everything that is intelligible and at all persuasive by way of defences of the practice of punishment, and also to pay some attention to persistent obscurities. These defences and obscurities are principally the work of a succession of moral philosophers.

I have, necessarily, found myself dealing with the several large moral attitudes which come into clear conflict over punishment and may, indeed, be appraised by way of it. I have also dealt with subject-matters that require for their most satisfactory handling something other than philosophical awareness. Here one finds the

statistician's questions about the efficacy of punishment as a deterrent, the many questions about conceptions of criminality as disability or disorder, the jurisprudent's questions about strict liability
in the law.

Answers to the question of why we punish, where that is not the
question of what reasons we can give, but rather a question about
causes, are no part of my concern. It may be, as some say, that
punishment derives from a dark motive to find scapegoats for all
our personal guilts, but I do not consider the question. No one, I
trust, has argued that punishment can actually be defended by this
supposition.

The first chapter sets out the fundamental problem. The next
three deal with traditional 'theories of punishment', for their intrinsic importance and also because they persist in contemporary
doctrines. The fifth chapter is about human freedom and responsibility and their relevance to punishment. The sixth chapter is
concerned with the contemporary doctrines just mentioned, the
seventh with the general question of what behaviour of individuals
should lie beyond the reach of the law. One problem taken forward through these chapters, but at last escaped, has to do with
the analysis of desert or retributive justice.

The postscript deals in part with what has sometimes seemed to
be a new college industry. It turns out theories of retribution.
Also, as remarked, the postscript advances what are at least
developments of views of mine in the seven chapters.

I am especially indebted to Professor H. L. A. Hart, whose
writings have contributed a great deal of enlightenment, and to
Professors P. H. Nowell-Smith and Richard Wollheim. I wish also
to thank Professor Patrick Corbett, whose idea it was that the
book should be written, and Nicola Lacey, Carlos Nino, John
Finnis, and Peter Morriss.

CHAPTER ONE: PROBLEM

1. The Need for Justification

The problem of punishment arises mainly, but not only, for the reason that the practice involves what traditionally has been called suffering. It involves a deliberate and avoidable infliction of suffering. Apologists have sometimes said that it is in part an automatic reflex of society, like that of a living body to injury.[1] This is at best darkening metaphor, and any suggestion that punishment is wholly an ungoverned reaction would be absurd.

It is certainly true that by comparison with penalties visited on offenders in the past, many of our present penalties are humane. Is it then inappropriate to describe contemporary penalties as giving rise to suffering? We are told by one defender of the practice that

most punishments nowadays are not inflictions of suffering, either physical or mental. They are the deprivation of a good. . . . Imprisonment and fine are deprivations of liberty and property. The death sentence is deprivation of life; and in this extreme case every attempt is made to exclude suffering. . . . We have taken the . . . important step of substituting the removal of something desired for the infliction of positive suffering.[2]

This less than reassuring distinction between deprivations and inflictions of suffering need not detain us. What is unlikely to be disputed is that penalties now imposed on offenders, whether or not they are to be described as causing suffering, do raise a question of moral justification. For one thing, more is now known of their destructive consequences, both for the offender and for others related to him. The question would correctly be raised, however, even by a practice which did no more than deprive a man of his usual liberty, or his usual resources, in some exceedingly sensitive fashion.

The moral problem arises, secondly, with respect to any system of punishment, as a consequence of a different fact: that others, as well as those punished, are coerced by it. Freedom is curtailed. One need not, in order to regard this as a consideration of importance, believe the laws of a society to be bad ones. Finally, and more vaguely, the moral problem arises because the whole quality of life in a society, the quality of its public and private institutions and relationships, is influenced by the existence of a central practice of an authoritarian and repressive nature.

The general claim, that one cannot but regard punishment as in need of justification, is itself a judgement of a moral nature. Like many to follow, it is an integral part of this inquiry. What cannot also be a part is the general problem of the nature of such judgements and the support they can have. I shall adduce no general arguments about their validity or invalidity. However, although the subject is one of complication, I see no reason to admit that what will be said here is a consequence of 'subjective responses' or 'individual moral attitudes'.

It is an arguable proposition, if not about all men then about many men, that their impartial evaluations of actions begin from two fundamental attitudes, one having to do with securing human welfare and avoiding its opposites, the other with the distribution of welfare and its opposites. Certainly, although this appears to be the origin of particular evaluations, they are often inconsistent with it. Often when they are regarded as logical consequences, they are not such. Between origin and particular conclusions come consideration of facts, imagination, and operations of derivation. Each of these allows, to say the least, for error. It is a work of practical, philosophical reflection to clarify judgements, to test them for consistency with others and with fundamental principles. Given the assumption that we share such fundamental attitudes, anyone who feels that he has arrived at true consequences of them, however novel, will take the view that these consequences are not peculiarly his own.

In the past, single reasons have often been given for the rightness of punishment. One of these reasons, which may be expressed with deceptive simplicity, is that punishment is *deserved* by offenders. Punishment is retribution. Another claim, historically associated with utilitarianism, is that punishment serves to *deter* others from offending. We are usually too simply told that men are made fearful of breaking the law or that they keep it out of a prudent awareness of the possibility of punishment. A third claim is partly that punishment, or a practice of treatment, secures that fewer offences will be committed in the future, but not through deterrence. It was once the case, but is no longer, that all views of this third kind could be positively described as recommending the 'moral regeneration' of individuals as an end in itself and also a means to the prevention of crime.

These three claims, each with variants and complexities, have been known as *theories* of the justification of punishment. This is so, perhaps, partly because it has been assumed that punishment or some closely related practice is an indubitable social necessity whose justification is beyond doubt. Given this seeming fact, what is to be done is to provide a hypothesis or theory in explanation, as one provides theories about facts of the physical world. I shall keep the usage for its usefulness, not for this implication.

More recently, philosophers and others have contended that none of these three reasons taken by itself is sufficient to justify punishment or related practices of enforced treatment. Two or even more are needed in combination. Sometimes a number of reasons are mentioned but one is accorded a very secondary importance. We are told that the traditional retribution theory is correct since punishment is justified because it is deserved, and then reminded that punishment also has the recommendation that it deters. It may be that these are no more than the standard compromises just mentioned, variously disguised in an attempt to keep an old flag flying, or an old feeling respectable.

In order to clarify what is involved in each of the three original claims and their later unions, I shall begin by looking at them separately. That is, I shall consider each one, as historically it was regarded, and in several cases still is by enthusiasts, as sufficient by itself to show the rightness of punishment. This procedure will have the advantage of demonstrating why it has been thought that no single claim is sufficient. More important, as I have said, it may bring into clarity the elements of the ensuing compromises.

The inquiry in hand is in a certain sense theoretical. Supporters of the deterrence theory are not committed *by their theory itself* to the support of *any* existent practice of punishment. They are committed to a practice only if something else is established as true: that the practice *does* satisfy the requirements stipulated by the theory. They are unlikely to have the detailed factual knowledge about, say, punishment in England or the United States which would enable them to make authoritative judgements on the actual state of things. They may be undeterred by this (as others with a greater factual awareness are undeterred by a lack of examined principles). None the less, whatever their factual knowledge, their theory does not by itself dictate such judgements. Precisely the same is true of the retribution theory and the other mentioned doctrines. What is also true, of course, as I have implied, is that theory or a set of general principles is a prerequisite of judgement.

2. Description

There is one other preliminary matter of importance. For a number of reasons we must have a definition or at least a useful description of punishment.

It is not treatment, although some patients, like offenders, are subjected to deprivation or distress. Anything we describe as punishment *must* involve some such thing as deprivation or distress, which, indeed, is reasonably described as its aim. This remains true, although the aim is not the final end, when punishment is imposed as a deterrent and thought to be justified as such. Treatment, obviously, has no such aim but rather seeks to avoid distress whenever possible. It mostly does.

Punishment, secondly, is not revenge, although certain of its supposed justifications would go some way to justifying revenge, and some of those who punish share motivations and needs with those who take revenge. A man who has been injured by another and then revenges himself upon him is not *authorized* to act as he does. That is, he is not empowered by generally accepted rules, as a judge is empowered by the law, to fix and enforce penalties. If there are practices governed by generally accepted rules, where the injured man or his family exacts the penalty, these approach to being practices of punishment. Punishment, thirdly, is obviously not something done to a man chosen at random and without regard to his previous conduct. Punishment, or so we habitually think, is imposed on an offender, someone who is found to have broken a rule, to have done something prohibited.

It may then seem, given these rudimentary differentiations, to be *an authority's infliction of a penalty*, something involving deprivation or distress, *on an offender*, someone found to have broken a rule, *for an offence*, an act of the kind prohibited by the rule.

Is this description true of all practices which we are ordinarily willing to call practices of punishment? If our description does not cover everything it might, this is so partly for the reason that not all punishments take place within a society's ordinary legal and penal systems. It may be said, against the description, that punishments are not always the work of the authorities: persons or groups of persons empowered to act by rules that have something like a general acceptance. 'War criminals' are said to be punished despite doubts as to whether the tribunals of the winning side count as authorities. It may also be denied that punishment is always preceded by an offence, assuming an offence to be an action that goes against a specific rule previously stipulated. Certainly a father is unlikely to have announced, before his son does some astonishing and unpredictable thing, that no one was to do *that*. Perhaps he may be taken as having announced something so general as that his son wasn't to behave in outrageous ways. Might there be similar cases which we would call cases of punishment and where the point was to teach a quite new rule?

If there are such cases as these latter ones, where there have not been offences, are these also cases where the person punished is not an offender: that is, someone found to have broken a rule? They are indeed such cases, given the understanding we shall adopt of what it is to find that someone has broken a rule. We shall take *finding* in this context to be like *knowing*, so that what is found must be true. There has to have been a rule, and someone has in fact to have broken it, for him to be *found* to have done so. Furthermore, incidentally, to find that someone has broken a rule is to decide in good faith, and by way of certain procedures, that he has broken it. A judge cannot find someone to have broken the law, in this sense, if he is convinced that he hasn't done so. Nor can he find him to have broken the law if he does not investigate the matter in certain ways.

It may also be suggested on the basis of quite different examples that punishment is not always *of an offender*. We speak of collective punishments of groups, such as classes in schools and villages in wars, some only of whose members have offended. More importantly, in English and American law, a shopkeeper who sells adulterated food, without intending to do so and without having been careless, may none the less be penalized. So may a motorist who without being negligent runs into a pedestrian under certain circumstances. An English publican who sells whisky to an intoxicated man, without knowing the man's state or being careless about finding out, is in the same position. It is also an offence under certain circumstances to seduce a girl under sixteen, and remains one if the man made an honest mistake in thinking she was older. That he did not intend to break the law is not a defence. These are offences of 'strict liability', which even now are not a merely peripheral part of the law and may be more pervasive in the future.

There is also 'vicarious liability'. A shop owner may be responsible if his clerk sells adulterated food. The owner of an English theatre could until recently be successfully prosecuted if without his knowledge or carelessness a play was presented which contravened the censorship rules of the Lord Chamberlain. Employers generally may be responsible for certain acts of their employees. Surely, it may be said, none of these could be regarded as offenders in the given sense.

What difficulties do these various cases raise for our description of punishment? Do they show we have not captured the ordinary notion of punishment? They are put forward as instances of punishment, instances of what we would ordinarily regard as punishment, and also as instances where some feature required in the given description is missing. On further reflection, most people may be inclined to say of them either that they *do* possess the feature in question and *are* punishments, as ordinarily conceived, or that they lack it and should not be regarded as punishments: that is, the cases in question do not show a conflict between our definition and ordinary usage.

What is done to 'war criminals' may be taken to be punishment by those who accept that the tribunals count as authorities. Those who do not accept this will give some other description to the practice, or to particular instances of it. So perhaps with the father-and-son case. If it is accepted that there was *no* antecedent rule of a relevant character it will go against the grain to call the case one of punishment. One can deal in a related way, perhaps, with 'collective punishments'. Strict and vicarious liability are much the same. Some people may, after reflection, be ready to name as punishment what is done in such cases, perhaps out of a kind of determined orthodoxy. Others will not be willing to regard what is done as punishment.

Fortunately, we need not set out to discover majority opinions. What we want is a description of punishment convenient for our purposes. It must certainly be in line with the ordinary understanding of the term, but over cases where there is no agreement, or where any existing agreement is not obvious, we may make our own decisions to suit our convenience. Nothing of a substantial nature follows from this with respect to the main question we shall be considering. It will be convenient to take up a description or informal definition which allows us to use the term 'punishment' of cases of strict and vicarious liability, whatever may be true of ordinary usage. We need not trouble about war tribunals, fathers and sons, and collective reprisals. The description we have, however, where punishment is *an authority's infliction of a penalty on an offender for an offence*, does not cover cases of strict and vicarious liability. This will be evident enough if we think a bit more about the requirement that there be an offender, as so far understood.

Suppose we take it to be established beyond any doubt that a man's action in selling adulterated food in no way resulted from a relevant intention of his or from carelessness. In a certain sense it would be mistaken to say he broke a rule. This is the sense which carries the implication that the person who broke the rule was at fault or responsible. It is the ordinary sense of the words, and precisely the sense of the words, which has entered into our definition of an offender. Hence, it would be mistaken to regard the man as an offender. There is something else to be noticed, however, of which we shall make use in a moment. There is a different sense in which he *did* break a rule. After all, one can break a rule unknowingly. The man, then, may be understood to have broken a rule although not to have done so with intention or negligence. Vicarious liability is another matter. One could not without absurdity exhibit the theatre owner or unfortunate employers generally as individuals who have broken rules in any way.

Our description as it stands has another quite different disability. It specifies that punishment is *for an offence* and so may be taken to imply that the moral justification of punishing a man is that he deserves it for what he has done. If we were to use this description, it might appear that we had so described punishment that the principal question before us, 'What, if anything, justifies it morally?', was already answered by the description. The answer might appear to be built in and anyone who disputes it, or anyone else for that matter, might protest that the outcome of the inquiry could hardly be in doubt. Is there anything to be said for the inclusion of the words 'for an offence'?

They are significant in two ways. They suggest certain necessary features of what we normally count as punishment, to the effect that a man must be found to have committed an offence. This, however, is already implied by the very mention of an offender. Secondly, as I have said, the words suggest an *attitude* to a man's having committed an offence. The words 'for an offence' suggest that the penalty is justified because he deserves it for the offence. This attitude is not itself a necessary feature of what we shall take to be punishment. We shall not regard something as other than punishment if the judge, who seems to be the relevant person, does *not* hold the view that the penalty he imposes is morally justified because it is deserved. We shall not be bothered if, through a certain mistaken enlightenment, he takes the view that the existence of an offence is important in *only* another way: merely as an indication that the man is one who is likely to offend in the future if he is not deterred.

Given this, and the difficulties raised by strict liability and by vicarious liability, let us change our minds. Let us describe punishment as simply *an authority's infliction of a penalty on an offender*, and now allow an offender to be a man who has broken a rule out of intention or negligence, or a man who has broken certain rules out of neither, or a man who occupies a certain position of authority with respect to a rule-breaker in either of the preceding senses. There is no need, I think, to be more specific about the mentioned positions of authority, which have to do with cases of vicarious liability.[3] They are in the main positions of employers who are legally responsible for certain acts of their employees.

Our description, so interpreted, is reasonably satisfactory for our purposes. Perhaps it does not fit everything that is ordinarily called punishment, whether by parents, teachers or irregular tribunals. It does fit the subject in hand: one of the dominant practices of control within democratic societies. The *authorities* in question are, in England, the magistrates and judges of the Magistrates' Courts, Quarter Sessions, Assize Courts, the Court of Criminal Appeal and the House of Lords. The *offenders* are most[4] of those judged to be legally responsible with respect to offences. The latter are crimes of violence to persons, including murder and assault, crimes involving the property of others, including theft and damage, crimes gathered under the heading of 'nuisance', crimes consisting of certain acts considered to be immoral, and finally certain crimes against the state and some of its institutions, including treason and the subversion of justice. The *penalties* are those fixed by law. In the main, the law sets down maximum penalties for offences. The choice in a particular case, fine or imprisonment or worse, is made by the magistrate or judge.[5]

If the given description is suitable for our purposes, it is also true that it departs from most or all of the many definitions provided by philosophers who have considered the question of punishment.[6] This is so for several reasons, one of them that almost all philosophers have attempted to capture the most common or ordinary notion. Most people do have the feeling that at least part of the justification of punishment is that it is deserved, and this attitude finds expression in their use of the term. Some such implication is thus present in most definitions. Also, of course, given this genesis of definitions in ordinary life, and a want of awareness there of the existence of strict and vicarious liability, the definitions have excluded a part of their intended subject-matter. This has issued, if not in clear mistakes, at least in an overlooking of things of relevance. Finally, let me admit what will be obvious to some, that I have by some comparisons[7] been casual in formulating my description. It has been safe to assume, I hope, that readers do not need reminding by explicit clause that punishment is not a matter of fortuitous misfortune. There would be better reason for demanding a fuller specification of, say, the nature of the authority involved. What has been said seems to me sufficient for the arguments I intend to consider and to put forward.

1. Ernest Barker, *Principles of Social and Political Theory* (Oxford, 1951), p. 182.
2. J. D. Mabbott, 'Professor Flew on Punishment', *Philosophy*, 1955, pp. 257–8.
3. For accounts of strict and vicarious liability see Glanville Williams, *Criminal Law, The General Part*, second edition (London, 1961), chapters six and seven.
4. Having defined 'offenders' partly as those who *have* broken rules, not all of those individuals who are adjudged guilty, and who thus are offenders in a strictly legal sense, are offenders in our sense. Judges make mistakes. Our definition has this inconvenience but avoids greater ones.
5. The offences, penalties, principles and practices of English law are concisely surveyed in P. J. Fitzgerald, *Criminal Law and Punishment* (Oxford, 1962).
6. Philosophers have given a good deal of attention to the definition of punishment, partly because some arguments about its justification have been supposed to rest on how it is defined: Antony Flew, '"The Justification of Punishment"', *Philosophy*, 1954; A. M. Quinton, 'On Punishment', *Analysis*, 1954; K. Baier, 'Is Punishment Retributive?', *Analysis*, 1955; John Rawls, 'Two Concepts of Rules', *Philosophical Review*, 1955; H. L. A. Hart 'Prolegomenon to the Principles of Punishment', *Proceedings of the Aristotelian Society*, 1959–60; K. G. Armstrong, 'The Retributivist Hits Back', *Mind*, 1961; H. J. McCloskey, 'The Complexity of the Concepts of Punishment', *Philosophy*, 1962; Thomas McPherson, 'Punishment: Definition and Justification', *Analysis*, 1967.
7. ' . . . a person is said to suffer punishment whenever he is legally deprived of some of the normal rights of a citizen on the ground that he has violated a rule of

law, the violation having been established by trial according to the due process of law, provided that the deprivation is carried out by the recognised legal authorities of the state, that the rule of law clearly specifies both the offence and the attached penalty, that the courts construe statutes strictly, and that the statute was on the books prior to the time of the offence.' Rawls, op. cit., p. 10.

CHAPTER TWO: RETRIBUTION

1. The Traditional Retribution Theory

One of the most influential statements of the retribution theory was given by Immanuel Kant in the eighteenth century. The following three passages, central if not entirely clear, are from his *Philosophy of Law*.[1]

... Punishment can never be administered merely as a means for promoting another Good, either with regard to the Criminal himself or to Civil Society, but must in all cases be imposed only because the individual on whom it is inflicted *has committed a Crime*. For one man ought never to be dealt with merely as a means subservient to the purpose of another, nor be mixed up with the subjects of Real Right [i.e. goods or property]. Against such treatment his Inborn Personality has a Right to protect him, even although he may be condemned to lose his Civil Personality. He must first be found guilty and punishable, before there can be any thought of drawing from his punishment any benefit for himself or his fellow citizens.

... If Justice and Righteousness perish, human life would no longer have any value in the world. – What, then, is to be said of such a proposal as to keep a Criminal alive who has been condemned to death, on his being given to understand that if he agreed to certain dangerous experiments being performed on him, he would be allowed to survive if he came happily through them? ... a Court of Justice would repudiate with scorn any proposal of this kind if made to it by the Medical Faculty: for Justice would cease to be Justice if it were bartered away for any consideration whatever.

Even if a Civil Society resolved to dissolve itself with the consent of all its members – as might be supposed in the case of a People inhabiting an island resolving to separate and scatter themselves through the whole world – the last Murderer lying in the prison ought to be executed before the resolution was carried out. This ought to be done in order that every one may realise the desert of his deeds, and the bloodguiltiness may not remain upon the people; for otherwise they might all be regarded as participators in the murder as a public violation of justice.[2]

It is not said in these passages merely that we are *justified* in punishing an offender: that we have a moral right to do so but may, without moral failing, choose not to exercise it. Rather, we are told, we have a *categorical obligation* to impose a certain penalty: it would be wrong not to impose it. This is so, we are initially told, 'only because the individual on whom it is inflicted *has committed a Crime.*' These words, as well as other expressions of the supposed reason for punishment, are likely to call up several ideas.

(1) They may be taken to amount to the claim, as on occasion they have been, that we have a moral obligation to punish a man simply because his act was against the criminal law as it stood. We have an obligation to punish simply because of an act contravening a law, without taking into account the moral nature of the act or the law.

(2) A judge may be *legally* obliged, or more likely, permitted, to punish a man simply because his act was against the criminal law. This is to say no more than that the law lays down certain possibilities for the judge in such cases. For him to be under a legal obligation, or for him to be legally enabled to act, is for there to be a covering law. We, on the other hand, are *legally* obliged not to interfere in the course of justice in certain ways.

(3) A judge has a kind of moral obligation, presumably one that may be overridden by other moral obligations, to administer the law as it stands. He has undertaken to do this. We may be under a similar kind of moral obligation, perhaps one more easily overridden, to support the law as it stands. It may be said that breaking even a bad law may have dangerous social consequences.

None of these three considerations comes close to resulting in the conclusion that we are morally justified in punishing offenders, let alone morally obliged to punish them. None of the three considerations, however, is the principal one intended by Kant. To consider them briefly anyway, it cannot be (1) that we are morally justified in punishing, or under an absolute obligation to punish, simply because of the existence of a law making an act a criminal offence.[3] It is notorious that there have been odious laws and hence completely unjustified punishments. That, however, is not the main point. When a man is punished under a law, however acceptable the law, a moral justification may be dependent upon the morality of the law but not upon the fact that there *is* a law. It will not depend on the fact that a particular procedure has been carried out by the correct authority, and hence that a certain act has become an offence. As for (2) it is obvious enough that the legal obligations of judges, and our legal obligations, do not result in the conclusion that anyone is morally permitted or obliged to punish. As for (3) the secondary moral obligations in question are clearly insufficient to provide us with a justification of punishment or an obligation to engage in it. It cannot be that a judge is justified in punishing a man simply because he has promised to do so.

(4) Kant's words, that we must punish a man only because he 'has committed a Crime', require another interpretation if they are to be taken seriously. Such an interpretation is suggested in several places, notably by the assertion in the third passage that we are obliged to support a man's punishment *because it is his desert for his deeds*. In part the point is that he has acted wrongly or immorally, as distinct from only illegally.

Notice, before we consider more fully the meaning of what I shall call *desert claims*, the nature of the supposed obligation. We are to observe (as we are elsewhere told explicitly) the *lex talionis*: 'an eye for an eye, a tooth for a tooth.' A man *must* be punished if he has performed an act for which he deserves a penalty. Further, he must not be given a lesser penalty than he deserves for his action even if it is true, as sometimes it is thought to be, that some lesser penalty will reform him or benefit others while the penalty he deserves will make recidivism likely. The obligation, however, is two-sided. A sane man who has obeyed the law must *not* be made to suffer even if this would have the good effect, for example, of keeping him from committing offences he otherwise is thought likely to commit. Further, given that every man must be treated exactly as he deserves, an offender's penalty must not be increased over what he deserves even if it is believed that a more severe penalty is needed as an example to deter others from the same offence.

It is worth reiterating, to avoid confusion and to distinguish this version of the retribution theory from others, that it is not a reminder that certain legal obligations exist, which is to say that there are laws which bind judges and also our own interventions in their procedures. Nor are we being reminded of moral reasons for support of the existing law, moral reasons of a relevant but not a conclusive kind. Nor are we being told that we are morally obliged to punish simply because there is a law against something. What *is* intended is partly that legislators, who regulate the practice of punishment partly by fixing scales of penalties, are obliged to arrange that men get what they deserve for the wrongfulness of their actions, *simply because they deserve it.* Legislators are not to take into consideration, in this respect, the well-being of offenders or of society as a whole. Judges are to proceed similarly in the fixing of particular penalties, again because they are deserved. We, finally, are obliged to support our legislators and judges, again because of desert.

To contemporary sensibilities and judgements this is harsh and unrealistic. Is there, perhaps, some misunderstanding? More than one philosopher has thought so. One asks: 'Does a person who advocates the retributive view necessarily advocate, as an *institution*, legal machinery whose essential purpose is to set up and preserve a correspondence between moral turpitude and suffering?' The answer given by the asker of the question is: 'Surely not.' Rather, we are told, 'what retributionists have rightly insisted upon is that no man can be punished unless he is guilty, that is, unless he has broken the law'.[4] That is, perhaps, desert is a necessary condition of a justified punishment, but not in itself a sufficient condition. It is necessary, but not enough by itself.

As we shall come to see, not everyone who holds what he calls a retribution view of punishment advocates a practice whose sole and supposedly sufficient principle is to preserve some relation between immorality and suffering. It would be bizarre to suppose, though, that Kant's view in the quoted passages is no more than that desert is only a necessary condition of justified punishment. Certainly this prohibition on punishing individuals who do not deserve it is present. Equally certainly, there is the supposed obligation to punish those who are said to deserve it, and to punish them as much as they deserve. In other passages of the *Philosophy of Law*, by the way, one hears other notes, but I shall not consider them. My concern is not really with exegesis but with the clarification and appraisal of one possible view about the justification of punishment. That it has been the view of many men is to me a certainty but not something for which I shall argue.

2. *Desert*

Let us now take one side of the supposed obligation, that we *must* punish to a certain degree in certain circumstances, and examine the reason given for it. The reason is that men deserve penalties. This has sometimes been given as a sufficient reason for the conclusion that we are justified or right in certain punishments, as distinct from being under an obligation to impose them. What will be said is as relevant to this more tolerable argument. We must begin by getting clear what may be meant by the claim that a man deserves a penalty. This will take some time since the claim may be taken to mean a number of things. I shall discuss nine possibilities. To my knowledge no adequate differentiating analysis has ever been provided by either the defenders or the critics of the retribution theory. What is offered here will be supplemented in later chapters when we have considered certain relevant matters.

(1) Sometimes people say that a man deserves something and intend no more than that it is right that he get it. To attempt to argue that a man's punishment is justified, by saying in this sense that he deserves it, is obviously pointless. Any desert claim that reduces to the assertion that it is obligatory or permissible to impose a penalty cannot, of course, be offered as a reason for the proposition in dispute, that it is obligatory or permissible to impose the penalty. This is a simple fallacy where the supposed reason is identical with the supposed conclusion. It is a simple fallacy which may sometimes be concealed, as we shall see.

(2) What may also be intended by a remark that a man deserves a penalty, as we have already noticed in connection with Kant, is simply that he did act wrongfully. More precisely, he performed

an action of a certain culpability. This by itself has not been regarded by retributivists as a sufficient explanation of the supposed justification of particular punishments. I shall include it, after clarification, in more adequate interpretations of desert claims, where it plays a part.

(3) What is usually meant or implied when it is said that a man deserves some particular penalty is that there is some relationship between it and something else. People may once have meant that imposing the penalty would involve an action of the same kind as the man's action in his offence. A murderer might in this sense be said to deserve execution. What a man who commits rape or breach of promise deserves, in this sense, is a question which leaves room for reflection. A more important difficulty is that any retribution theory that is worth discussion allows that certain defences may be offered by an accused man. They include the defences that he was grossly provoked and that his action was unintentional. Such defences would be entirely ruled out by the principle that a man is to be punished as he deserves, *given this present notion of desert*. All that would matter would be the kind of action he performed. This notion of desert, then, must be discarded.

(4) Someone may mean in saying that a man deserves a certain penalty for an offence that the penalty would cause roughly as much distress to him as he caused to someone else by his offence. This different contention about a relationship is in the neighbourhood of something interesting. As it stands, however, it could not be part of any tolerable retribution theory. The reason is the same as before. Two men who by their offences cause the same distress, one intentionally and one accidentally, would be said in this sense to deserve the same penalty. No reflective retributivist has intended this notion of desert.

(5) To say that a man deserves a certain penalty may mean that there is a relationship between the culpability of his behaviour and the distress of the proposed penalty. This particular relationship has been and still is commonly regarded as one of 'equivalence'. Whether it can sensibly be regarded in this way depends on the terms of the relationship. The culpability of an offender in his offence, we may briefly say, depends on two things: the harm

caused by his action and the extent to which he can be regarded as having acted responsibly. Greater culpability attaches to violent assault than to pilfering, given equally responsible agents. Greater culpability attaches to intentional as against accidental wounding. Given some such understanding of culpability, it is clear that no penalty can be regarded as either equivalent or not equivalent, in any factual sense, to a man's culpability in his offence. This is so because the distress of a penalty and the culpability of an offender are not commensurable. There are no common units of measurement.

(6) Reflection on forms of expression used by judges and others in place of 'because he deserves it' may bring to mind yet another relationship. 'The punishment is right because he owes it.' 'He is to be punished because he must pay his debt to society.' I shall take it that what lies behind such claims, although disavowals may be expected, is that a man is rightly punished because his punishment brings satisfaction to others. In particular, but certainly not exclusively, it satisfies desires of the person or persons he has offended against. For a number of reasons of a cultural nature which we need not consider, this argument is rarely made explicit.[5] To ignore it is none the less to ignore what has given force to the retribution theory.

The relationship may be described as holding between the grievance caused to the victims of the offence and others, on the one hand, and, on the other hand, the satisfactions given them by the offender's penalty. 'Grievance' may seem an odd choice of word here, but I think it the best one. It would be mistaken, for example, to talk of the injury or the deprivation caused to individuals as one term of the relationship in question. This is so for the reason that we want something which varies with the extent to which a man may be regarded as responsible for his action. The grievances I have in mind are those which a person may *have* rather than have done to him. They are feelings, not injuries. They are, we may say, desires for satisfaction, satisfaction which comes via the experiences of certain individuals.

Penalties may be regarded as *equivalent* to grievances in the sense that they precisely satisfy them. The distress caused to the man who is penalized is neither less nor more than is required to satisfy the grievance. It is important to see, however, that to defend a man's punishment as deserved, in this sense, is not simply to rest one's case on an equivalence. It is to defend the punishment as giving satisfactions. That they *are* satisfactions is more important than that they can be displayed as equivalent satisfactions. Why should these satisfactions be given? The argument must be, in the end, that grievances exist. They are desires, and like other desires they must be taken into consideration. That a man wants something is itself a reason for his having it. It is equally certain, of course, that it is a reason that may be outweighed by others.

To construe desert claims in this last way as an element of the retribution theory is to run contrary to a prevailing orthodoxy. All recent discussions of that theory have defined it as a doctrine which finds justification for punishing a man wholly in his past action and a relationship between that and the penalty *in so far as it affects him*. If, it is said, anything else is in question, such as the effect of the penalty on others, the doctrine is not the pure retribution theory.

This is to fall under the thrall of a definition and into misdescription. It is to misdescribe the attitudes and arguments of retributivists. They cannot much protest because they have not been self-aware or explicit. Their reticence, whatever is finally to be said of their argument, is misplaced: there is no reason for *ruling out of discussion* the claim that a course of action will lead to the satisfaction of desires. There is no reason for keeping it dark. What is to be said for the orthodox interpretation of the retribution theory is only that it pays a somewhat scholarly attention to the self-descriptions of retributivists. The consequence is that the theory becomes mystery, a doctrine whose central proposition about equivalence, if not construed in such a way as to call out for dismissal, evokes mainly wonderment. It would be jejune to suppose, in this context if not in others, that the persistence and force of the doctrine in question had no basis in intelligible argument.

(7) In saying that a particular man deserves a particular penalty, people commonly allude to a certain system, a penalty system. Its supposed nature can more easily be made clear by considering a model of its construction. In doing this, I shall make use of the

intelligible and sensible notion of equivalence between penalty and offence.

To begin in constructing such a system we reflect on actions of considerable harmfulness. The grievance to which they may be regarded as giving rise, however, is a function not only of their harmfulness but also of the extent to which the agents involved are responsible for their actions. Hence we initially fix a particular penalty for actions of a particular harm, say killing, given that they are actions for which the agents can be held wholly responsible. We then fix lesser penalties for actions of this harm where the agents are to a lesser extent responsible. In each case, the intention is to fix a penalty whose distress brings satisfactions to others roughly equivalent to the grievance they have been caused. What this means, of course, is that the penalty does satisfy, and does no more than satisfy, the grievance.

What we have in the end is a set of rules which specify a particular penalty for each of a large number of actions. These are actions which cause grievance sufficient to call for satisfactions which can be had only by punishment. (Other actions which cause grievance may be the objects of practices analogous to judicial punishment, where the penalties are less severe.) It should be clear that the system need not involve the supposed equivalences, which we have already put aside as unintelligible, that are thought to hold between penalties and the culpabilities of agents in their actions ((5) above). A man's culpability or guiltiness may be judged, as we have seen, by the harmfulness of his action and the extent of his responsibility for it. These two considerations also determine in a different way what I have called the grievance he causes, and it is this very different thing that is in question. It is this that *can* intelligibly be regarded as equivalent to something else.

A number of objections may be raised against this account of the construction of a penalty system. Some of them are not relevant. No attempt has been made to do more than sketch a model. Many things are left out that would be essential to anything like a factual depiction of the actual development of penalty systems. Such a depiction is not the object of the enterprise. The object is only to bring into view the underlying principle.

It may be objected, more relevantly, that the construction assumes an assessment of grievances and satisfactions and there can be no 'objective' measure that can be used. What can be said in reply to this? The construction involves, centrally, the picturing of a situation involving (1) a certain offence, generally considered, (2) the grievance to which it gives rise, and (3) the penalty that would satisfy the grievance. Let us take these in turn.

The offence is identified by way of the harm caused and the degree of responsibility of the agent. To say as we ordinarily do that a man has been harmed in some way is to describe his state and also to do *something like* express an attitude of disapproval. 'Objectivity' objections, such as they are, are in place at this particular point. That a man's car has been taken away is as 'objective' a fact as that he is now on a bus. But has he been *harmed*? This is in part an evaluative question, and one that must be answered. Retributivists, in facing such questions, are no worse off than their critics and the holders of other theories. It is worth remembering that we are in considerable agreement as to what constitutes a harm.

As for judgements about responsibility, they may be described as factual. We recognize a considerable range of conditions which may reduce a man's responsibility for a particular action. He may be compelled to do something, perhaps in such a way that what he does barely counts as a case of action at all. He may do a thing without intending it, or fully intending it. He may act only after having been subjected to extreme provocation, or as a consequence of illness or disability. There are many more such excusing conditions and we can order them as to their excusing capacity. Needless to say, it will not be a simple list.

The point that emerges is that there is no insuperable difficulty, of the sort envisaged by our objector, in the specification of an offence. It is not, in any fatal sense, a procedure of 'subjectivity'. If we turn now to the estimation, in general, of the grievance caused by an identified offence, there again is no such serious difficulty. That a man has a certain response to the disappearance of his car is a consequence, in part, of attitudes. What response he does have, what grievance he feels, is a question of fact. It is a difficult question but not an evaluative one. It is partly to be answered, and this brings us to item (3) above, by consideration of what satisfies him, what puts an end to his grievance. Here again, in judging satisfactions, we have what is fundamentally a question of fact, or at least can be. So too, finally, is *our* question of equivalence: whether a penalty satisfies, fails to satisfy, or more than satisfies a grievance.

Let us remember where we were. We were considering one of a number of interpretations of the claim that a man deserves a particular penalty. Under this interpretation, the claim is that *his penalty is in accordance with a certain system of penalties*. Even given all that has been said, this remains in a way ambiguous.

The claim cannot reasonably be, although sometimes this seems intended, merely that a certain system of penalties exists, that it has been worked out or enacted as law. It often seems, secondly, that in referring to a penalty system a defender of punishment means to accept or to underwrite it. He implies its moral acceptability. Given this, his argument for punishment is similar to something mentioned above, in connection with the very first understanding of desert claims. It involves a form of the fallacy of *petitio principii*. Very simply, he argues that punishment is justified in a particular case because it is justified in all cases of this kind. But exactly this is what is in question. There is a third and very different way in which the reference to a penalty system is of significance. As I have implied already, to say a man's punishment is justified partly because it is in accordance with a penalty system may be to say that other men who have caused similar grievances have been *similarly treated* and that the same will be true of those who do so in the future. This *is* something (the first of two) to be taken into consideration.

One final comment here. Our actual practice of punishment is undeniably governed by a certain system of rules. These rules in some manner or other connect particular offences with particular penalties and may be classified in different ways. The description and justification of these rules, unlike their existence, is a matter of question. A retributivist may regard them as the outcomes of a construction of the sort just suggested, or at any rate he should.

A very different account, as we shall see (in chapter three, section three), may be given by proponents of another theory of punishment.

(8) There is also another acceptable understanding of desert claims which sees them as referring to a penalty system. It is an understanding that is of sufficient impórtance to be listed separately. It may be implied of a man said to deserve a penalty that he was aware of two options and free to choose between them. He knew of the existence of a penalty system, which is to say he knew of an intention and indeed an undertaking on the part of society to penalize certain actions. He was aware, too, of the intention and undertaking *not* to penalize other forms of behaviour. He knew of these options and chose between them. He 'knew what he was getting into and needn't have got into it.' He was responsible for his action.

(9) Suppose, finally, that two men have been given the same opportunity to commit an offence, perhaps a theft in conditions where discovery is highly unlikely. One succumbs to the temptation and the other does not, and it is said that one deserves a penalty and the other does not. What this may be taken to mean, in part, is that it is in a certain sense fair that one man and not the other be penalized. The offender has presumably gained some satisfactions from his offence while the other man has forgone satisfactions and perhaps even been distressed by his renunciation. What we have, it may be argued, is a situation where punishing the offender and not the other man will be a move in the direction of equality of welfare and distress. To say that one man deserves a penalty while the other does not may be to convey, in part, just this.

3. Defences and Criticisms

Let us now salvage from our survey the most defensible and complete interpretation of the claim, as ordinarily made, that a man deserves a particular penalty for a particular action. It may be taken to have five parts.

(1) He behaved culpably,
(2) the penalty will give satisfactions equivalent to the grievance caused by his action,
(3) similar penalties have been and will be imposed on similar offenders,
(4) he was responsible for his action and performed it with a knowledge of possible consequences according to a penalty system, and
(5) unlike non-offenders he has gained satisfactions attendant on the commission of an offence..

This might be complicated in various ways to avoid misunderstandings and objections but I shall not make it more cumbersome than it is. As it stands, it is worth consideration as a sufficient argument for punishing a man. It has never been advanced by a supporter of the retribution theory, partly for the reason that supporters of the theory have commonly tried to defend their conclusions in ways we have already rejected. (Untenable suppositions about factual equivalence between offence and penalty have been curiously persistent.)

If the argument as it stands is worth consideration, attempts might be made to strengthen it. Whatever use they have tried to make of notions of desert, retributivists have also appealed to certain very general moral principles in support of their view. These have almost always been principles of justice, and they might be said to be relevant to our present version of the retribution theory. Consider this:

There are many positive considerations in support of the retributive theory of punishment, if it is construed as the theory that the vicious deserve to suffer. Firstly, it is a particular application of a general principle of justice, namely, that equals should be treated equally and unequals unequally. This is a principle which has won very general acceptance as a self-evident principle of justice. It is the principle from which the more celebrated, yet opposed accounts of justice, are derived. It is a principle which has wide application and which underlies our judgements of justice in the various areas. We think of it as applying – other things being equal – to fair prices, wages, and treatment generally.

It is in terms of such a principle that we think that political discrimination against women and peoples of special races is unjust, and that against children, just. Justice in these areas involves treating equals equally, unequals unequally – where the equals are equal in the relevant respect, and the unequals unequal in the relevant respect. Hence we think it just to deny women some jobs because of their weaker physique, but unjust to exclude a woman from a post such as a librarian or a violinist if she is more proficient as such than other candidates for the post. So too with justice and punishment. The criminal is one who has made himself unequal in the relevant sense. Hence he merits unequal treatment. In this case, unequal treatment amounts to deliberate infliction of evils – suffering or death.[6]

Notions of justice are difficult to handle with clarity, as this passage indicates. We might take it that the argument advanced is that there is a general moral principle that *individuals who are equal in some respect are to be treated equally and in a way different from others*. Does this provide support for the claim that those who can be said to deserve punishment, in our present sense, should be *treated differently* from those who cannot be said to deserve it? It may, since those who deserve punishment are different in given ways from others. Does it provide support for the claim that those who deserve punishment should be *punished* and those who do not deserve it should not? It does not. The mentioned general principle would be satisfied, equally well, if we were to punish those who do not deserve it and not punish those who do. The principle would also be satisfied if we did no punishing at all and, say, repeated three times to ourselves the names of those who do not deserve punishment. *All* that the stated principle requires is that individuals who are equal in some respect should be treated equally and in a way different from others.

Let us try again. Perhaps the fundamental principle of justice in question is *that individuals of the same desert are to be given their desert and that individuals of different desert are to be given their different desert*. The principle would be a general one, applying to all of life and not only that part to which punishment pertains. This is of relevance, at least, but the argument attached to it is hardly compelling. We are said to accept some such general moral principle and so to be committed to accepting a particular application or consequence of it, a particular justification of punishment. *One* reply is that we obviously are not governed in all our actions and attitudes only by such a principle. We are also governed, if that is the word, by fundamental considerations of benevolence. We often think it right to forgo exaction of a man's deserts. There is thus no possibility of claiming that in consistency we must support punishment when it is deserved. What we must do, in this as in other problem-situations, is consider the force of arguments about desert among others. This will be our procedure.

There is yet another interpretation of the passage that we can try. It may be said that we share a principle to the effect that *all people or all members of certain groups should be equal in satisfactions. If they become unequal in some respect, then some of them may be treated unequally in a certain way: a way that will restore equality of satisfactions.* Those who commit offences gain in satisfactions. If we assume that a state of equality of satisfactions existed before the offences, what we must do is punish the offenders in order to restore the state of equality. Punishment will deprive the offenders of certain satisfactions and satisfy the grievance-desires of others.

One quite sufficient reply that may be made to this argument is that it depends upon a patently false premise. It is not true of our societies that their members are at any time equal or even roughly equal in satisfactions. As often as not the imposition of a penalty will make for less rather than more equality. Given our societies as they are, the general principle that individuals ought to be equal in satisfactions would direct us in at least a great many cases to the conclusion that we ought *not* to punish offenders.

Let us forget about more general principles and return to our fundamental retributivist argument for punishment, that men deserve it, taken by itself. What can be said against it? Much is, and much of it mistaken.

The enterprise of punishing men as they deserve, as we have seen, involves assessments of their responsibility for their actions. It has often been objected[7] that such assessments are impossible or exceedingly difficult. The objection, already alluded to, can do with more attention. To assess adequately a man's responsibility, we are occasionally told,[8] we would require introspective knowledge of his state of mind at the time of his offence. We cannot enter into his consciousness. In the necessary absence of this, we have only his reports, and these are fallible and may be dishonest. A second objection is that we would require a full knowledge of his past development. We would require this to be able to determine to what degree his past excuses him.

In reply, it can be pointed out that it is easy to deny the possibility or practicability of judgements of whatever kind by setting an impossibly high standard for acceptable ones. If what we must have in order to assess a man's responsibility adequately is knowledge by introspection or by something like indubitable report, we can rarely if ever assess his responsibility adequately. But there is no reason for thinking that we need such knowledge. However, we do need a knowledge of his past. We must safely assume or know a good deal of his history in order to decide what he could, at any moment, have avoided doing. With respect to a number of the excusing conditions mentioned already, we must know of his past in order to decide if they obtain. The objection is that we require more than we can in practice have. In reply it must be admitted that there are effective limits to what can be learned by a judge of a man's past life. He may make use of inquiries but only to an extent fixed by a reasonable allocation of social resources. However, it may be said, it is at least possible to picture a workable procedure by which a judge or jury could be supplied with a sufficient knowledge of the histories of defendants. It is important to remember that retributivists are not committed to the defence of any actual judicial system in all its shortcomings.

It seems to be supposed, sometimes, that one can arrive at the same objection to the retribution theory by reflection on a particular difficulty.[9] There has long been a controversy over the definition of those offenders who are to be regarded as mentally ill or incapacitated and thus not legally responsible for their actions. The McNaghten rules in English law, until modified, specified that a man was to be held responsible for an act unless he was labouring under such a defect of reason, from disease of the mind, as not to know the nature and quality of his act, or, as not to know that his act was wrong. The effect of this formula was to count as legally responsible those individuals who are incapable of acting on the knowledge they possess. The effect was hence to count as legally responsible many individuals generally regarded as ill and in fact not accountable for their actions. Other difficulties, however, attach to other conceptions. I shall have more to say of relevance to this dispute in another place.

What is at present of importance is this question: Do difficulties of definition, in this borderline area, constitute a conclusive objection to the retribution theory? It seems that they do not. To grant that there are difficult or even undecidable questions about responsibility goes no way to committing one to the conclusion that all or even many questions are undecidable or even particularly difficult. A retributivist impressed with the problems of judging responsibility where mental illness is a possibility might well dismiss the possibility of punishment. He could, in perfect consistency, maintain his doctrine with respect to the vast majority of offenders.

So much for objections to the retribution theory involving responsibility. A second kind of argument against the theory is that to say a man deserves a penalty is not to give anything that *could* count as a reason for punishment. That a man deserves a penalty is not a morally insufficient reason, but something that is not a reason at all, good or bad. A retributivist like Kant, we are told, refuses to consider such consequences or advantages of the practice of punishment as deterrence and reform.

It is therefore virtually impossible for him to answer the question, 'What justification could there be for rules requiring that those who break them should be made to suffer?' except perhaps in theological terms. For appeals to authority apart, we can justify rules and institutions only by showing that they yield advantages. Consequently, retributivist answers to the problem can be shown, on analysis, to be either mere affirmations of the desirability of punishment or utilitarian reasons in disguise. To the first class belong assertions of the type 'It is fitting (or justice requires) that the guilty should suffer.' For to say 'it is fitting' is only to say that it ought to be the case, and it is just this that is in question. To say, with Kant, that punishment is a good in itself, is to deny the necessity for justification; for to justify is to provide reasons in terms of something else accepted as valuable. But it is by no means evident that punishment needs no justification, the proof being that many people have felt the need to justify it.[10]

Consider three claims made here. The first is that an institution such as punishment can only be justified, if one forgets about appeals to authority, as we shall, by showing that it has advantageous consequences. The second, slightly wider, is that such an institution is only to be justified by giving reasons in terms of something else accepted as valuable. The third is that it is pointless to argue in such a way that one's argument reduces to the assertion that something is right because it is right. This third claim is a truism. What of the others? Is it true that an institution can be justified, appeals to authority aside, *only* by giving reasons for it in terms of something other than itself?

It is worth reiterating at this juncture that these are not intended as moral appraisals. It is not being maintained that no *morally adequate* justification of punishment can be given except in the way in question. Rather, what is advanced is a contention about the meaning or logic of a term, a contention about what sorts of thing can count as *justifications* at all, adequate or inadequate. There are several logical points that might usefully be made about the notion of justification[11] but this is not one of them. To ask for a justification, in the way we are, is to ask for a sufficient reason for the acceptability or obligatoriness of something. Why should it be supposed that a description of whatever is being considered, as against a reference to its effects or whatever, cannot count as a reason for its acceptability? Why should it be thought that a feature of a thing itself, or several features as in the case of punishment, cannot be the basis of its justification?

It is a familiarity that various states of affairs, notably certain possible ends of human life, have been argued for in precisely this way. There is no reason for thinking that the same cannot be true of rules and institutions. Of course, to do so is now unfamiliar. Most people hold the moral view that the only adequate justification of a rule or an institution takes into account its effects, but there is nothing to be gained by confusing this with a claim of another kind. It seems then that even if the retribution theory is so construed as to exclude all references to the effects of punishment, excepting those on offenders themselves, it cannot be put aside by a merely logical consideration.

The argument, redescribed, is that one must regard the retribution theory as not offering a logically possible justification at all, or else as consisting in a certain disguised utilitarianism, a disguised attempt to justify punishment by its supposed deterrent or reformative effects. To take the second alternative would also be mistaken. It is not necessary to discount the often fervent claims of retributivists that they do not take punishment to be of value for its supposed deterrent and reformative effects. If there are cases where it is necessary to discount such denials, these are quite atypical.

This mistaken supposition that retributivism must often be taken in the suggested way, however, may derive in part from a truth. It is the truth already noticed that retributivism has been a forceful and widely held doctrine because it *does* imply that punishment gives a benefit. This is the benefit, as we have seen, of satisfactions produced by the imposition of penalties. We have construed the claim that men deserve penalties as implying, among other things, that the penalties will give satisfaction. We have taken the retribution theory to include this argument. To do so, obviously, is not to regard it as a theory of deterrence or reform under considerable disguise.

Consider now a third and more common-sensical argument against the belief that we are obliged or permitted to punish men in so far as they deserve it. Is it not *inconsistent* to condemn one man for injuring another and then to claim that society is morally correct to injure the offender in turn? Both the offender's act and the act of punishing him, it may be said, are contraventions of some principle, perhaps one of benevolence. The fact that the victim, in the case of punishment, has himself injured somebody else should not be regarded as making a sufficient difference between the two cases. If the first action was wrong, so is the second.

Nor is there a sufficient difference to be found in the fact that in one case the injury is the work of a private individual and in the other the work of officers of a society acting in accordance with the law. Given this fact, punishment is not revenge. But if it can be defended only by considerations of desert then it, like revenge, is unjustified.

A retributivist can oppose this argument in a number of ways. He may insist that there is a fundamental difference between a private action of one individual and the lawful actions of society. He need not but might introduce into the argument principles of democracy. He may say, further, that there is a fundamental difference between striking and striking back.[12] One may think a little or a lot of these considerations. What cannot be disputed is that the retributivist can rebut any charge of inconsistency. *His* principle of benevolence, he may say, includes a distinction between private actions and those of a society's authorities. Or, he includes in his principles, in addition to one having to do with benevolence, another having to do with desert. Injuries are wrong except in certain circumstances when they are deserved. Here there is no inconsistency. He might be asked by a critic, of course, to imagine a state of affairs where he himself was being punished. Would *that* be right? If the answer forthcoming is no, the retributivist may indeed have fallen into inconsistency. It is highly likely that he will accept that his own punishment, in the imagined case, would be justified. If so, his position is consistent.[13]

If these criticisms of the theory of retribution are mistaken or insufficient, at least two others are not such. It is proposed to us in the theory that a man's punishment is justified or obligatory because (1) he has behaved culpably, (2) his penalty will give satisfactions equivalent to the grievance he has caused, (3) it will be similar to those imposed on other offenders who have caused similar grievances, (4) he was responsible for his action and knew of the possible consequences under a system of offences and penalties, and (5) unlike non-offenders he has gained satisfactions attendant on the commission of an offence. The first effective criticism is in a sense an external one. It has become increasingly apparent that there are many offenders who cannot be said to deserve penalties, in the sense just stipulated. The proportion of offenders who may be said to have been responsible for their actions is not so large as once was supposed. Over the past half-century or so, it has come to be accepted that a considerable proportion of individuals who break the law cannot do otherwise. Given this, the retributivist must supplement his proposal for the control of criminality. Other practices than punishment are required. None the less, it may still be maintained, with respect to those offenders who can be said to deserve punishment, that their punishment is justified by the fact that they do deserve it.

One cannot make the familiar reply that this contention, as we have understood it, runs against the conviction that men cannot be made to suffer, or be deprived, if no good in human welfare comes of it. The retribution theory does recommend a practice partly on the basis of accruing benefits. It would be difficult to explain its appeal, I have argued, if something like this was not true. One *can* reply, as I shall now explain, that the theory runs against the conviction that benefits in the satisfaction of desires, to say nothing of other 'goods', must not be purchased at too great a cost.

Let us proceed by considering in turn the five elements of the retribution argument. We are first given as a reason for punishment that some men have behaved culpably. I have included this supposed reason out of a desire for completeness and with misgivings. It seems, on reflection, not to be a moral reason for action at all, good or bad. The fact, *taken entirely by itself*, that a man has caused a certain harm by a responsible action, seems to have no moral consequences. That is, as I shall come to explain more fully (see p. 80), it cannot be connected with any recognizably moral attitude. The fact might be offered as an *explanation of revenge*, but that is entirely different.

The second element of the retribution argument, that punishment satisfies grievances, must be neither disregarded nor overestimated. The third is that a man's penalty will be similar to those imposed on other offenders who have caused similar grievances, and different from the penalties of offenders who have caused different grievances. Taken in the context of the retribution theory, this is in a way a secondary consideration. That is, a reason is advanced for choosing a particular system of punishment, one which is fair or consistent, if we are going to have some such system at all. Consider an analogy. If food is to be distributed to a group of people, some of whom are very hungry and some of whom are slightly hungry, we are likely to give a larger amount to each of those who are very hungry and a smaller amount to each of those who are slightly hungry. That we do anything at all, however, and that we feel that we ought to distribute any food, is not to be explained by the fact that all the members of one sub-group are in *one* state and all the members of the other in a *different* state. It is that they are all hungry. Suppose that there is a reason why all of the people in question should not eat for a given period. All of them are going to have surgical operations. We would not give them food, or feel we ought to, although some were very hungry and others slightly hungry. Similarly, the fact that some individuals have caused similar grievances, while others have caused dissimilar ones, is not in itself a reason for action.

The fourth element of the retribution argument is that offenders have been responsible for actions which they knew to be offences and to carry with them certain possible consequences. This has usually been taken to be a reason for punishment although its nature has been left unclear. I shall for the present accept that it is a reason and postpone until later (see p. 81 ff., p. 166 ff.) a fuller consideration which depends on acquaintance with doctrines so far undiscussed. (The index, under 'desert', gives a guide to all analyses.) Fifthly, we have it that offenders, unlike non-offenders, have gained satisfactions through their offences. Punishing offenders and not non-offenders, it may be said, contributes to the re-establishment of some earlier state of equality of satisfactions and distress. *One* adequate reply, as may be anticipated from our examination of the relevance to the retribution theory of general principles of justice, is that this is entirely untenable in our societies as they are. They are not societies of equality to start with.

What emerges from this further procedure of elimination is that we must in the end regard punishment as defended by the facts that *it gives satisfactions to victims of offences and others, and that offenders have freely and responsibly taken the option of committing offences.* This, fundamentally, is what the retribution theory comes to. Obviously, if this is all that can be said for punishment, not enough can be said for it.

We share a conviction that wants should be satisfied, and that they can justifiably be frustrated only under certain conditions. They may sometimes be frustrated if this course of action leads in the end to greater satisfactions. They may sometimes be frustrated in the interest of greater equality. Neither of these considerations applies in the present case. It is not seriously arguable that the deprivations imposed by punishment on offenders and others is outweighed by the grievance-satisfactions gained by victims and others. Nor can it be argued that the course of punishment can be defended by the principle of equality. It is not arguable either that the deprivations of punishment are outweighed by the satisfaction of grievance *and* the value, whatever it may be, involved in the fact that those who are punished have freely and knowledgeably offended. This seems to me indubitable, but it should not be taken for any other conclusion than it is.

Quite often it is supposed that *all* doctrines mentioning desert have been exposed as masks for vengeance, that in our enlightenment we need pay them no attention. An entirely general attitude, one which takes all talk of desert to be pointless in all contexts, cannot be sustained. This is a matter considered in the following chapters. I should add that I will there give further accounts of what is being appealed to when individuals are distinguished according to whether or not they have acted freely and responsibly in the commission of an offence. There is a good deal more to be said, but it will not substantially affect the argument just given.

One final point to be made concerns strict and vicarious liability. It will be apparent that the retribution argument which we have considered would not justify punishment where a man neither intended to commit an offence nor was negligent. Such a man could not count as deserving a penalty in the given sense. Nor, of course, could the retribution argument justify punishing a man who merely occupied a certain position of authority with respect to someone who performed a certain action. This man, although 'vicariously liable' to conviction, could not count either as deserving a penalty. Strict and vicarious liability, however, of which I shall have more to say, are themselves matters of controversy.

4. *Annulment and Rights*

There is another retribution theory of very secondary interest. We are obliged to punish, according to its first part, since to do so 'is to annul the crime, which otherwise would have been held valid, and to restore the right'.[14] A punishment is an annulment, a cancellation or a return to a previous state of affairs. This alone is what justifies us.

> If crime and its annulment . . . are treated as if they were unqualified evils, it must, of course, seem quite unreasonable to will an evil merely because 'another evil is there already'. To give punishment this super-ficial character of an evil is, amongst the various theories of punishment, the fundamental presupposition of those who regard it as a deterrent, a preventive, a threat, as reformative, etc. What on these theories is sup-posed to result from punishment is characterised equally superficially as a good. But it is not merely a question of an evil, or of this, that or the other good; the precise point at issue is wrong and the righting of it. If you adopt that superficial attitude to punishment, you brush aside the objective treatment of the righting of wrong, which is the primary and fundamental attitude in considering crime. . .[15]

All this, of course, is obscure. It is by Hegel. Marriages, con-sidered as contracts, can be annulled, but crimes cannot be, in any ordinary sense. My death or imprisonment, after I have killed a man, does not make things what they were before. In what way can my death or imprisonment be seen as an annulment? Hegel's argument begins from a conception of moral principles, such as the principle against taking another's life except, as we say, in certain circumstances. An act of murder is not merely a contra-vention of this principle but also a denial of its rightness. Such a denial is said to 'infringe' the principle. We must 'restore' it and this can be done only by punishing the offender. We are not to regard the crime as a harm done to someone, a mere 'evil', but rather as a denial of what is right. Nor do we 'restore' the principle because it is important for its effects in guiding conduct. We do what we do because the principle is right.

To reproduce this doctrine more faithfully and intelligibly would require a considerable and tedious excursus into the philosophy of Absolute Idealism. The doctrine, incidentally, has found a home elsewhere as well, in a tradition of English judicial thought. James Fitzjames Stephen, the Victorian judge and law historian, finds a justification of punishment in its 'ratification' of a morality which has been violated.[16] Lord Denning has observed that 'the ultimate justification of any punishment is not that it is a deterrent but that it is the emphatic denunciation by the community of a crime.'[17]

How are we to take Hegel's suggestion that offenders not only break moral principles but also deny their rightness? They speak, perhaps, a language of action. How are the principles 'infringed'? Are we to understand that they become more open to question by individuals? The argument would then be that because a principle is differently regarded we are justified in punishing. This would not be the argument that the new attitude to the principle may issue in certain effects, notably the commission of offences. It would then be tantamount to a version of the arguments from deterrence and reform.[18] We are to punish, rather, simply because of a change of attitude. This is nonsense.

However, it is pretty clear that the supposed infringement of a principle has to do with more than individual attitudes. Hegel's intention, as distinct from those of some of his followers, is to be understood only by way of reflection on his view of moral principles. They are embodiments of Spirit. Not a great deal of advantage can be had at this point by consulting the related views of the English Idealists. Bosanquet, for example, speaks of crime as having a bad effect on 'the general mind', which is not to be confused with even the collection of individual minds, mere 'atomic states of consciousness'.[19]

Let us recall that we have taken the position that individuals should not be deprived or made to suffer, no matter what they have done, if insufficient good in the form of human welfare or equality comes of their experience. We now have the claim that punishment has the consequence of restoring a moral principle which itself has a kind of independent 'spiritual' or 'personal' reality. We are not to count in any possible effects on human conduct of this restoration. We might in reply question the truth, or more likely the meaning, of the metaphysical doctrines in question. The conclusion might be that punishment does not have the restorative consequences attributed to it, for there are no consequences of that kind. Another course is to assume what can be assumed of the suggested view of moral principles. The question then arises as to whether the restoration of a moral principle so conceived is something sufficient to justify the practice of punishment. It is difficult to bend one's mind to the question.

A second part of Hegel's account of punishment, so far unmentioned, concerns the 'rights' of offenders to be punished. One line of argument proceeds from the assumption that men are in some part of themselves rational. They recognize the supposed obligation to punish offenders, presumably the supposed obligation based on the need to restore a principle. They recognize this obligation even if they are offenders. They have a right, furthermore, to be enabled to fulfil this obligation. So we must punish them. (This part of Hegel's doctrine, incidentally, like the first part, continues to find supporters. 'If we respect personality,' we are told, 'we must respect responsibility. If we respect responsibility, we must respect the right of offenders to be punished for their offences.'[20])

One's response to this, of course, is that a right that cannot be escaped is an odd right. Essays in the psychoanalysis of argument are not often profitable but it is hard to resist the feeling that the claiming of rights to punishment on behalf of others is most interesting as a projection of one's own feelings of guilt. Let us admit, for purposes of economy of thought, that offenders have such a right *if* there exists the supposed obligation. The obligation, however, has not been established, and so the argument comes to nothing.

A second line of reflection about rights, sometimes confused with the first one, is mentioned by Hegel in the following passage.

The injury [the penalty] which falls on the criminal is not merely implicitly just – as just, it is *eo ipso* his implicit will, . . . his right; on the contrary it is also a right established within the criminal himself, i.e. in his objectively embodied will, in his action. The reason for this is that his action is the action of a rational being and this implies that it is something universal and that by doing it the criminal has laid down a law which he had explicitly recognised in his action and under which in consequence he should be brought as under his right.[21]

Implicitly, in his rational self, the offender accepts that punishment is obligatory and demands the right to fulfil this obligation. This is the proposition we have just considered. By his act, however, we are now told, he *explicitly* establishes a certain principle: that it is right to injure others. In consistency, again since he is rational, he accepts that this principle should be observed even when it leads to himself being injured – by punishment. Again, he claims a right. We need not exercise ourselves over whether an offender can be supposed to assert such a principle. Nor need we wonder about what sense can be attached to the resultant demand that he be treated according to the principle. Let us suppose he makes the demand, or can be said to have a right. The question then arises of whether or not we ought to meet the demand or act on the right. That we ought to has not been shown.

It is worth noting, finally, that one Hegelian scholar[22] has presented a different interpretation of the arguments about rights, an interpretation which might indeed be extended to cover the previous argument about annulment. It is that an offender may be *reformed* by punishment, and that he claims this reformation as his right. It is not that punishment, perhaps imprisonment, provides authorities with an opportunity to reform a man by one means or another. It is that punishment itself, the experience of suffering or deprivation, has a reforming effect. This interpretation of Hegel has often been accepted. Certainly it requires a curious reading of the first passage quoted above as well as others. It produces a supposed justification of punishment of a kind to be considered below.

1. Translated by W. Hastie (Edinburgh, 1887).

2. op. cit., pp. 195–8.

3. Something like this view was taken to have been advanced by J. D. Mabbott, 'Punishment', *Mind*, 1939, and criticized by C. W. K. Mundle, 'Punishment and Desert', *Philosophical Quarterly*, 1954. A related doctrine, to the effect that to accept a law as both validly enacted and also immoral is self-contradictory, is espoused by Hans Kelsen, *General Theory of Law and State* (Cambridge, Massachusetts, 1946), pp. 374–6, 407–10. Mabbott, whom I discuss in chapter six, has subsequently put forward what appears to be a revised view.

4. John Rawls, 'Two Concepts of Rules', *Philosophical Review*, 1955, p. 7.

5. That this consideration having to do with grievance-satisfaction is fundamental to retributivism is further defended in chapter ten of my *A Theory of Determinism: The Mind, Neuroscience, and Life-Hopes* (Oxford 1988).

Hermann Lotze, the nineteenth-century German philosopher, speaks of the vindictive satisfactions given to individuals, particularly the victims of offences, by punishment. He continues: 'Were these persons all so organized that they were incapable of feeling pleasure and pain, then it is self-evident that there would no longer exist . . . any right of punishment. . . . It is only the unhappy condition of feeling which takes place in the soul of the injured person that explains and forms the basis for new actions which aim to obviate the same.' *Outlines of Practical Philosophy*, translated by George T. Ladd (Boston, 1885), p. 98.

James Fitzjames Stephen, the Victorian judge, writes: 'The punishment of common crimes, the gross forms of force and fraud, is no doubt ambiguous. It may be justified on the principles of self-protection, and apart from any question as to their moral character. It is not, however, difficult to show that these acts have in fact been forbidden and subjected to punishment not only because they are dangerous to society, and so ought to be prevented, but also for the sake of gratifying the feeling of hatred – call it revenge, resentment, or what you will – which the contemplation of such conduct excites in healthily constituted minds. If this can be shown, it will follow that criminal law is in the nature of a persecution of the grosser forms of vice, and an emphatic assertion of the principle that the feeling of hatred and the desire of vengeance above-mentioned are important elements of human nature which ought in such cases to be satisfied in a regular public and legal manner.' *Liberty, Equality, Fraternity* (London, 1873), pp. 161–2. (Also, New York, 1968.)

6. H. J. McCloskey, 'A Non-Utilitarian Approach to Punishment', *Inquiry*, 1965, p. 260. The view advanced here is not wholly retributivist; this does not put in question the use I make of the passage.

7. See A. C. Ewing, *The Morality of Punishment* (London, 1929), p. 36 ff.; W. D. Ross, *The Right and the Good* (Oxford, 1930), pp. 58–9; W. G. Maclagan, 'Punishment and Retribution', *Philosophy*, 1939; C. H. Whiteley, 'On Retribution', *Philosophy*, 1956; S. I. Benn and R. S. Peters, *Social Principles and the Democratic State* (London, 1959), pp. 186–90. Brief attempts to defend retributivism are to be found in J. D. Mabbott, 'Punishment', *Mind*, 1939; C. W. K. Mundle, 'Punishment and Desert', *Philosophical Quarterly*, 1954; H. J. McCloskey, 'A Non-Utilitarian Approach to Punishment', *Inquiry*, 1965.

8. A. C. Ewing, op. cit.

9. See Barbara Wootton, *Crime and the Criminal Law* (London, 1963). Cf. H. L. A. Hart, *Punishment and Responsibility* (Oxford, 1968), chapter eight.

10. S. I. Benn and R. S. Peters, op. cit., pp. 175–6.

50   Retribution

11. See Antony Flew, '"The Justification of Punishment"', *Philosophy*, 1954.

12. K. G. Armstrong, 'The Retributivist Hits Back', *Mind*, 1961.

13. An illuminating account of this sort of argument, involving among several things an appeal to someone to imagine himself in someone else's shoes, is given by Professor R. M. Hare, *Freedom and Reason* (Oxford, 1963).

14. G. W. Hegel, *Philosophy of Right*, translated by T. M. Knox (Oxford, 1942), p. 69.

15. ibid., pp. 69–70.

16. As Professor Hart has pointed out in *Law, Liberty and Morality* (London, 1963), p. 63. (Also, Stanford, 1963.)

17. *Report of the Royal Commission on Capital Punishment*, s. 53.

18. In the passage just quoted it seems plain enough that Hegel finds no justification of punishment in its practical effects. However, interpretation involves difficult appraisals of his many reflections. In one of the additions made to the text of *Philosophy of Right*, on the basis of lecture notes, he is represented as saying that in some states of society 'an example must be made by inflicting punishments since punishment is itself an example over against the example of crime' (p. 274). Deterrence seems to be in the air, to say the least.

19. Bernard Bosanquet, *Some Suggestions in Ethics* (London, 1918), pp. 190–96.

20. Ernest Barker, *Principles of Social and Political Theory* (Oxford, 1951), p. 179.

21. *Philosophy of Right*, p. 70.

22. J. M. E. McTaggart, *Studies in Hegelian Cosmology* (Cambridge, 1901), p. 137.

CHAPTER THREE: DETERRENCE

1. Factual Presupposition

The retribution theory is often characterized as an account of the justification of punishment which looks to the past. It is contrasted in this with the deterrence theory, and also reform theories, which are truly said to look to the future. The retribution theory as we have conceived it, however, is not an argument that a man's punishment is justified wholly by an event in the past, his offence, or a relation between that and his penalty. It includes the contention that a man's punishment provides satisfactions. It must be taken to include this if we are to have a realistic characterization of one persistent attitude, or a related set of attitudes, to offenders and their punishment. Given this, the retribution theory is to some extent similar to the deterrence theory. It does rest, albeit in a different way and to a lesser extent, on supposed consequences of punishment.

The two differ in this: the deterrence theory finds no justification for action in a past offence, which has no more than a certain evidential importance, and it depends upon consequences of punishment other than the immediate satisfactions given to victims of offences and others. It need not ignore these satisfactions.[1] It rightly finds them of relatively small importance. What is taken to be of supreme importance is that punishment prevents offences.

General prevention ought to be the chief end of punishment as it is its real justification. If we could consider an offence which has been committed as an isolated fact, the like of which would never recur, punishment would be useless. It would be only adding one evil to another. But when we consider that an unpunished crime leaves the path of crime open, not only to the same delinquent but also to all those who may have the same motives and opportunities for entering upon it, we perceive that punishment inflicted on the individual becomes a source of security to all. That punishment which considered in itself appeared base and repugnant to all generous sentiments is elevated to the first rank of benefits when it is regarded not as an act of wrath or vengeance against a guilty or unfortunate individual who has given way to mischievous inclinations, but as an indispensable sacrifice to the common safety.[2]

The writer is Jeremy Bentham, the founder of Utilitarianism. He goes on to suggest that punishment may prevent the occurrence of offences in these ways: (1) by making it impossible or difficult for an offender to break the law again, at least in certain ways; (2) by deterring both offenders and others; (3) by providing an opportunity for the reforming of offenders. Some but not all punishments prevent offences in the first way, by incapacitation. Imprisonment tends to rule out the possibility of more offences by the offender for a time, except those he can commit in prison. The death penalty does, and fines generally do not, incapacitate. With respect to the second way of prevention, if we describe it in the usual insufficient way, punishing a man may make him less likely to offend again because of fear or increased prudence and may act in the same ways to deter others. As for the third way of prevention, punishment may be a means to changing a man's character or personality so that out of some motivation like consideration for others he obeys the law. In this chapter we shall be concerned with only the first and second reasons for punishment, incapacitation and deterrence, considered as sufficient by themselves. It will not be seriously misleading, I hope, to refer to them together as the deterrence theory.

It is a supposition or at least not an established truth that punishment does in fact deter. Are many people deterred? If so, are they deterred from *all* offences or is some other explanation to be given of why they do not commit such offences? Philosophers have very rarely if ever considered such questions. Most often this has been a consequence of an assumption that punishment does deter to some significant extent. Recently it has been a consequence of a general reluctance to engage in factual controversy, controversy which can be settled (if at all) only by other than philosophical methods. I share this reluctance, but it has been overborne by an unwillingness to leave wholly unconsidered an essential part of the argument in hand as well as arguments to come. I shall say relatively little.[3]

What is in question? It is maintained as part of the deterrence theory that (1) because of the possibility of punishment some significant number of potential offenders, individuals contemplating possible offences in a serious way, do not in fact go ahead. (2) Other individuals who find themselves in situations which they did not anticipate or intend, perhaps situations where they are provoked, are said to be restrained by the prospect of a penalty. (3) Others who do commit certain offences are restrained from more serious ones because of the greater possible penalties. They sometimes take self-preserving steps, such as not carrying weapons. The individuals in each of these three classes may not have been punished in the past. The explanation of their behaviour may be fear of punishment, some other aversion to it, or a prudential calculation. What is typically not mentioned is the further proposition (4) that the practice of punishment may have a role in the creation, transmission, and reinforcement of the unreflective attitudes of many people for whom the question of breaking the law never or rarely arises in a serious way. Certainly *any* single-factor explanation of this common behaviour would be mistaken. At the same time, it would be rash indeed to ignore the factor of punishment.

There are some statistics of a certain relevance.[4] It is very evidently the case that much more crime is committed by the young. Among men and boys in England and Wales in one recent year the age-group with the largest number of convictions for indictable offences was that of the fourteen- to sixteen-year-olds. There were 3,199 offenders per 100,000 of the population. In the age group of those seventeen or over and under twenty-one, the rate was 2,944. In the group of those twenty-one or over and under thirty, the rate was 1,867. For those thirty and over, the rate was a mere 385 per 100,000. The conclusion is inescapable that a very large number of offenders do not come back to the attention of the courts after the age of thirty or over. The different conclusion that these statistics 'prove' the factual assumption of the deterrence theory, of course, *is* disputable. In considering the question, there are several things to be kept in mind.

The figures have to do with men and boys who have been found guilty, which is not to say punished. Large numbers of convicted offenders, particularly in the lower age ranges, are discharged or placed on probation. What we can safely say, then, is that very large numbers of individuals do not come back to the attention of the courts after either having been punished or having been made particularly aware of the prospect.

The figures are for those found guilty, not for all men and boys who commit indictable offences. It might be said that the figures are consistent with the supposition that many offenders, as they grow older, continue to break the law but avoid apprehension or conviction. Perhaps a sufficient reply to this is that while older individuals may be more capable of avoiding apprehension and conviction, those who are younger are often not charged at all but dealt with in other ways.

The figures do not establish what proportion of offenders become law-abiding as they grow older *because of* the experience of punishment or of having been made particularly aware of the possibility. The figures are consistent with the supposition that a large proportion of young offenders become law-abiding adults because of something having nothing to do with punishment. Perhaps there is a process of maturation which leads to law-abiding behaviour and would do so as effectively without punishment or a heightened awareness of it. One of the things we need, and have not got, is statistics on boys who break the law but are never apprehended or convicted. What is their later behaviour?

If we stick with the statistics we have, our response to them must depend on the conviction that is carried by alternative explanations of them. The explanations open to the deterrence theorist, the propositions mentioned above, are certainly not obvious losers. The boys in question, he may say, are *by their experiences* made more fearful of or averse to punishment, or simply more prudent.

One very common reply is that such explanations, or some of them, involve a fallacious assumption, 'that we are rational beings, who make a careful calculation of possible gains and losses before deciding upon our actions'. It is fallaciously assumed, 'in the Benthamite phrase, . . . that we always act in accordance with our own "enlightened self-interest"'.[5] On the contrary, individuals do not approach the law as such rational calculators. Some commit offences for the excitement, and it is hardly a surprising fact given the quality of their lives. Others, the victims of guilt-feelings unrelated to crime, are not deterred by the prospect of punishment but positively attracted to it. Still others, in varying ways 'abnormal', are equally far from any prudential consideration of possible consequences of their actions. Only one third of discovered murderers are sentenced as 'mentally normal', it may be said, and of these a large number act in conditions or situations where 'rationality' is anything but likely. Finally, it may be added, it is a truism that people do not choose between possible courses of action in a prudential way if the possible consequences of one course are distant in time and the consequences of the other immediate. A penalty is a distant possibility; the gain from an offence is usually immediate.

This is confusion if intended, as it sometimes seems to be, as *a general reply* to the explanations of the deterrence theorist. He may admit without reluctance that many of those who commit offences are for one reason or another not influenced by the possibility of punishment. It certainly does not follow, however, that those who *do* obey the law are not deterred. It can hardly be claimed that the possibility of punishment must be as uninfluential in the conduct of the majority who obey the law as it is, in different ways and degrees, in the conduct of the minority who do not. The fact that 'non-rational' factors govern the behaviour of some individuals is not good evidence that they govern the behaviour of all or many others. Moreover, it is clearly a mistake to suppose that the claim of deterrence must simply be that individuals 'calculate' and compare the possible gains of offences and the possible losses through punishment, that they judge what is in their best interests and act on their judgements. That punishment leads to law abidance through 'non-rational' processes is quite as important as part of the deterrence claim.

That a man never thinks of offending may in good measure be explained by the existence of the institution of punishment. If the institution plays no part in securing that young offenders become law-abiding, what alternative explanation can be given? There is no explanatory value in passing references to the possibility of 'spontaneous recovery'. To say that there occurs a 'process of maturation' is similarly unhelpful.[6] Doubtless, something of this sort does occur, but would it have the supposed consequence, obedience to law, in the absence of an institution of punishment? In the absence of an adequate alternative explanation, it is difficult to resist the belief that young offenders are affected by their experience. It is also difficult to resist the belief that individuals who never offend are influenced in a related way. Such conclusions, however, require qualification. They are, as they stand, much too general.

As I have implied, the argument would be improved if a positive correlation could be shown between youthful law-breaking, *without* apprehension, and later law-breaking. One should not expect, given the deterrence supposition, a *strikingly* high correlation. The supposition is in part that the practice of punishment has a deterring effect on individuals other than those convicted of offences. It is reasonable to suppose that this effect is also a function of such things as expectations, obligations, and settled wants that increase in strength and number during early life. None the less, one would expect some correlation of the kind mentioned. Statistics are unavailable here because those who conduct research cannot get hold of the relevant control group: young unapprehended law-breakers. There is a bit of evidence of a related kind, however, related in that the situation in question involved a belief on the part of offenders, a well-founded one, that the possibility of punishment was remote. It supports the claim that punishment deters and also is one of several considerations that suggest that a considerable modification of that claim is necessary.

A unique opportunity for making an evaluation of the deterrent approach to crime was presented by Danish experience during the war. In 1944, the German occupying forces deported the Danish police, and for some time the country had only a local guard force invested with police authority. There followed an immense rise in the number of robberies, thefts, frauds, etc., but no comparable increase in murder or sexual crimes. While this experience does show that crime is reduced very considerably by the prospect of detection and presumably punishment, it suggests that deterrent methods are of less value in reducing the incidence of those crimes in which strong passions or deep psychological problems are involved.[7]

One might raise questions about this case, which is one of behaviour in an abnormal situation, the occupation of a country in wartime. One might also resist any implication that it is only rarely that robberies, thefts, frauds, and other 'ordinary' offences are the product of 'strong passions or deep psychological problems'. None the less, there is some support to be had here for the contention that the prospect of punishment has a considerable deterrent effect with respect to many offences. That it does not have this effect with respect to *other* offences is a probability as well supported by general psychological theory. In this connection one might also remark that punishment's having a deterrent effect with respect to many offences is at the very least consistent with a good deal of psychological theory. The practice of punishment, one may say, gives support to the super-ego.[8]

I shall have more to say of relevance to the claim that punishment does deter many potential offenders. Many reformative theories of punishment rest a good deal on a denial of it. My present inclination, in which I shall persist, is that there are adequate grounds for supposing that the practice of punishment does greatly reduce the incidence of a large group of offences. To take the view that it does not have a comparable effect with respect to another considerable group of offences, however, is to accept that the application of the traditional deterrence theory is much more limited than has been supposed. That theory, as I shall explain more fully in a moment, has always been that punishment is justified only under certain conditions, one of which is that it must in fact deter to a certain extent. It is a traditionally recognized consequence that some offenders should *not* be punished. What is now evident, however, is that Bentham and other supporters of the theory considerably underestimated the numbers of offenders whose punishment is unlikely to have an acceptable deterrent effect.

A first conclusion of our discussion, then, one that will be given more support when we come to reformative accounts of punishment, is that the contemporary deterrence theorist is left with a significantly large class of offenders whose punishment is of doubtful value. He must then add something to his recommendations and in effect depart from a programme for dealing with offences based only on deterrence. It does remain a possibility, despite what has been said, that the punishment of many offenders is morally justified on grounds of deterrence alone. For all that has been said, punishment as a part of a larger programme may be acceptable simply because it deters.

2. Economical Deterrence

That it is not so justified is the conclusion of a number of moral rather than factual arguments, most of them to the effect that punishment governed only by the intention to deter is inhumane or unjust. Despite its notoriety, it is said, the retribution theory is more humane. Some of these criticisms derive from taking into consideration a parody of the deterrence theory. They suppose that what is being claimed is that *any* punishment is justified if it serves to keep the offender and possibly others from committing offences in the future. It is said that this is the deterrence principle *per se*, and that if we acted on it we would be perfectly justified in attaching savage penalties to certain minor offences if such penalties were required in order to deter potential offenders.[9]

It has been remarked, for example, that the principle would justify flogging a man for a parking offence, since flogging would certainly have the effect of deterring him and others from parking their cars in the wrong places.[10] It is quite true that such repugnant consequences follow from the simple principle that any punishment is justified if it deters. For that reason such a principle is far from morally acceptable. No one would regard it as a defensible principle, and it would be absurd to suppose that Bentham, for example, puts it forward. Whether or not it can be correctly described as the deterrence principle *per se* is unimportant.

Bentham's view, partly, is that a penalty may be justified only when the distress it causes to the offender and others is *not greater* than the distress that would result if he and others, undeterred, offended in the future. Punishment is an 'evil' because it causes pain both to those who suffer it and others, and also because it limits the freedom of those who obey the law because of it. Offences, obviously, are an evil to the victims. Both evils, that of the punishment and that of the kind of offence in question, must always be considered. 'If the evil of the punishment exceed the evil of the offence, the punishment will be unprofitable: the legislator will have produced more suffering than he has prevented; he will have purchased exemption from one evil at the expense of another.'[11] We then have it that punishing a man is justified if it deters and if the suffering, misery, or anxiety involved is not greater than that which would result if he were not punished. One further addition is desirable. It may be true that any of a number of possible punishments would deter and in so doing cause less distress than would otherwise occur. If this is the case, of course, only that particular punishment is justified which causes the least distress.

We then have the principle that a man's punishment is morally justified if the following conditions are satisfied:

(1) it does indeed deter,
(2) it does not cause more distress than would occur if it were not imposed,
(3) there is no other punishment that would deter as effectively at a cost of less distress.

Punishments which satisfy these conditions have been called *economical deterrents* or punishments that *deter economically*. The usage, of course, does not have to do with the economics, in the sense of financial cost and profit, of punishments.

I shall use the term 'economical deterrent', and speak of

punishments deterring economically. References simply to deterrent punishments and to deterrence are also to be understood as references to economical deterrence. It may be of use to reiterate, in anticipation of later arguments, that punishments may fail to satisfy the given conditions in several ways. If they may cause too much distress to the offender, they may also cause too much to persons other than the offender who are affected by the fact of his punishment. The connection, as we shall see, may be very indirect. It is also to be noticed that the conditions have other consequences. Penalties must be sufficiently severe to deter effectively. It has sometimes been true that offenders regarded the penalties for their offences as like licences: an unavoidable feature of conduct of a certain kind and not so undesirable as to be a deterrent. Such penalties, on the view we are considering, have no justification.

Of the pertinent criticisms of the deterrence view, a vague one advanced by Kant is that to punish a man simply because this will deter him and others from offences in the future is to treat him only as a means and not as an end. This might be taken to refer to several supposed moral errors and it is important to distinguish them.

(1) To treat all men as ends and not merely as means may be to take into account, in any particular situation, the personal welfare of each and every individual involved. We should, that is, consider the interests of each individual affected by a different possible course of action before coming to any decision. Under this interpretation of the rule that all men are to be treated as ends, it is at least arguable that the deterrence theory observes it. According to the theory, certainly, the degree of suffering caused to the offender is relevant to the question of whether or not his punishment is justified.

(2) What may be intended, however, by a critic who employs Kant's rule, is that the deterrence theory does not give *sufficient* attention to the interests of the offender. Such a claim has sometimes been advanced by some of those who argue for a justification of punishment in terms of a supposed reformative function. They suppose that punishment protects the interests of others by reducing the number of offences, and serves the interests of the

offender by reforming him. Punishment is not justified simply by the prevention of offences. We are not yet in a position to assess the claim about means and ends when so interpreted. It amounts to a version of the reform theory.

(3) Sometimes the rule about treating men as ends is at least partly intended to convey the injunction that men are to be treated as responsible moral agents, which they are supposed to be. What is recommended here is a general attitude, difficult to encapsulate, which takes as supremely important the supposed fact that men make free decisions for which they are accountable and which place limits of a certain nature on our treatment of them. This attitude issues naturally in support for the retribution theory of punishment and in particular criticisms of the deterrence theory. These and other criticisms I shall now make clearer and consider in more detail. There is nothing to be gained by retaining Kant's terminology.

The criticisms attempt to display the deterrence theory, even in its reasonable form, as having entirely unacceptable consequences. Unusual and well-worn cases are produced where punishments that may seem *unjustified*, given our ordinary moral convictions, appear to be justified by the principle of economical deterrence. We are asked to suppose, often, that on a particular occasion a judge knows that the man before him is innocent of the offence with which he has been charged. He knows too that there is no possibility of apprehending the actual offender. Finally, he knows that the offence that has been committed will be followed by others of the same kind unless the potential offenders are deterred – unless, that is, someone thought to be guilty is punished for the offence that has been committed. Given all this, we are invited to conclude that the judge would be justified by the stated principle in *pretending* that the man before him was the actual offender and imposing a penalty on him. Why not punish him? This would, we suppose, have the effect of preventing other offences, which would involve more distress than that caused to the innocent man by his punishment. This effect would follow from the belief on the part of others that justice had been done; that the man was not really guilty would be irrelevant to this fact.[12]

In short, if one maintains that punishment is justified by deterrence alone one seems committed to the immorality of punishing the innocent. It seems that one is committed to denying the rule that only the guilty may be punished. Surely, then, the deterrence theory is unacceptable.

The traditional rejoinder to this traditional criticism is that imposing a penalty on an innocent man, first appearances to the contrary, would *not* result in *economical* deterrence. We shall consider this, but let us first look at two more recent attempts to dismiss the criticism summarily. The first amounts to the reminder that the deterrence principle of punishment is about punishment and that it attempts to justify this and nothing else.[13] That is, the principle is about an authority's infliction of distress *on an offender*. The principle, it is said, simply does not apply to the case imagined, where a man known to be wholly innocent is made to suffer. Since the man is not thought to be an offender by the judge it is quite mistaken to suppose that this is a case of punishment. In calling it such, we have been forgetful of the description of punishment given above in the first chapter, one of a kind stipulated by defenders of the deterrence theory. We might better say, although the term may have some misleading connotations, that the imagined case is one of *victimization*. The deterrence principle has nothing to say about victimization. It is not the principle that imposing a penalty on anyone, if it deters economically, is justified. It is that *punishment*, the imposing of a penalty on a man who is an offender, is justified if it deters.

This forceful reply has been thought inadequate by a number of philosophers, although they have not done much to despatch it. We are told, for example, that the given reply prevents us from considering the question of whether the deterrence theory does justify the imprisonment of innocent men. So it does, and for a given reason which must be considered. It is true that the deterrence principle as ordinarily expressed does not appear to commit one to sending innocent men to prison when this would serve the end of deterrence. This seems odd. One expects that it is at least a possibility, if no more, that the deterrence theory has such a consequence. Can it be that the contrary seems true only because the view has been expressed in a particular way? That this is so can be shown.

According to the theory, punishment is justified by the fact that it deters *and for no other reason*. The anticipated result, a state of affairs involving fewer offences, secured at a certain cost of distress, is by itself a sufficient justification. It is not the case that the means to this end, punishment by itself, has any separate and additional justification. The contrary is explicitly said to be true by utilitarian defenders of the theory, for the simple reason that punishment consists in the causing of distress to offenders. Punishment is valuable only as a means to a desirable end. If one keeps these facts in mind, it becomes apparent that the following formulation, '*Punishment* is justified when it deters economically', is misleading as a formulation of the deterrence theory. By referring only to punishment, which necessarily is of offenders, it implies a falsehood. That falsehood is that the deterrence theory taken by itself has some feature such that its holders could not possibly be committed to acts of victimization. There is no such feature. All that is relevantly impossible is that they are committed to acts or practices that do not serve as economical deterrents. The theory can be formulated in a way that overtly excludes this false implication. For all that has been said so far, there can be no objection to expressing it in the following more general way: 'A society's practices or actions in dealing with criminal behaviour are justified if they deter economically.' So expressed, it is at least a possibility that acceptance of the view commits one to victimization in certain circumstances. If it can be established that certain victimizations would deter, and if we accept that such victimizations are not morally justified, the conclusion follows that the view which sanctions them is unacceptable.

This argument may give rise to an uneasiness, one which can be dispelled. It may be thought that there is an arbitrariness about the reformulation of the deterrence theory. Might it not be defensible for a proponent of the theory simply to persist in his own formulation, that *punishment* is justified only by the consideration that it deters economically? This and only this, he says, is what he means. He may do this, but without gain. His intention is to give a justification of punishment but evidently he is bringing to light only part of what he counts as its justification. It is impossible to avoid the conclusion that he regards punishments as justified not only because they deter but because those who suffer them have in fact committed offences. If this were not the case, then certain victimizations too would be acceptable to him. It must be that he refuses to defend them because they lack a feature had by punishments. He has implicitly abandoned a straightforward deterrence account for something else. He can *either* take up a compromise view of the justification of punishment, one which includes some requirement of guilt, and so avoid accepting the possibility of certain justified victimizations, *or* he can take up the deterrence view and accept the possibility of such consequences. Our present concern is with the latter view.

Let us now consider a second attempt to deal summarily with the speculations about victimization to which the critic of the deterrence theory has recourse. One cannot but feel a certain suspicion about the producing of cases where it is claimed that judges, according to the theory, would be committed to secret acts of victimization. The suspicion, misidentified, may issue in the comment that if we are to keep in touch with social realities, something better must be found by way of criticism. What might better be offered, it may be suggested, are descriptions of social practices that might actually be established in the usual way.

Might we have 'an institution . . . which is such that the officials set up by it have authority to arrange a trial for the condemnation of an innocent man whenever they are of the opinion that doing so would be in the best interests of society'?[14] The officials might be judges of the higher courts together with police authorities, the minister of justice, and members of the legislature. But, we are told, when we consider the possibility of such an institution, which would be established by law and a matter of public knowledge, we see that it would involve very great dangers. There would be the possibility of abuse of power and the creation of a general insecurity among members of the society. It cannot seriously be supposed that someone who defends punishment by the argument that it is an economical deterrent would be committed to the institution we have imagined. It is entirely too likely that the losses would exceed the gains.

Such a reply begins from a misconstruction of the traditional objection to the deterrence theory. That objection does not involve, nor need it, the specification of some social institution different from punishment. There is no reason why the objection should proceed by specifying some possible publicly known practice and by arguing that such a practice would have a justification given the deterrence theory. All that is required is that the objection isolate some possible action and relate it to the deterrence theory. The logic of the argument does not require even that the action in question be one by an officer or officers of a society.

We are told by the deterrence theorist that the one and only, and a sufficient, justification of punishment is that it deters economically. There are *no* other justifying features. If so, *any* action or practice which does deter economically must be morally acceptable. If it is not, then a question arises about the claim that punishment is justified *solely* in virtue of being deterrent. The simplicity of the objection reflects the simplicity of the theory. What I am maintaining, then, is that in criticizing the deterrence theory one is in a way free to choose one's counter-examples. One need not initially meet *any* demand but that they be examples involving victimizations which might be of an economical kind. *Reductio ad absurdum* arguments are not essays in social theory.

Certainly this is but the first step of the argument. One must go on to establish that in the examples in question it *would* be true that victimization would prevent more distress than would otherwise occur. The traditional position of those who hold the deterrence theory, to which we now turn, is that this cannot be shown. The suspicion one does feel about the cases in question is that in the end the suggested victimizations would not be economical. This suspicion, we are told, is not merely reasonable but very well founded.

3. The Consequences of Victimization

We have on the one hand defenders of the theory, who have maintained that it does not in fact ever issue in victimization. They agree, however, that victimization would never be morally acceptable. We have on the other hand the critics, who maintain that the theory does, or would in certain circumstances, justify victimization. They declare, of course, that victimization is not and would not ever be morally acceptable. Their reason for the latter belief is that victimizing a man is *treating him in a way that he does not deserve*. As we shall see, both defenders and critics are in error, defenders with respect to both of their propositions, critics in supposing that it is absolutely impossible that a victimization should be morally justified.

Our practice of punishment is taken to be governed by certain rules, such as the rule that the guilty but not the innocent are to be penalized. Other rules are to the effect that offenders of greater culpability are to receive greater penalties. Grievous assault carries a heavier penalty than petty theft, injury that is fully intentional a heavier penalty than inadvertent injury. For the retributivist, as we have seen in some detail, the point of these rules is that they secure that men are treated as they deserve. The rules are taken to comprise a penalty system of the kind whose construction was sketched in the first chapter. To the traditional deterrence theorist their point is quite otherwise. They are rules whose observance secures that we deter economically. To depart from them, in one direction, is to engage in what we have been calling victimization. Victimization, according to the argument, is never justified by the deterrence theory because it is never economically deterrent.

Let us look at the details. With respect to the general rule about punishing only the guilty, one insufficient claim has its origin in the truth that if we are to prevent offences by punishment we must direct our efforts toward the right individuals, those likely to offend in the future. One kind of evidence that a man is likely to break the law in the future is that he has done so already. To act on this evidence in picking out potential offenders is to obey the rule about punishing only the guilty. It may also be added that it is by punishing those who have already performed certain actions that we affirm or reaffirm to others what actions are offences and thus to be avoided. These considerations may serve to give an explanation of why in many cases we should abide by the rule in question. But let us return to the first case of possible victimization mentioned above.

Here, a judge reasonably believes that secretly victimizing an innocent man is necessary if other individuals are to be deterred. We assume he has good grounds for thinking they will commit the offence in question unless they are deterred. Admittedly, there may be no evidence that the defendant needs deterring, but that cannot settle the question. A standard rejoinder by the deterrence theorist is that such an act of victimization is unlikely to have good results on the whole, despite the possibility or even the certainty that sentencing the man might in the short term deter a number of potential offenders. Sentencing the man would be to take an exceedingly dangerous step, one whose distant consequences are all too unpredictable. It *might* happen that one victimization would lead to others, and it might become *known* that innocent men were being penalized for offences committed by men never apprehended. It might then be supposed that actual offenders escaped punishment with considerable regularity. One upshot would be that potential offenders of all kinds would cease to be deterred to the same extent as before by the possibility of punishment. A man is the less deterred the less certain it seems that he will be punished for an offence.

Another result, one of several, might be that the law would be brought into disrespect. This claim, never long forgotten in this context by defenders of deterrence, is in part that people respect the law because they believe it deals fairly with individuals. This respect would be lessened by a belief in the existence of victimizations. Who can say what the consequences of such a lesser respect for the law might be? All these are no more than speculations, certainly. But who, we are asked, could be reasonably certain that developments of this sort would *not* follow from the judge's action in breaking the rule that only the guilty are to be punished? If one could not be reasonably certain, one could not accept that such

an action would in the end make for economical deterrence. This
is little more than a sketch for an argument, obviously; the processes by which victimization might issue in the supposed consequences would be complex.

Let us suspend judgement for a time and consider something
else. Penalizing the wholly innocent is but one possible kind of
victimization. Other kinds involve infractions of the other rules
of punishment. These can be divided, artificially, into two groups,
and we shall concentrate on the second. There are the rules which
preserve heavier penalties for offences involving greater harms, for
example, grievous assault against petty theft. Here, the deterrence
theorist explains, economy is obviously the justification and
infractions of the rules would be uneconomical and hence not
justified by his theory. The other rules, which may be roughly
described as having to do with the responsibility of agents, have
been divided into three kinds.[15] There are those, first, which allow
that in certain circumstances a man is *justified* in a kind of action
which in other circumstances would be criminal, and so is not to
be punished at all. Killing in self-defence is sometimes an example.
Secondly, there are rules which specify that a man is to be *excused*
in certain circumstances and not punished at all. He may be
excused if his action was in some way quite involuntary or unintentional. Finally, there are rules specifying that a man's punishment is to be *mitigated* under certain circumstances. If he can
establish, for example, that he was subjected to extreme provocation, he may receive a lesser penalty. In choosing the particular
penalty from the range fixed by statute for offences of the kind in
question, a judge is to take into account provocation.

The explanation and justification of these three kinds of rules,
according to the deterrence theorist, is also that observing them
serves the end of economical deterrence. Their explanation and
justification has nothing to do with desert. Breaking the rules
would not be sanctioned by his theory.

A man who injures another in self-defence on one occasion
gives no evidence that he is likely to injure others again unless he
must do so to defend himself. He is no more a danger to the community than most other men. If it does happen that he is attacked

again, then he will be justified in defending himself: we do not take the view that he should be deterred from doing so. The same is true of anyone else who is attacked. Thus there would be no point whatever, on the deterrence view, in punishing the man on this occasion. In general, to follow rules of justification is to act in accordance with the principle of deterrence. Somewhat similar considerations apply to actions covered by rules of excuse. A man who injures another by an entirely unlikely accident gives no indication of being a generally dangerous character. Nor would punishment on this occasion prevent either him or others, obviously, from causing accidental injuries in the future. There is no point in punishment, given the deterrence view, where rules of excuse apply.

As for the rule of mitigation having to do with provocation, a man who retaliates only under extreme provocation is unlikely to offend again, since extreme provocations are few. There is some possibility, nevertheless, that he will be provoked in the same way again. What is required to make it likely that he will resist this future provocation, if it occurs, is no more than a lighter penalty on the present occasion. We suppose, that is, that a man who has resisted a good deal of provocation before succumbing on the first occasion will need only a slight additional motive derived from a relatively mild punishment in order to resist a bit more in the future. Thus there is no need for a heavier penalty on the first occasion: it would be wrong to impose it since it would cause more distress than is necessary. One can present much the same argument, such as it is, with respect to other potential offenders, who must also be considered. One supposes that they are unlikely to be subjected to such a provocation. In general, the danger is small. If they are so provoked, one supposes that they will be deterred from giving in if they have been influenced by no more than the example of a relatively mild punishment. If we are to deter economically, then, we must not victimize by breaking rules of extenuation.

Such considerations go some way to showing that abiding by rules of the three kinds is in accord with the deterrence theory. Nevertheless, they have a general and considerable weakness.[16] Consider the argument that observing a rule about provocation is a necessity if we are to deter economically. It hangs together, or appears to, only because certain of the future possibilities and not others are considered. This can be brought out by way of a model. Brown injures a man who has provoked him by harming his dog. Brown's penalty is reduced, according to the deterrence argument, partly because there is little danger of his offending again. People are unlikely, we suppose, to be after his dog very often, or to be doing things that are similarly provocative. We suppose, furthermore, that Brown will not need very much by way of a new motive to keep him from repeating his offence *if the same sort of occasion arises again.* Looking to other possible offenders, they are unlikely to be provoked to the same extent in the future, since such provocations are relatively rare. If they are so provoked, they will not succumb to the provocation if they know Brown has been lightly penalized – *if, that is, they are as self-controlled as Brown.* But what if we look to other possibilities in the future? What if Brown's dog is harmed *and*, true to form, his flowers are trampled? Perhaps he would resist the temptation to retaliate by inflicting a serious injury if in the past he had been given a heavier rather than a lighter penalty for injuring someone who kicked his dog. What of other potential offenders who are not as self-controlled as Brown? Suppose one of them was to see his dog being harmed or was provoked to about the same extent. Perhaps he would retaliate even if he knew Brown had been given a relatively light penalty but would not do so if he knew Brown had been given a heavier one.

When we consider such possibilities, and there is no reason for ignoring them, it is not at all clear that sticking to the rule of mitigation in question is called for by considerations of economical deterrence. Indeed, it seems that the principle in question might demand infractions of the rule. It is equally arguable that if deterrence is our only guide we might be committed to breaking rules of excuse, to punishing a man who injured another by accident. Our severity might well have the effect of preventing possible offences in the future. It might serve to prevent intentional offences and to make avoidable accidents more rare. Something of the same sort may be argued in connection with some offences covered by rules of justification.

Are there effective rejoinders to argument of this kind? In the case of the first imagined rule-infraction, that of penalizing a wholly innocent man, it was open to the defenders of the deterrence view to argue that such a victimization might in the long run issue in more rather than fewer offences. Our present cases are different. We suppose, for example, that a judge believes on good grounds that potential offenders will be deterred only if he makes a striking example of a man, which involves breaking the rule about mitigation. Here it is not so open to holders of the deterrence view to suggest that the outcome, in the long term, may be more rather than fewer offences. We cannot readily suppose that if the judge's action becomes known, potential offenders will be the less deterred. On the contrary, they may be more deterred by the fact of the judge's rule-infraction. However, we may still worry about the possibility of disrespect for the law.

There is also another argument to which the deterrence theorist can retreat. Rules of excuse and mitigation, aside from those of them having to do with certain special classes of offenders such as children, have the effect of excusing, wholly or partly, actions that are less than wholly voluntary or deliberate. This means that to a considerable extent the possibility of a man's being penalized, or heavily penalized, depends on his deliberate and voluntary actions, those over which he has control. He thus can be reasonably confident, if he wishes to be, that his life will not be disrupted by judges. Precisely this security would be endangered if the rules of excuse in particular were sometimes suspended. The danger, although distant, would exist. It *could* come about that a man could no longer be reasonably confident of an undisrupted existence if his intention was to obey the law. Accidents happen. It can thus be argued that while breaking the rules of excuse and mitigation might sometimes have a greater deterrent effect than keeping them, the cost in anxiety or something like it which might result from breaking them would outweigh the profit.

(Such an argument, which is also relevant to our earlier case of a wholly innocent man, is open to anyone who takes up the position that punishment is justified when it deters economically, although it has sometimes been suggested otherwise. It has been supposed, perhaps, that anyone who makes use of it must be appealing to retributivist considerations. It has been supposed that the argument is rooted in a principle of justice or fair play. Quite obviously, an argument *could* be presented which would begin from the premiss that each man should get what he deserves and proceed to the conclusion that the rules ought to be observed. This is quite distinct from what has been presented.[17])

Despite everything that has been said on behalf of the deterrence theory, however, it seems that in the end a certain admission is necessary. It is that we can at least *conceive* of a case of a very special nature where a judge would be committed by the deterrence principle to an act of victimization. It can be one involving a wholly innocent man or one involving a disregard for the rules of justice we have been discussing. Indeed, the conceivability of such a case has occasionally been allowed by deterrence theorists. All that we require is an imagined case which has such peculiar features as to rule out the possibility of all the long-term dangers we have considered. In this case, for example, there will for some reason be no possibility of its becoming known that a man has been victimized.

If the conceivability of such a case has occasionally been admitted, it has also been maintained that it is entirely unlikely that there will ever be an *actual* case which satisfies the imagined conditions. This latter fact has then been used in an attempt to escape the argument. We are told that

... if one considers ... fantastic situations ... one does of course consider them as a person with certain moral sentiments, the strength of which, in society as it is, is an important Utilitarian good. These sentiments are offended. A Utilitarian will see no point in trying to imagine oneself looking with approval on the imaginary situation, since this is likely to weaken the feelings while not serving as a preparation for any actual situation. If in fact punishing the innocent (say) always is and always will be harmful, it is likewise harmful to dwell on fanciful situations in which it would be beneficial, thus weakening one's aversion to such courses. Thus the Utilitarian shares (quite consistently so) in the unease produced by these examples. Although he may admit that in such a situation punishment of the innocent would be right, he still regards favourably the distaste which is aroused at the idea of its being called right.

Certainly if one imagines the world as other than it is, one may find oneself imagining a world in which Utilitarianism implies moral judgements which shock our moral sentiments. But if these moral sentiments are quite appropriate to the only world there is, the real world, the Utilitarian is glad that moral judgements in opposition to them seem repugnant. He sees no need for moral acrobatics relevant only to situations which in fact are quite out of the question.[18]

The objection to the deterrence theory that we are considering involves three considerations which I shall state in order to comment on the quoted rejoinder. They are:

(1) the proposition that in a certain conceivable case victimization would deter economically,
(2) the consequence that such a victimization would be called for and justified by the principle of economical deterrence,
(3) the acceptance that such a victimization would not be morally acceptable.

How does the argument in the quoted passage function? Does it attempt to call into question (1), (2), or (3)? One might think, confusedly, that (1) is the object of the argument. But it is not being maintained that in such a case victimization would not deter economically. It is simply being claimed that to *accept now* that such a victimization would deter economically may have bad effects. Given a commitment to the deterrence theory, one would have to accept that the imagined victimization would be right. Accepting this, it is supposed, might weaken one's general aversion to victimization, which aversion is perfectly in place with respect to actual cases. The speculation may be that one might be led not to disapprove of victimizations in actual cases, where they are not economical.

We can accept all this without comment. It leaves undisturbed the hypothesis that in a conceivable case the action of victimizing a man would deter economically. We can suppose, if with reservations, that a utilitarian judge who contemplates our conceivable case comes thereby to approve of or to bring about victimizations that do not deter economically. This does not matter; we can still conceive of the case we want.

Can it then be that the argument is intended to falsify (2), that the principle of economical deterrence would justify the conceivable victimization? The argument cannot possibly succeed in showing this to be false. There is a logical connection between the principle, the specification of the case, and a conclusion that victimization would be justified by the principle. Finally, can it be supposed that the argument is aimed at (3), that the imagined victimization would be wrong? On the contrary, it is accepted that the victimization in question would be without moral justification.

There is one further possibility. It might be thought that while the argument does not disturb any of (1), (2), or (3), there is implicit in it another forceful criticism. Is the objection to the deterrence theory in a way toothless? All that it establishes, it might be said, is that in a case which is unlikely ever to obtain the principle of deterrence would give us a consequence we regard as unacceptable. This, it may be said, should not trouble us. The principle remains acceptable, for all that has been said, for the real world, and that is what we are concerned with.

The reply is that we are indeed concerned with the real world and in particular with our practice of punishment. The objection against the deterrence theory, involving a merely conceivable case, appears to tell us something about a possible justification of that practice. It is that the practice cannot be justified by considerations of economical deterrence alone. We have been offered the principle that our practice has no justification whatever other than that it deters potential offenders at a certain cost of distress. This by itself, none the less, is said to be sufficient. *If* this were true, then a certain conceivable case of victimization would be justified. If we do not accept this, and *do* accept that punishment may be justified, then it must have more to recommend it than merely that it deters economically. It should be clear that the fact that this argument rests on a conceivable rather than a likely or an actual case is of no importance. What is important is the specification of the case and the moral view that is taken of it.

4. Necessary Distinctions

We have now surveyed, in something like its own terms, a persistent dispute. Sadly enough, it ignores certain very relevant facts. As has been pointed out,[19] we already *have* within the law what are regarded by many as *justified* victimizations. We *have* departures from rules of excuse and mitigation. Precisely what is true of a defendant charged under a strict-liability statute is that he is *not* excused because he did not intend to commit an offence and was not careless. The shopkeeper who sells adulterated milk, in complete ignorance of the fact and despite having taken reasonable care to avoid doing so, cannot offer this as a defence. The rationale that is given for this, of course, is that the dangers of adulteration are so considerable that they must be avoided even at the cost of certain victimizations. Some of those who regard rules of excuse as essentially rules for securing that men get their deserts and only their deserts would claim that the dangers are so considerable that they must be avoided at the cost of treating some men in a way that they do not deserve. Convictions where defendants are vicariously liable are defended in the same and other ways.

Quite as important, we are familiar with victimizations where strict and vicarious liability are not in question. They are, indeed, absolutely common. Defendants who have been found guilty of certain offences are given penalties which judges announce to be 'exemplary' ones, penalties calculated to satisfy what is taken to be a considerable need for deterrence. In England cases involving train robbers and espionage agents provide outstanding examples. More everyday examples result from the theft of coins from telephone kiosks and acts of physical assault. It would be a work of benighted piety to argue that the penalties which are imposed are in general precisely those called for by the rules of justice ordinarily thought to govern our practice of punishment.

I wish, at the moment, to say two things about these facts. The first is that it is arguable that we do here have *actual* victimizations which deter economically. The last persuasive objection to their being such cases, it may be recalled, was that victimizations would give rise to a general insecurity and anxiety which would make them, in the end, uneconomical. This has not been the effect of the creation of offences of strict and vicarious liability. Nor has it been an effect of exemplary penalties. The second thing to be said, although I wish to put off a final consideration of strict and vicarious liability, and also exemplary penalties, is that it is arguable that these victimizations do have a moral justification. With respect to exemplary penalties, it is at least sometimes true that they are not much greater than the penalties that would be imposed given a strict adherence to the rules. Also, the need for deterrence may be regarded as substantial. Many of the penalties imposed under statutes of strict and vicarious liability are relatively small ones, or relatively easily borne by the defendants. As I have said, the dangers to be avoided may be regarded as great.

Given these circumstances, obviously, the argument about the deterrence theory must take a different form. The defenders of the theory need not labour to maintain that any conceivable victimization would be uneconomical. If certain victimizations would be economical, *but also* have a moral justification, they constitute no objection to the deterrence theory. Critics of the theory, on the other hand, must do more than show that certain victimizations would be economical. They must establish (as we so far have not) that these lack moral justification. Is it possible to produce such cases?

We can proceed to an answer by seeing more clearly what it is that makes certain victimizations at least possibly justified. With respect to at least some strict-liability offences, it can be said that there exists a great danger to *each* of a considerable number of individuals. Offences of selling decayed foods are an example. Also, the penalty imposed on the shopkeeper is certainly such as to cause him less distress than would be caused to each of a number of individuals if they were poisoned. When a man is given an exemplary penalty, once again, it can be argued that there exists a great danger to each of a considerable number of individuals. Also, it may be argued, the additional distress caused to the offender, over and above what he may be said to deserve, is usually relatively small.

There is also something else to be kept in mind. It is not essential that for a possibly justified victimization the penalty in question must be a relatively small one. Utilitarians in their zeal to avoid the traditional objection to the deterrence theory have not seen one clear possibility of defence. In that objection, as we have seen, it is vaguely said that in a certain case a judge would be justified in the secret victimization of an innocent man. Instead of hurrying to reply that this would be uneconomical in the long run, one might reasonably demand a further specification of the case. Is it one where the judge may literally be said to *know* that a considerable number of offences will be committed unless there is a deterring example? Is it certain too that nothing else would work? The answers must be in the affirmative, it may be said, if the objection is to be coercive. Let us also suppose that the penalty imposed on the innocent man would cause him extreme distress, and something like the same distress as would be caused to each of the victims if the potential offenders were not deterred. If *this* is what we are to consider, we have a situation in which there exists a choice between very considerable distress for one innocent individual or roughly the same distress for each of a considerable number of innocent individuals. The commendable response of most people, given such a situation, is to look for some other option. *If* there is no other option, however, it seems undeniable that the victimization of the defendant would be morally preferable. We have not got an economical victimization that is morally indefensible.

What brings us, however unwillingly, to admit the possibility of justification in all these cases is that (a) there is a considerable danger to *each* of a group of individuals to be avoided, and (b) the distress that would be caused to the victimized individual is relatively small or no greater than that which would be caused, if there were no victimization, to each of the group of individuals.

Obviously we *can* conceive of a case without these saving features, a case of grossly unequal treatment. It will be one where there is a great danger to be avoided, and which can be avoided *only* by a victimization involving very great distress to the individual in question. Most important, it will be one where the distress that would occur, without the victimization, would be *widely spread*. That is, the great danger in question is that *each* of *very many* people would suffer relatively little. In total, which is all that is important given the deterrence view, the distress would be such as to make the victimization, despite its severity, economical. Here it is not an arguable proposition that the victimization would be morally tolerable. We do not think that an extreme imposition of distress on one individual is tolerable if the alternative distress for others, however great in total, is for any particular individual bearable. We are governed in this, clearly enough, by a principle of equality. Given that distress is inevitable, and that all the individuals in question are equally vulnerable or undeserving, we choose that distribution which most closely approximates to an equal one. In our present case, that distribution is the one which involves no distress for the single individual in question, the defendant, and not a great deal for anyone else. What remains is to see what final conclusion can be drawn from this sequence of argument.

We do have a case of economical victimization, it seems, which would not be regarded as morally justified. It must then be that punishment if justified has some recommendation other than that it deters economically. That recommendation, obviously, is that it excludes the possibility of a kind of grossly unequal treatment. We may conclude that any acceptable justification of punishment must rest in part on its being *deserved*, in a somewhat unusual but not unreasonable use of the term where it means no more than that the practice does exclude grossly unequal treatment.[20]

Many objectors to the deterrence theory are likely at this point to want to argue for a more general conclusion: that punishment is partly justified because it is deserved in the sense defined above in the first chapter. There we supposed in the end that to say a man deserves a penalty is to say (1) he has behaved culpably, (2) his penalty will give satisfactions equivalent to the grievance he has caused, (3) it will be similar to those imposed on other offenders who have caused similar grievances, (4) he was responsible for his action and knew of the possible consequences under a system of offences and penalties, and (5) unlike non-offenders he had gained satisfactions attendant on the commission of an offence. Let us consider this.

5. *Comparisons*

We might to do so by considering directly the proposition that we are opposed to the victimization because the victim does not deserve a penalty, in the sense of the words defined by way of the five propositions just mentioned. He did not behave culpably, and so on. That the victim does not deserve the penalty in this sense, it might be said, mainly explains our opposition. That some offenders *do* in this way deserve penalties, it might be said, contributes to the justification of punishment.

In order to gain a certain expositional advantage in considering this matter, let us follow a somewhat different procedure. We have until now followed a traditional line by considering cases of victimization where it is supposed that there is no possibility of securing a similar deterrent effect by punishment. Why not consider situations in which there is a choice between punishment and victimization? It seems indubitable that if we were to have a choice between a punishment and a certain victimization, each being thought likely to deter to the same extent, we would prefer the punishment. Why is this true?

. Is it to be explained, more adequately than in the traditional utilitarian arguments, by the fact that the punishment would be more economical? Perhaps there are better arguments of the same general character. Is it to be explained, rather, by the claim that the punishment would be, in our full sense, deserved? *To what extent is this latter claim distinct from the claim that punishment would be more economical?* In order to answer these questions, and in particular the last one, I should like now to attempt the further analysis of arguments about desert which was promised in the first chapter. Such a further analysis is now possible or at any rate easier since it depends in part on utilitarian considerations with which we are now familiar.

It is worth while and perhaps essential to imagine a case in which one's responses would be the stronger and clearer for reasons of personal involvement.[21] The dangers are obvious enough to be avoidable. If a friend were the victim I would in opposing his victimization certainly assert that it was undeserved. I would mean in part, according to our account of desert, that he had not acted culpably. He did not cause a harm by an action for which he could be held responsible. Would this constitute a moral objection? On what feelings would this part of my claim rest? The answer can be anticipated from what was said in the second chapter. The claim would rest, it seems, on feelings which derive from something like instinctual responses both to injury inflicted on oneself and injury inflicted on others.[22] It seems undeniable that we share such responses. Furthermore, when there is no question of someone's having inflicted injury, of being an assailant, it is not that we have *no* related feelings about he himself being injured. It is rather that we feel an opposition to his being injured, one which derives from the desire to retaliate against actual assailants. A good deal might be said of a psychological nature in explanation of these facts. More relevant is the question of whether these feelings can be regarded as giving rise to a moral claim. It seems to me that they cannot. It approaches certainty that the retaliatory response to assailants cannot be regarded as generating a moral argument. (I have such responses when it would generally be granted that my assailant is in the right and I am in the wrong.) My inclination is to take a similar view of those *related* attitudes to individuals *which depend entirely on their not being assailants.*

Could I reasonably intend, secondly, in saying that the victimization would not be deserved, that it would not give satisfactions equivalent to *the grievance caused by the victim*? Assuming that the victim did not commit an offence at all, there is no such grievance: that is, one caused by him. None the less, a grievance exists, the one caused by whoever did commit the offence in question. *This* grievance might indeed be satisfied by the victimization, if the individuals who feel it take the victim to have been the offender. It seems, then, that in opposing the suggested victimization I *cannot* say that it is undeserved where this means it would not provide certain satisfactions.

Consider now the third contention that might be contained in the judgement that the victim would not deserve the penalty: if he were imprisoned he would be being treated in a way different from the way in which other non-offenders are treated. Why do I resist this? Let us suppose that neither in this victimization nor in the possible punishment would the distress caused to the victim or offender be considerably greater than that caused to each of the victims of future offences in the absence of a deterring effect. We do not have a case, as before, of what was called grossly unequal treatment.

My resistance to the victimization, nonetheless, in so far as I am thinking of unlike treatment, is clearly based in part on *a* consideration of equality. My friend is being treated differently from, and worse than, other non-offenders. There is not much that can be said, or needs to be said, in explanation. It is surely clear, however, that my resistance is also based on the following facts. As a consequence of the general truth that apprehended offenders are treated as they are, and non-offenders left to go about their lives, members of each class have certain expectations or regard certain things as possibilities. The non-offender in question, in being treated as offenders are treated, would be subjected to a special distress: shock, frustration, continuing apprehension. He would, as a consequence of his expectations as a non-offender, be subjected to a particular distress that would not be experienced by the offender if he were punished. Certain other things being equal, he would experience a greater distress. What we can conclude, I suggest, is that in opposing the victimization on the ground that it would not be deserved, I would in part be opposing it as *uneconomical* when compared with the punishment. *In part, I suggest, arguments from desert dissolve into arguments to the effect that deterrent punishments should cause as little distress as possible.*

Fourthly, I should have in mind in opposing the victimization that the victim was not responsible for the commission of an offence, that he did not knowingly choose one of two options offered to him by society. What would make this a reason against the victimization? *It seems to me that it is a reason simply in virtue of the existence of certain expectations. The victim acted in accordance with the law and as a result had certain normal anticipations. To treat him as if he had broken the law would give rise to special distress.* Before saying more of this explanation, which is likely to give rise to resistance, I should like to complete the particular inquiry in which we are engaged.

In opposing the victimization as undeserved, I could be taken to be maintaining, lastly, that the victim did not gain satisfactions attendant on the commission of an offence. That is, he did not disrupt any state of equality of satisfactions by committing an offence. The difficulty about this argument, as may be anticipated on the basis of what has already been said, has to do with the assumption of states of equality. It is perfectly possible that if we took into account the actual lives of members of the given society, the victimization *would* have an equalizing effect.

I take it that what is likely to be most resisted is my suggestion about the fourth element of the desert argument. Can it be that in opposing the victimization on the ground that the victim did not perform such an action, was not responsible for such an action, one can only be arguing that the punishment would for a particular reason cause less distress?

Consider another case, and another choice with which we might be faced. It is again between a victimization and a punishment but here it is strictly true that each would cause the same distress to the individual involved. The victim, we suppose, would undergo a distress consequent on his having had certain expectations. However, because the offender is somehow more vulnerable, offender and victim would experience about the same distress. We shall also assume, of course, that the distress caused to others in the two cases, perhaps family dependants, would be roughly the same, and that punishment and victimization can be taken as equally effective with respect to the prevention of offences in the future.

It remains true, I think, that one's immediate response is that the punishment would be preferable. It is also unquestionable that many people would defend this preference by saying that the offender deserves and the victim does not deserve a penalty. One can readily imagine someone going on to explain: 'The victim simply did not do what the offender did. There is an immense difference between his past conduct, which was lawful as a consequence of a decision or resolve of his, and the conduct of the offender, who did make a choice or decision to break the law. Either of them could have broken the law and one did not.'The point in this imagined case is that the offender has freely contributed to the situation in which he finds himself and the victim hasn't.'

This crucial case leaves me in some small doubt. We have it urged that *the fact alone* that the offender unlike the victim 'freely contributed to his situation' is of moral relevance. It is difficult to see what this relevance can be. One cannot but suspect that the objector is in one way or another so construing the case as to change it. He may, out of a kind of rooted habit, be persisting in the generally justified supposition that victims suffer more than offenders. He may have in mind some factor of a utilitarian kind so far unmentioned. He may have in mind that the victimization will involve a lying imputation of guilt. This lie, of course, is likely to bring a particular distress to the victim. *However, our case necessarily involves taking into account all such factors.* Given all of them, it remains true that for other reasons the victim would experience no more distress than the offender. It is important, particularly so at this fundamental level of moral reflection, to enter imaginatively into this supposition. To do so, perhaps, one must have in mind features which might explain the unusual vulnerability of the offender. One must not tacitly suppress consideration of him and his situation.

If one takes the case precisely as intended, can it really be argued that the offender's choosing to offend is itself a fact of moral relevance? I cannot see that it is. One may have considerably different attitudes to offender and victim, but they seem not to issue in specifiable moral reasons for action. If they were of such a kind as to do so, one would expect greater resistance than one actually gets to someone's saying that a victimization is preferable in a closely related case, the last one we shall consider. I have in mind a choice between victimization and punishment where, all things considered, the victim would experience somewhat *less* distress than the offender. Let me spell this out. Suppose Brown, who did nothing, would suffer less distress from a penalty than Green, who actually did commit the offence. Someone argues that Brown should be penalized and shows that the situation is otherwise as in the previous case: the deterrent effect would be the same, the effect on secondary parties the same. He also makes very real for us the greater distress that Green would experience if he were penalized. I suggest that our resistance to his recommendation, that Brown be penalized, would be greater than it is likely to be if in fact we did attach moral relevance to past actions by responsible agents, taken by themselves. That our resistance would be low indicates that we do not feel this way about past actions. However, I shall reconsider the question in chapter six, where it arises again.

My general conclusions about the deterrence theory are these.

(1) Since, as we saw at the beginning of this chapter, there are classes of offenders who are not deterred by the prospect of punishment, it cannot be acceptable that a society should attempt to prevent all offences by punishment. If deterrence is an essential part of a justified punishment, then certain offenders must not be punished.

(2) Punishment cannot be justified by the argument alone that it is economically deterrent. If this and this alone were a sufficient justification, then the grossly unfair victimization described in the previous section would also be acceptable. This conclusion is not affected if we take into account what we have tended to ignore, that punishment may *incapacitate* a potential offender.

(3) In anticipation of the discussion to come, we can say that punishment *may* be justified by being both economically deterrent and also deserved. To defend it as deserved, however, is in good part to reiterate the claim that it is economical of distress. For the rest, as several of our conclusions suggest, it is to argue from a premiss about equality.

6. *Rule-Utilitarianism*

The deterrence theory of punishment is a logical consequence of the morality of utilitarianism. In rejecting it we reject that morality as well, one which may be cursorily expressed as the principle that *an act is right or justified if it is likely to produce the best welfare-consequences: more satisfaction or at least less distress than any other act that might be performed instead.* There is another morality, supposed to have been intended by Mill,[23] which is regarded as a form of utilitarianism. It is labelled rule-utilitarianism and it would be claimed that it issues in a theory of punishment which does not justify the unacceptable victimization we have imagined. Furthermore, the punishment theory in question is apparently regarded by some philosophers as that of economical deterrence. If it *is* the deterrence theory, and it does not justify the victimization, then the argument of this chapter must be mistaken.

. Rule-utilitarianism may be expressed as the principle that *a particular action is right or justified if it is according to a rule which itself has a utilitarian justification, even if the action is likely to produce less satisfaction or more distress than some other action that is possible.*[24] The principle is a result, in part, of reflection on punishment. Traditional utilitarianism, as we have seen, was thought to issue via the deterrence theory in the justification of certain victimizations, infractions of the rules of punishment. Victimizations were assumed always to be morally mistaken, and utilitarianism thus to be in question. Rule-utilitarianism has been regarded as a satisfactory alternative by those of the opinion that the rightness of conduct has to do only with the maximization of satisfactions and the minimization of distress. The rules of punishment were taken to have utilitarian justifications and therefore, given the new doctrine, to be inviolable.

I wish to maintain two things, both of which seem obvious. Rule-utilitarianism is not a utilitarianism at all if one regards utilitarian moralities as those which have to do solely with satisfaction and distress, their maximization and minimization. Secondly, the theories of punishment in which it can issue do not include the theory of deterrence.

Rule-utilitarianism is expressed, very vaguely, as the view that an action is right if it is according to a rule *which itself has a utilitarian justification*. What does this mean? What is it that justifies us in taking up a particular rule as something to follow even if doing so on a particular occasion will result in less satisfaction or more distress than is necessary? Let us have in mind that rule or principle of equality which is infringed in the extreme case of victimization where the victim's distress would be far greater than any distress to any particular individual if there were no victimization.

Can it be that we are to accept this rule because *usually* or *almost always* following it has the effect of producing more satisfaction or less distress? We can assume this to be true. It clearly does not provide a sufficient reason for accepting that we should *never* break the rule. Given *this* reason, it seems that we should *not* keep the rule on those occasions when breaking it would have the best welfare-consequences. Can it then be that we are to accept the rule because following it *always* has the best welfare-consequences? We know this isn't true. Indeed, the belief that certain victimizations would have the best welfare-consequences was precisely a reason for taking up rule-utilitarianism.

These are the only possible grounds, in terms of best welfare-consequences alone, for adopting the rule in question. Neither is satisfactory. Whatever the ground for taking up the rule as always binding, it must involve more than a commitment to maximizing satisfaction or minimizing distress. It may involve, obviously, some fundamental commitment to equality. Also, of course, if the ensuing theory of punishment does involve an embargo on breaking the rule in question, it is not the deterrence theory. It is an attempt to justify punishment by reference to several values taken together. It is a compromise theory, to be considered in due course.

1. See Bentham, 'Principles of Penal Law', p. 383, in *The Works of Jeremy Bentham*, volume one, edited by John Bowring.
2. op cit., p. 396.
3. A more extended discussion may be found, for example, in Nigel Walker, *Crime and Punishment in Britain* (Edinburgh, 1965), chapter twelve.

4. Criminal Statistics for 1966 (Home Office, London). Difficulties in the use of criminal statistics, which I do not consider, are excellently surveyed in Barbara Wootton, *Social Science and Social Pathology* (London, 1959), chapter one.

5. Howard Jones, *Crime and the Penal System* (London, 1956), p. 140.

6. See Wootton, op. cit., chapter five.

7. Jones, op. cit., pp. 141–2.

8. See for example J. C. Flugel, *Man, Morals and Society* (London, 1955), p. 208.

9. A. C. Ewing, *The Morality of Punishment* (London, 1929), p. 52.

10. K. G. Armstrong, 'The Retributivist Hits Back', *Mind*, 1961.

11. Bentham, op. cit., p. 397.

12. 'In point of utility apparent justice is everything, real justice, abstractedly from apparent justice, is a useless abstraction, not worth pursuing and, supposing it contrary to apparent justice, such as ought not to be pursued.' Bentham, 'Principles of Judicial Procedure', *Works*, volume two, p. 21.

13. Anthony Quinton, 'On Punishment', *Analysis*, 1954. For a view similar in some respects see John Rawls, 'Two Concepts of Rules', *Philosophical Review*, 1955. See also S. I. Benn, 'An Approach to the Problems of Punishment', *Philosophy*, 1958, and Benn and R. S. Peters, *Social Principles and the Democratic State* (London, 1959), pp. 182–3.

14. Rawls, op. cit., p. 11. The argument I am considering is combined with several others in this paper. I treat of them separately.

15. H. L. A. Hart, 'Prolegomenon to the Principles of Punishment', *Proceedings of the Aristotelian Society*, 1959–60. See also Richard Brandt, *Ethical Theory* (Englewood Cliffs, New Jersey, 1959), chapter nineteen. Notice, incidentally, that the kinds of victimization now in question (as against penalizing the wholly innocent) also count as punishments.

16. See also Hart, op. cit.

17. Hart, op. cit., argues that it is impossible to explain the rules of excuse and mitigation by reference to deterrence and then goes on to explain them by the consideration, for example, that they increase 'the power of individuals to identify beforehand periods when the law's punishment will not interfere with them . . .'

18. T. L. S. Sprigge, 'A Utilitarian Reply to Dr. McCloskey', *Inquiry*, 1965, p. 274.

19. First, to philosophers, by Hart, op. cit.

20. As has has been pointed out by a reviewer, the conclusion might have been based, just as well, on a conceivable *punishment*.

21. Cf. R. M. Hare, *Freedom and Reason*, especially chapter six.

22. Cf. John Stuart Mill, *Utilitarianism*, chapter five.

23. See J. O. Urmson, 'The Interpretation of the Moral Philosophy of J. S. Mill', *Philosophical Quarterly*, 1953.

24. It is true, certainly, that traditional utilitarianism also makes use, rather puzzling use, of rules. What is certain is that the rules are guides and we are not enjoined to stick to them in all cases, no matter the consequences. For discussions of rule-utilitarianism see Urmson, op. cit.; J. Rawls, 'Two Concepts of Rules', *Philosophical Review*, 1955; J. J. C. Smart, 'Extreme and Restricted Utilitarianism', *Philosophical Quarterly*, 1956; H. J. McCloskey, 'An Examination of Restricted Utilitarianism', *Philosophical Review*, 1957. Richard Brandt presents a justification of punishment in terms of rule-utilitarianism in *Ethical Theory* (Englewood Cliffs, New Jersey, 1969), chapter nineteen.

CHAPTER FOUR: REFORM

1. Punishment as Reformative

There are a number of views which recommend particular practices for dealing with criminality on the grounds that they would reform offenders, or improve or help or 'socialize' them, and thereby reduce offences. Too often these doctrines are ill-defined or presented as group-orthodoxies beyond the need for explanation. They differ very considerably in character and assumptions. The traditional ones, but certainly not their successors, can be described as recommending the inculcation of moral principles. Some of them are so much concerned with the state of the offender as to give little attention to the prevention of offences. All of them, for different reasons, include rejections of retribution and deterrence.

Of those to be mentioned here the first two recommend the practice of punishment while the others, which conceive of criminality as disorder or disability, recommend some practice of treatment. I shall have relatively little to say of any of them, partly for the reason that they are in a certain respect similar to the deterrence theory and so open to a familiar objection. The following chapter, however, is given over to consideration of the dogmas of freedom and determinism and determinism enters into conceptions of criminality as disorder or disability requiring treatment.

'Punishment,' it might be said, 'is justified because it provides an opportunity for us to take steps to reform offenders and so to reduce offences.' It seems unlikely that anyone has ever believed punishment to be justified *solely* by the supposed fact that imprisoned men are morally improved and made law-abiding by chapel services, exhortatory chats, and regimens designed to build character. There has been a certain amount of faith in such things but those who have had it have been inclined to defend punishment by such other beliefs as that it is deserved. If one takes this first possible reformative doctrine by itself, it is open to immediate dismissal. It is impossible to have anything remotely like conviction about the supposition that men are reformed by traditional ministrations and so become law-abiding. Furthermore, the conclusion which is drawn requires another premiss, which is indubitably false.

What we are told is that certain steps may be taken which reform men and make them law-abiding, and the conclusion is drawn that punishment is justified because it enables us to take these steps. What also needs to be established, of course, is the additional premiss that *only* punishment would give us the opportunity, or the best opportunity. This is false. It may be admitted that some form of control or restraint would be necessary if we were to attempt reformation in the suggested ways. This is not to say that we would have to *punish*. Punishment is a practice which aims to cause distress. A practice which does not have this feature is not punishment. This difficulty is avoided by the second doctrine we shall consider, one of greater familiarity.[1]

Here, it is punishment itself which is claimed to have a reformative effect. It is said to have this effect in three indirect ways. It deters men from breaking the law, and thus they are inclined to become habitually law-abiding. They do obey the law, but not from 'moral motives'. However, they are said to be more likely to advance from here than from elsewhere to a state in which they do obey the law from 'moral motives'. Secondly, and more important, punishment may have the effect of emphasizing to a man his immorality:

> It is not only pain that is characteristic of punishment, it is pain inflicted because of wrong done and after a judicial decision involving a moral condemnation by an organ representing society. It is not only that the man suffers pain, but that he suffers as a consequence and sign of the condemnation of his act by society as immoral and pernicious. Now this surely is a striking way of bringing home to him, so far as external symbols can, the wickedness of his conduct. It is generally admitted that recognition of one's sin in some form or other is a necessary condition of real moral regeneration, and the formal and impressive condemnation by society involved in punishment is an important

means toward bringing about this recognition on the part of the offender.[2]

Thirdly, punishment has a moral effect on individuals other than those who actually experience it:

If it may help the offender to realise the badness of his action, may it not help others to realise the badness before they have committed the kind of action in question at all? This must not be confused with a purely deterrent effect. A man who abstains from crime just because he is deterred abstains through fear of suffering and not because he thinks it wicked; a man who abstains because the condemnation of the crime by society and the State has brought its wickedness home to him abstains from moral motives and not merely from fear of unpleasant consequences to himself.[3]

The second and third propositions do not rest precisely on the mistake that members of a society could not or would not regard offences as wrongful without the demonstration of punishment. They do rest on some such assumptions as this one, that if an action is not one that is punished by the state, individuals may not realize the extent of its wrongfulness. We are said[4] to be inclined to allocate wrongful actions to two classes: those that may sometimes be excused and those that are absolutely prohibited. When an action is made a crime, and those who commit it are punished, the effect is to locate it firmly in the second class.

Punishment, then, to sum up, is both a deterrent and an effective condemnation, and as both it has reformative consequences. It contributes to a change in the beliefs of offenders and others as to the wrongfulness of certain actions. It thereby contributes to a change for the better in behaviour.

A good many things may be said about and against these claims. What is advanced is certainly a considerably simplified conception of the relationships between morality and the practice of punishment. It seems fairly evident that an effective creation of criminal law, in the societies with which we are familiar, usually depends upon an already existing consensus as to the wrongfulness or undesirability of certain behaviour. It cannot be in general true that the making of an action into an offence results in a moral reallocation of the kind suggested. In certain cases, no doubt, making an action into an offence serves to increase and fortify beliefs as to its immorality. I wish, however, to avoid a difficult and inessential discussion of the relations between punishment and accepted morality.

Let us suppose the existence of a society, very different from ours, where punishment does contribute greatly to law abidance by influencing beliefs and attitudes as to the immorality of offences. The suggestion we are considering is that punishment would here be justified *solely* by these effects. This can be shown to be mistaken in precisely the way in which the deterrence theory has been shown to be mistaken. To accept a principle to the effect that punishment would be justified solely in virtue of its influence on moral beliefs and the further consequences in behaviour would be to commit oneself to unacceptable victimizations. No doubt it would be difficult to conceive of a victimization in which the victim was led to morality and lawfulness. His victimization might be justified, none the less, by its effects on others. Given the unacceptability of this victimization, the conclusion would follow that even in the imagined society punishment could not be justified by the suggested principle of reformation alone.

The deterrence theory, according to our argument, fails because it places insufficient limitation on what may be done to individuals in order to secure certain behaviour. It fails to take into account a limitation having to do with equality of treatment. This limitation is observed by our actual practice of punishment. The doctrine we are presently considering fails because it places insufficient limitation on what may be done in order to secure changes in belief and attitude and consequent behaviour. It does not take into account a feature of our practice of punishment which is essential to any justification it may have. What would have to be true in order for the present doctrine to escape the objection? It would have to be true that in any conceivable situation we would prefer (1) a course of action which would result in certain moral beliefs and lawfulness to (2) a course of action having other results. This, I take it, can be shown to be false. To do so would require both a detailed development of the doctrine and also a repetition of essentially the sequence of argument of the last chapter.[5]

There is also a special objection to the reformative doctrine we are considering and to others like it. If we attempt to deter by punishment, our intention is to affect behaviour, but not by changing certain beliefs and attitudes. If we attempt to reform by punishment, the changing of beliefs and attitudes is an end in itself as well as a means to fewer offences. But just what will be the consequences if we succeed? What will be the consequences if we change the beliefs and attitudes of members of society with respect to certain actions? Those who are quick to suppose that a great deal will be gained usually make the assumption, so evident in the quoted passages above, that *whatever* is punished at present is certainly wrong. They assume, that is, that punishment will always create or reinforce attitudes that certainly are right.

This is simple error. The history of the law is littered with moral barbarities. At *any* time, indeed, the law includes elements which are open to question. What is required, with respect to these elements, is not that members of society should be influenced in some direction by the practice of punishment. What is desirable, rather, is both that the law as it stands be obeyed, and that there be unrestrained discussion of the issues in dispute. Such discussion, after all, gives us the best assurance we can have of rational decisions and moral progress. Discussion should not be impeded, with respect to the issues in question, by a practice of punishment that coerces judgement in one direction. One might then maintain that given a choice between punishment of a reformative kind and punishment of a deterrent kind, where the preventive effect would be the same, the deterrent punishment would be preferable.

Someone may object at this point that there cannot be any doubt about the moral correctness of some core of the law. Would it not be a good thing if at least certain offences were regarded by more people as wholly wrong? We are here in the neighbourhood of a number of considerable difficulties, including the ancient problem of the moral agent. Out of what grounds does the good man act? What is suggested to us by the theory of punishment we are considering is that one takes an important step on the way to becoming such a man by being impressed by condemnations issued by others. It is not, of course, that one is impressed by their reasons or their arguments, but rather by the declarations in which they issue. These are punishments. But surely this is not a way to becoming a good man. Surely I am most admirable as a moral agent if I obey the law out of a sympathetic and impartial awareness of the effects on others of its being broken. My first major step toward this state will involve an awareness of the victims of offences rather than the condemnation of offenders.

2. *Illness and Treatment*

'Those who break the law,' we are often told, 'do so as a consequence of illness and so we should treat them rather than punish them.' These judgements are expressed or implied in a good many books but not, I think, satisfactorily explained or defended.[6] Cogency is generally in short supply. The inherent assumptions are that the mental illness or disability, however conceived, is as much a matter of discovery and description as physical illness, and that it explains and excuses criminal actions. Punishment, almost invariably regarded as necessarily retributive in character, is thought to be out of the question. All of this, needless to say, while orthodoxy to some, is questioned or denied by other psychiatrists and psychologists concerned with the law.

It seems an obvious truth, and one worth remembering, that the influence on the law of the social studies, medicine, psychology, and also certain theories of personal development, has been humanizing and entirely beneficial. That we now do less punishing and more of other things is in accord with discoveries made in these inquiries and the recommendations associated with them. None of the traditional theories of punishment, or at least none of the associated beliefs about the numbers of people who rightly may be punished, can avoid serious emendation at the hands of psychiatrists, sociologists, and others. That we should, because of their evidence, do even less punishing and more of other things seems a likelihood. Should we, however, give up punishment entirely and substitute treatment? Are all offenders ill? Whether or not one thinks so, of course, depends on one's conception of illness.

In English law, from 1843 until 1957, the McNaghten rules in unamended form provided a specification of mental abnormality: the abnormality required as a defence against a criminal charge. As we have noticed already, for a man to have been mentally abnormal in this sense, with respect to a particular act, he must at the time have suffered as a consequence of disease of the mind from a defect of reason such that he did not know the nature of his act or that it was wrong. The 'diseases of the mind' in question are traditional madnesses or incapabilities, or some of them. Not to know the nature of one's act, in this context, is for example not to know that what one is attacking is a human body. A wrong act is taken to be an illegal act.

Clearly enough, given a conception of mental illness based on the McNaghten rules, one would be a long way indeed from the generalization that all offenders are mentally ill. The rules, certainly, have since their inception been criticized as too narrow. In the main, this narrowness consists in regarding a man as sane who knows what he is doing, and that it is wrong, but lacks the emotional capacity even to begin to act in any other way. Such men, it is said, are often obviously and classically mad and it is absurd that they should be held responsible for actions which are the consequence of their illness. In 1957 a relatively trivial step toward widening the English legal conception of mental abnormality took place. In other countries there have long been much wider conceptions.

One might try at this point to arrive at a more inclusive idea of illness by putting aside consideration of the law and its history and turning directly to the doctors, or to some doctors.[7] Abnormal mental life, we are told, although endlessly various, can be divided into forms of illness which are dependent on some distinct bodily disorder and forms of illness which are identified at the psychological rather than the physical level and for which organic causes have not yet been isolated.

In the first group are to be found dementia and also the various forms of mental defectiveness. The confusion, delirium, and loss of intellectual capability that is typical of states of dementia may result from physical sickness, injury, kinds of intoxication, or inheritance. The forms of mental defectiveness, including idiocy, imbecility, and feeble-mindedness, are also of known physical basis. As for the second group of conditions, it can be broken down into a number of sub-groups, the first of which takes in disorders of emotion. Central here are states of anxiety, of depression, and of mania. A second sub-group includes schizophrenic states, marked by disordered thinking, emotional excesses and incongruities, hallucinations, odd or bizarre conduct. A third sub-group includes states of obsession and compulsion, various forms of hysterical illness, and also psychopathic states. Among psychopaths one finds a significant number of offenders, recidivists in particular.

None the less, given even a determination to make the fullest possible use of the notions of this schema, it seems fairly clear that not all offenders can be regarded as falling under it. If this is the extent of sickness, not all offenders are sick. This, of course, is the attitude of many medical authorities. If a man is to be regarded as mentally ill or incapacitated, he must exhibit some established syndrome, where 'established' means something like 'included in standard textbooks of psychiatry'.

There remain other ways in which one can attempt to show that all offenders are disabled. Several of these are more promising. One can begin with one of the related but competing theories of personal development and arrive at a host of disorders. I have in mind those theories of which Freud's is the exemplar. It encompasses, among its fundamental concepts, those of the unconscious mind, basic instinctual drives, such early sexual phases as the anal-sadistic, sublimation and repression, the Oedipus conflict and its resolution, the pleasure principle and the reality principle, the formation of the Super-Ego. It would be pointless to attempt any encapsulation of the theory. Given it, one can display the actions of offenders as consequences of emotional states which are themselves the results of deviations from a normal course of development.[8] There are many possibilities.

Offenders, it may be said, are individuals suffering from character disorders, and these consist in faulty relationships between Id,
Ego, and Super-Ego. Mainly because of unsatisfactory emotional
environments or simply inconsistent treatment in early life, no
adequate Super-Ego or conscience has been developed. Offenders
are like children whose instinctual drives for immediate gratifica-
tion have not come under control. Or, it may be said of some individuals that their experience of the Oedipus conflict was not satisfactorily resolved and they have been left with an ungovernable
reaction to figures of authority and indeed authority in any form.
Alternatively, some men may offend because they desire punishment. The feeling of guilt which issues in this desire may have its
origin in early sexual experience. Or, a man's behaviour may be
explained by the fact that there was no successful emergence from
the stage of anal-sadism, or by the fact that through a certain
experience he has regressed to that stage. Or again, it may be said
that an individual has become fixated in that common illusion of
children, the family romance, and steals in order to try to maintain it.

Whatever else may be said of the enterprise, the notions of the
theory seem to be such as to allow it to be put to very wide use. It
is not obvious that it cannot be applied to all offenders. Rather, it
is a matter of argument whether all offenders suffer from personality or character disabilities resulting from abnormal emotional
development. There are also related doctrines which offer similar
possibilities of general application. Some of them are found attrac-
tive for their relatively common-sensical air. It is supposed by a
good many people that there is a causal connection between anti-
social conduct and separation from one's mother in infancy, rejection by her, or a loss of affection.[9] One or more of these experiences
gives rise to a personality disorder and it in turn produces criminal
behaviour.

There is another less familiar alternative to be found in a
strictly physical account of personal development.[10] Here too, our
attention is drawn to inherent dangers of disorder and its consequences. In this account we are reminded, for example, that when
an external stimulus excites a sensory surface of the body, excita-

tion is passed on through synapses to the brain and then to other parts of the body. There is also inhibition, which is a kind of resistance to excitation. These two processes enter into another one which is of fundamental importance to the individual's development. This is conditioning, the process of establishing responses to stimuli. If a puff of air is directed at the cornea of a man's eye, he blinks. If he hears a particular sound each time he feels a puff, then, after sound and puff have occurred together a number of times, a conditioned reflex is established. That is, some percentage of times when he hears the sound and there is no puff, he blinks. The extent to which the reflex is established may be said to be determined by the degree of inhibition of his nervous system and the number of times he has experienced sound and puff together.

As with the development of the blink-response, so with human behaviour in general. A child misbehaves in a particular way and is then punished in some way. His response to the punishment is fear and pain. By a process of conditioning exactly parallel to that one which produced the blink-response, he comes to respond with something like fear and pain to misbehaving itself, and indeed to the thought of it. As a result the child comes to avoid the behaviour in question to some particular extent. This is a matter of conditioning, not a making of conscious choices.

It is not supposed that all individuals who have nervous systems of such kinds that they condition badly do in fact become offenders. Two other requirements must be satisfied before it becomes a probability or better that a particular child will come to break the law. It is also a consequence of inheritance that an individual be of a certain degree of emotionality or neuroticism. He has a place on a personality scale. Persons at one extreme of the scale, who are very high in emotionality, have such qualities as aggressiveness, restlessness, moodiness. Persons at the other extreme are likely to be calm, reliable, carefree. A high degree of emotionality in the suggested sense is the second condition of criminality. The third requirement is environment and in particular childhood punishments and disapprovals.

Criminality, then, is reducible to conditionability, emotionality, and 'input'. If the possibility of certain other factors is sometimes mentioned by behavioural psychologists, it is not seriously considered. Certainly there is no room for free decisions as usually conceived:

> The deduction which may be made from our general theory is relatively uncompromising. We would regard behaviour from a completely deterministic point of view; that is to say, the individual's behaviour is determined completely by his heredity and by the environmental influences which have been brought to bear on him.[11]

There are still other ways in which criminality may be described and explained in terms of disorder or incapability. 'Deviant syndromes' are explained by sociologists as primarily a consequence of environment rather than individual development. Offenders, on one view, have simply acquired the common pattern of behaviour of the neighbourhood or of some peer group. 'When persons become criminal, they do so because of contacts with criminal patterns and also because of isolation from anti-criminal patterns.'[12] They, like everyone else, have norms imposed upon them. The norms in question happen not to call for obedience to the law, or to all laws. Indeed, they sometimes call for infractions.

With respect to both this and the other kinds of explanation of criminality, incidentally, it is not always true that the supposed sickness or disorder or disability is thought to *give rise to* criminal behaviour. Rather, there is an evident tendency to regard the behaviour itself as the sickness, disorder, or disability. To be mentally healthy is to behave in certain ways; to be unhealthy is to break the law or to act in other anti-social ways.[13] Given this point of view, it is pointless to attempt to explain the behaviour by the disability, but not pointless to try to explain the behaviour, whether or not conceived as a disability, by some independent factor or factors, perhaps the social environment.

Finally, of course, there are some combinations of these several doctrines. Offenders are what they are, it may be said, as a consequence of both personal and social factors. One might try to explain a man's becoming a criminal in terms of both Freudian categories and the sociologist's notion of anomy. It seems possible that something like a spirit of compromise is growing among psychologists, sociologists, and others who concern themselves with the theory of criminality. It has not grown so far (to my knowledge) as to produce fruits. There has recently also been more emphasis on particular kinds of offenders and an increasing unwillingness to regard criminal behaviour as homogeneous stuff. Full-time thieves are very different from rapists and both of them are quite unlike the man who assaults the neighbour who has been annoying him for years.[14]

Several of the general doctrines, of course, are conjoined with quite specific recommendations as to treatment. If offenders are suffering from disabilities which are to be explained in a Freudian way, then it seems that psychoanalysis or psychotherapy is indicated. Often, for clear reasons, one finds a reluctance to propose such a treatment system. It is difficult to see an alternative, however, given the usual condemnations of punishment as barbarous or useless, a dismissal of the utility of other kinds of treatment, and the acceptance that we should try to prevent offences.

On the other hand, if offences are importantly the result of unsuccessful conditioning, or successful conditioning of an antisocial kind, then behaviour-therapy is presumably the answer or a major part of it. A shoe-fetishist may now be so conditioned that the sight of a shoe in certain circumstances, far from exciting him, produces nausea or terror. The same procedure could be attempted with all anti-social behaviour. We might also take steps to alter the conditionability of individuals. Something of this kind, involving the use of drugs, has been attempted with delinquent boys. Finally, whatever steps we choose to take later in their lives, we might consider the desirability of testing the conditionability of schoolchildren. 'Once this particular aspect of the child's nature was known, we could ... pick out those who, by virtue of their poor conditionability, are predestined to become criminals and delinquents, and recommend to their parents a kind of upbringing that would minimise that possibility.'[15]

There are, needless to say, other recommendations as to treatment attached to other diagnoses. Those who are impressed by the argument that offenders are the products of maternal deprivation sometimes advocate particular kinds of institutions, unlike prisons, where individuals can come to a kind of maturation earlier denied them. Finally, there are the less doctrinaire proposals to the effect that we should establish a treatment system comprising within it approaches of various kinds.

3. Objections

Great numbers of questions, most of them not open to settlement here, are raised by these doctrines. Consider, for a start, these three propositions, each of which has been asserted or at least implied. (1) All offenders, perhaps save some of the traditionally mad, are suffering from personality or character disorders resulting from a certain abnormal emotional development, and these disorders are the main causes of their behaviour. To misuse a familiar label, this might be called the Freudian position. (2) All offenders, perhaps save some of the traditionally mad, are the products of certain processes of conditioning, and their behaviour is to be mainly explained in this way. This is the view of some experimental psychologists. (3) All offenders, again excluding some of the traditionally mad, offend mainly because they have been formed by a certain social environment. This is a sociological view.

One might attempt to trim, amend, or interpret these propositions in various ways in order to make them consistent. If they are taken as they often have been intended, however, two at least of them must be false.

It is difficult to resist certain familiar suspicions about the first one, either if offenders are presented as the consequences of unsatisfactory relations between Id, Ego, and Super-Ego or if they are explained in terms of more particular hypotheses of a Freudian kind. General questions about psychoanalytic theory raise themselves. Without being drawn into the ideological conflicts between the analytical movements and their critics, one can question the nature and the extent of the evidence for the propositions put forward. One can also question the precision of the concepts at the base of the system. One can discard a number of worn defensive strategies, including the simple rejoinder that each criticism of psychoanalytic theory may be regarded as no more than resistance, in the technical sense.

As for the second proposition, that one based on the notion of conditioning, it would seem best taken as a simplification of some hypothesis yet to be clarified and tested. Here again, for good reasons, there is controversy among those who are engaged in the relevant disciplines. One good reason is that the theory flattens out what seem to be striking differences. At least certain human decisions, whatever phenomena they are, appear to be very different from blink-responses. Finally, with respect to the more testable assertions of the sociologists, let us notice only that again there is extensive disagreement among those most qualified to judge, and that the explanatory power of a number of familiar sociological claims is in doubt. It is difficult to accept, as a complete account of why some individuals offend, that they were members of a certain group, class, or society.

To mention these problems is simply to draw attention to what is certainly a fact. It cannot be regarded as anything like *settled* that *any* of the three propositions, or more discriminating versions of them, is true. It seems likely that each of them represents human behaviour by way of a too-simple or a distorting model. Nor can the efficacy of different modes of treatment be regarded as established. I shall not attempt any adjudication or, of course, any speculation as to a less doctrinaire theory. Instead, I should like to notice some difficulties that will have to be faced by *any* such theory and its attendant recommendations as to treatment. I take these difficulties to be insuperable. Before mentioning them, let us be clearer about the doctrine we are anticipating.

It will be distinguished, first, by a denial of free choice as ordinarily conceived. This is what is common to the views of criminality as sickness or disability enumerated above. The practice recommended in place of punishment, secondly, will be one of treatment, a practice in which characters, personalities, views and attitudes would be changed as a means to changing behaviour. These changes would not be brought about by what I shall call argument, or not wholly so. What will be the claimed justification? It will be that the practice recommended in place of punishment would in some way improve offenders and in that way prevent offences. The claim will be, in so far as the doctrine is of the single-principle kind we are discussing, that this in itself is sufficient to justify the practice.

One difficulty in accepting such a doctrine, as in the case of the reform theory of punishment, would be that one would be committed to what we may persist in calling victimization. Hitherto, we have understood victimizations to be departures from rules which govern our practice of punishment. Victimizations of the sort hitherto considered would be the work of judges. Let us extend the notion far enough to cover any impositions of distress not in accord with principles of equality. Someone may still object that one cannot have victimization as a consequence of treatment rather than punishment. The ground of the objection may be the supposition that treatment cannot be against the will of the patient. But this is not a logical truth, obviously, and in many circumstances unlikely to be a truth at all. It is mere utopianism to suppose that if punishment were replaced by treatment, of whatever effective kind, offenders would cheerfully present themselves for their remedies. The only realistic alternative to punishment, of the kind in question, would be a *coercive* system of treatment.

(This fact, incidentally, provides an answer to one quite different objection that might be made against a treatment system of the kind we are considering. It is objected, familiarly, that such a system would perhaps help offenders but would not sufficiently prevent offences. That is, it might change known offenders by treatment but it would not influence others against offending. The supposition is that the prospect of being treated would not be deterrent. For several reasons having to do with the fact that treatment would be enforced on individuals, this seems a mistake.)

To return to the main point, however, it seems obvious that a medical authority might impose too much distress on an individual either in the interest of curing him or improving his condition, or in the interest of that and of preventing offences. That, at any rate, would be a possible consequence if the practice in question was governed only by some principle to the effect that treatment was justified if successful in securing such ends. It is such a practice and principle that we are at present discussing. If a practice of treatment was established, and it did exclude victimizations, one would have to accept that any justification it had was not simply that offenders were treated and offences prevented.

A second difficulty, also one faced by the reform theory of punishment, would have to do with the changing of beliefs or attitudes mainly by means other than argument, a giving of reasons. The general case against other means is that there are values of the first importance in maintaining the place or rather the places in society of rational discussion. The effects of what may be called indoctrination are likely to be felt far beyond the area in which it is used. It is entirely mistaken to say[16] that our present practice of punishment succeeds in indoctrination or attempts to indoctrinate. What it primarily attempts to do is to change behaviour. It might reasonably be pointed out, on the other hand, that we certainly do influence children by other than rational means. This is so, and to some extent defensible. It might also be admitted that in certain cases behaviour-therapy for adults is justifiable, even against the wishes of the individuals in question. These would be cases in which there was a danger of very great harm to particular individuals and no other more tolerable way of avoiding it. It certainly does not follow that society could justifiably treat all law-breakers or potential law-breakers in this way.

There is also a third difficulty, one having to do with the allocation of a society's resources. One sometimes has the feeling that for reformists no expenditure could be too great if it secured an insignificant incidence of criminality. It is as if there was no question but that an army of therapists would be best engaged in dealing with those who commit criminal offences, about half of which are motoring offences. Surely the claims of other sectors and institutions in society must be considered. Should we have so many therapists or practitioners of whatever kind? If so, what numbers of them should be concerned with, say, the education of children rather than with criminality? Our practice of punishment is often said to be inefficient and wasteful. If we are far indeed from having one, there remains a possibility that a radically different system would be inefficient and wasteful in different ways. One can certainly conceive of two societies such that one with a higher incidence of criminality would be far preferable.

Finally, with respect to difficulties in the doctrine we are anticipating, it will involve the denial that offenders are free in their offences and responsible for them. If it is anything like those doctrines we already have, it will involve a quite general thesis of determinism. It will not be allowed that *anyone* chooses or acts freely, in an ordinary sense of the word, or is to be held responsible. For several reasons this large and all too enduring question calls for fuller consideration.

1. Dr A. C. Ewing considers and defends such a view in *The Morality of Punishment* (London, 1929). It is more briefly stated in 'Punishment as a Moral Agency', *Mind*, 1927. Related accounts are given by J. M. E. McTaggart, *Studies in Hegelian Cosmology* (Cambridge, 1901), chapter five; Hastings Rashdall, *The Theory of Good and Evil* (London, 1907), volume one, chapter nine; E. F. Carritt, *The Theory of Morals* (London, 1928), pp. 108–13. McTaggart, as I mentioned in the first chapter above, supposes Hegel to have held the view in question.
2. Ewing, *The Morality of Punishment*, p. 97.
3. ibid., p. 96.
4. ibid.
5. Ewing attempts some rejoinders to the traditional claims about victimization. His rejoinders rest, in my view, on a happy choice of cases. See *The Morality of Punishment*, p. 90 ff.
6. For an analysis see Antony Flew, 'Crime of Disease', *The British Journal of Sociology*, 1954.
7. My sketch is taken from David Stafford-Clark, *Psychiatry Today* (Harmondsworth, 1952).
8. See, for example, Kate Friedlander, *The Psycho-Analytical Approach to Juvenile Delinquency* (London, 1947). (Also, New York, 1960.)
9. For a careful discussion of these theories, see Wootton, *Social Science and Social Pathology*, chapter four.
10. See H. J. Eysenck, *Crime and Personality* (London, 1964).
11. Eysenck, op. cit., p. 177.
12. Edwin H. Sutherland, *Principles of Criminology* (Chicago, 1955), p. 78.
13. See Wootton, *Social Science and Social Pathology*, chapter seven.
14. A valuable essay on general theories of crime and their weaknesses, and an argument for particularized research, is to be found in Wootton, *Crime and the Criminal Law* (London, 1963), chapter one.
15. Eysenck, op. cit., p. 163.
16. Eysenck, op. cit., p. 173.

CHAPTER FIVE: FREEDOM

1. Freedom and Punishment

The argument for punishment in terms of retribution presupposes that men sometimes make free choices for which they are responsible. Indeed, as we have seen, the claim that a man deserves a penalty for an action may best be taken to mean, in part, that he was free in the action and responsible for it. The retribution theory, then, could barely survive a demonstration of the truth of determinism. Our main objection to that theory of punishment was of a moral kind. If men were never free and responsible, in certain common senses of the words, there would also exist an insuperable objection to the theory of a non-evaluative kind.

The deterrence theory is not in the same way bound up with the controversy about human freedom. Quite commonly its holders have been advocates of some doctrine of determinism. They have argued, by way of it, against the retribution theory. It is clear, though, that determinism is not a presupposition of their own justification of punishment in the way in which freedom is a presupposition of the retribution theory. Punishment might be justified in virtue of being an economical deterrent even if determinism was false. If it is true, of course, and the retribution theory thus unacceptable, the field is left to the supposed justifications in terms of deterrence and reform. In connection with the latter we have just seen that conceptions of criminality as disorder or disability are in ways determinist. Furthermore, the truth of determinism would provide at least a retort against one of our criticisms of the associated recommendations that we treat and not punish offenders. Let me say for the moment, simply, that the distinction upon which we insisted between rational argument and indoctrination may be thought to be put in danger by determinism.

In the chapter following this one, we shall consider justifications of punishment in terms of several principles. These typically contain a retribution argument and thus, like the traditional retribution theory, presuppose human freedom. Finally, it seems to me at least arguable that advocacy of all these doctrines about punishment, traditional and recent, requires an assumption of freedom in quite another way. The same is true of what I myself shall suggest is the best that can be said for the practice of punishment. For all these reasons the subject can do with attention. This chapter, none the less, gives it rather more than the central intention of the book requires. This indulgence on my part, I hope, will be found worth while.

2. Determinism

A number of philosophers who have considered the ordinary belief in human freedom have concluded that there is no opposing case to be met. They have held, that is, that there is no intelligible or coherent doctrine of determinism. This easy way with a problem is open to the easy and sufficient reply that we as much lack an intelligible and coherent account of what it is, or would be, to choose or decide freely. However, determinism *is* unclear and any discussion must begin with some examination or stipulation of the *meaning* of the claim that all or some events are the products of preceding causes. What is it for one thing to cause another?

Let us first put aside the central use of the word 'cause' in ordinary life. We say that the cause of a man's showing irritation was that he was ignored or that a house caught fire because there wasn't a screen in front of a fireplace, that someone couldn't find an address because of not knowing London and being unable to find a taxi, that the war went on because members of a government were entranced by an ideology. In each case, the cause would not by itself bring about the effect. It was necessary to the fire, for example, that the floor in front of the fireplace was inflammable, that there was oxygen in the room, and so on. Talk of a cause in this sense, then, is talk of *one* of a set of factors which only together are sufficient to give rise to an effect. Why do we single out one particular factor or condition and call it the cause?

Reflection on the examples will give the beginning of an answer. At least often, one factor is singled out because it is the only human action or human failure involved. At other times, one factor is chosen because, within a certain context or given certain expectations, it is abnormal or unusual.[1]

To say that all actions are caused, in this sense, may be to make a philosophically uncontroversial remark. To say in this way that someone was caused to write a book on some subject by some fact about his personality or his finances is not to say that his conduct was not free. Another equally important factor may have been that he willingly chose, every so often, to go on with it. We may use the word 'cause' in other and more consequential ways, to refer to some part or the whole of the set of factors which give rise to an effect. It is the latter use that is important at present.

The cause of a particular event, in this sense, is that set of factors sufficient to produce it. Their specification is a matter of considerable difficulty. One may say, however, that the cause in this sense[5] of the house's catching fire was the set of conditions including the absence of a fire-screen in front of a fireplace, an ember's falling from the grate, its resting on a wooden floor for a certain time and the presence of oxygen. This description may be criticized both as incomplete and as inclusive of redundancies. What is unlikely to be disputed is that *some* set of conditions was sufficient to produce the effect. But what more can be said of the relationship between such a cause and its effect? This is the traditional problem of causation and one important source of the unclarity of determinism. We are likely to say that given the existence of a cause in this sense, the effect is *certain* to follow or that it *must* follow. We may say that it *necessarily* follows. What relationship of necessity is this? It is not, of course, logical necessity. That is, to assert of a particular set of conditions that it did not produce what in fact was its effect is to fall into error but not self-contradiction. Nor do we know truths about causes and effects without recourse to experience. This is another mark of the absence of logical connection or logical necessity.

Hume and his many followers, of course, maintain there is *no* relationship of necessity whatever between causes and effects. To return to the example of the fire, we have a set of conditions or what I shall sometimes call a circumstance, C, and the event of the house's catching fire, E. What may be said of C and E, according to the Humean account, is only that C preceded E, that they were contiguous in space and time, and that circumstances similar to C are always related in these several ways to events similar to E. Circumstances like C, in the familiar philosophical phrase, are *constantly conjoined* with events like E. When we say that C caused E we can sensibly mean no more than this. Indeed, this is what we do mean. The traditional objection is that this cannot be so, since there are instances of constant conjunction that are not acceptable as instances of cause and effect.

A particular day, for example, is followed by a particular night and the two together constitute an instance of constant conjunction: days are always followed by nights. However, we do not regard the day in question as the cause of the night. There is no point in remarking, incidentally, that 'day' and 'night' may be given scientific definitions such that we *would* accept that days cause nights.[2] In the intended sense of the word, the day in question is a period of light on a part of the earth's surface. The night is a period of darkness. This day and night are an instance of a constant conjunction and would, if the account we are considering was correct, be cause and effect.

A second objection is that the given account makes all causal statements in a way general. Certainly we may use 'cause' and 'effect' to refer to classes of things, as when we say that poor brakes cause car accidents. It is also common, as we have seen, to use them to refer to particulars: a certain circumstance or set of conditions and a certain event, each with one place in space and time. On the given account of the language of causation, I do more than mention two particulars when I say that one was the cause of the other. To say that C caused E is to say that C happened and then the contiguous event E happened, *and* circumstances like C are always so related to events like E. This seems unlikely.

Defenders of the Humean account of causation have generally attempted to meet the first objection by maintaining that the supposed non-causal instances of constant conjunction are not really instances of constant conjunction in the intended sense. It has sometimes been explained that a class of circumstances is to be regarded as constantly conjoined with a class of events only if these situations and events have always been conjoined in the past and also *always will be*. This is ambiguous. It may be taken to mean something such that the proposed account of causation would still commit us to regarding a day as the cause of a night. This would happen if we were of the opinion that days will in fact always be followed by nights.

What seems sometimes to be intended in such an amendment is something like this: a class of circumstances and a class of events are to be regarded as constantly conjoined if they *would* continue to be conjoined even if certain things in the universe were to change. More particularly, an event of the kind in question would occur, given that a circumstance of the kind in question obtained, *no matter what else was true.*[3] Given some such explanation, it can be argued that yesterday and last night are not an instance of a constant conjunction. The occurrence of a particular day would *not* be followed by a night if the earth were to stop rotating. If we take an undoubted causal connection, on the other hand, it does satisfy this definition of constant conjunction. Take, for example, that circumstance which we do regard as the cause of a particular day. It will have among its factors the rotation of the earth and the burning of the sun. Given the obtaining of a circumstance of *this* kind, whatever else was true, a day would occur.

By some such means one can move toward accommodating the objection. Doing so, of course, involves a radical amendment or indeed a rejection of Hume's view. What we now have is this. To say a particular circumstance was the cause of an event is to say that the obtaining of the circumstance preceded and was contiguous with the event, that similar events are always so conjoined with similar circumstances, and that given such a circumstance an event of the kind in question would occur no matter what else was the case. Obviously, this faces the second objection, in that all causal statements are presented as general. However, we can preserve the strength of the account, and not open it to any new objections, if we simply drop the curious reference to circumstances and events other than the single pair with which we are primarily concerned.

We can drop the supposition that causal statements refer to whole classes of circumstances and events. We may say, simply, that to say that C caused E is to say that E followed C and that when C obtained E would have followed whatever else was true. No doubt we believe more than this when we assert a causal connection between two particulars, but there is no good reason for thinking that this belief is part of the content of what we assert. We need not think that what may be regarded as evidence for the causal assertion, a general belief about the conjunction of circumstances and events, is *part* of the assertion.

There will be a reluctance to accept this account of what we mean when we say that some circumstance was the cause of an event. Do we really mean, partly, that given the obtaining of the circumstance, the event would have followed *whatever else was the case*? Do we intend so strong a claim? Someone may say that we merely mean, rather, that the circumstance obtained and the event followed, the circumstance being 'sufficient' to produce the event. It seems that if we do mean this, we are also committed to the seemingly stronger claim. We have the idea of a set of conditions sufficient *by itself* to give rise to an event. If it *is* sufficient, we would get the same result if everything else was different save that the set of conditions did obtain. To suppose that E would not follow C if 'attendant circumstances' were in some way different and unfavourable is to suppose that C is *not* sufficient to give rise to E.

There remain a number of extremely difficult problems. What analysis can be given of a statement that given a certain circumstance an effect *would* have followed whatever else happened? Or, to choose another formulation I shall use, how are we to analyse the statement that given a certain circumstance, nothing other than a particular effect *could* have followed, whatever else happened? One cannot ignore these demands for explanation, certainly, if one's intention is to treat adequately of the problem of causation. My different intention has been to give a sketch of an account of what is meant by causal claims. It is, I suggest, sufficiently intelligible to provide one of the bases for further discussion. Certainly the causal relationship has not been finally clarified. It cannot be said, however, that it remains so obscure as to make useful discussion of determinism impossible. There are also other problems and obscurities, some of which attach only to forms of determinism other than the one upon which I shall concentrate. I allude below to some of those which are relevant but others must go unnoticed. None, I think, is insuperable: determinism can at least be adequately formulated.[4]

. Are all human choices, decisions and actions caused? Is each of them a *necessary consequent* of some antecedent circumstance? Is it true of each, that is, that it could not have been otherwise no matter what else happened, given a certain circumstance? Is each element of each circumstance also a necessary consequent itself? In the past those who have given an affirmative answer to these questions have often derived it from the Law of Causation, that all events without exception are caused. The inductive support for this major premiss is that multitudes of *physical* events, events not particularly related to human choice and action, do have causes. The whole argument, then, proceeds from knowledge of one kind of event to a claim about events of a very different kind. For this reason, it inspires something less than confidence. Physical and mental events are of different categories, as we are so often reminded, and at least caution is required in considering whether what is true of the former is also true of the latter.

More contemporary determinism avoids this and other difficulties. It is argued that some mental events can be shown to be caused, and that this is a sufficient basis for an extrapolation to the conclusion that all choices and decisions are caused. One line of argument here, of which we have already seen something, begins from the claim that some mental events can be shown to be consequences of mental causes. Rather more coercive for several reasons is the argument which begins from the premiss that some mental events have been shown to have *physical* causes. Over the past decade or two, there have been striking advances in neurophysiological knowledge. It is nowhere near true, of course, that causal accounts of a physical kind have been given of the mental events in which we are most interested. That is, there has been no specific causal explanation, in terms, say, of the firing of neurons in the brain, for choices and decisions. To get to the conclusion that these are physically caused, a considerable extrapolatory step is required.

What is true is that causal connections are established between other mental phenomena and chemical and electrical events and states in the brain. The possibility of producing feelings of ease, relaxation, joy, satisfaction, irritation, fear, or pain by electrical stimulation of brain centres is fairly familiar. There are established neurophysiological procedures for the alteration of states of mental illness. Memory has also been the subject of considerable investigation and a kind of sequential and detailed experiencing of past events has been produced recurrently by electrical stimulation of the cortex. Finally, to mention a different order of support for determinism, growing knowledge in the field of cybernetics has established that complex logical operations can be reduced to steps that can be carried out by relatively simple mechanisms.[5]

The ever-increasing number of such facts, which have analogues in quite ordinary experience, does seem to pose a threat to ordinary beliefs about choice and responsibility. It is difficult to resist the feeling that there is some considerable warrant for the deterministic extrapolation to the conclusion that all mental events are the necessary consequents of preceding causes. This feeling, perhaps not misdescribed as such, has greatly contributed to what has long been a philosophical familiarity, an attempt to have it both ways, to have both freedom and determinism. The strategy of many philosophers has been to accept that choices and decisions are or may be caused, and to argue that, none the less, we may be confident of our freedom. Their position, which I shall now consider, is that determinism is compatible with our ordinary beliefs to the effect that we sometimes choose and decide freely.

3. The Compatibility Theory

The problem of human freedom, we are persistently reminded, has long since been solved. Indeed, we have been told, it is 'really one of the greatest scandals of philosophy that again and again so much paper and printer's ink is devoted to this matter . . .'[6] The supposed solution was stated by Hobbes and has since Hume been a traditional part of what may be called the empiricist conception of man.[7] The problem is the seeming incompatibility of the belief that such things as decisions are caused and the belief that sometimes we decide freely. The solution of those who hold what we may call the compatibility theory is that these two beliefs, contrary to what is supposed, are perfectly consistent. They can both be true. To see this we need only be clear about the correct meaning of the word 'free' and related words. The word 'free' is taken, by those who hold the compatibility theory, to mean something like 'unconstrained' or 'uncompelled', and it is claimed without fear of denial that there is no incompatibility between the claim that all decisions are the necessary consequents of preceding causes and the claim that in general we are not constrained or compelled to decide as we do. A causal decision is not necessarily a constrained one. It in no way follows from the fact that my decision was caused, for example, that I did not want to make it.

It requires but little ingenuity, of course, to find a conception of freedom such that freedom and determinism are consistent. Let us notice some other examples. If to decide freely is defined as opting for something in the belief that some doctrine of determinism is true, then deciding freely and determinism are in no way opposed. Again, some of us may be both determined and free if free decisions are those made by men who live by the instincts of war, are indifferent to travail, and in other ways satisfy Nietzsche's requirements. The arguments advanced for the compatibility theory, which certainly is to be distinguished from these curiosities, are not arguments to the effect that decisions may be both caused and unconstrained. This may be assumed. Rather, they are arguments which purport to show that the particular meaning given to 'free' and many related words is the one *relevant* to the dispute about human freedom. Let us begin by looking more closely at several of the particular meanings that have been assigned.

Originally, within the tradition of thought we are considering, a man was said to be free when he was not kept from doing as he pleased by *a physical force external to him.*[8] The paradigmatic case of a lack of freedom was taken to be a man in fetters or in jail. This conception has the consequence, paradoxical at least to us, that a man who acts under threat is perfectly free in his action. On a revised view, to say that we sometimes act freely is to say that we have 'a power of acting or not acting according to the determinations of the will; that is, if we choose to remain at rest, we may; if we choose to move, we also may.'[9] This second conception also has its obvious disadvantage, at least to us. Hume, its author, says rightly at one point that 'it is commonly allowed that madmen have no liberty', and yet, according to the account, it would seem that at least some have. Certainly they may possess a power of acting as they will. Finally, consider a more recent version.

Freedom means the opposite of compulsion; a man is *free* if he does not act under *compulsion*, and he is compelled or unfree when he is hindered from without in the realisation of his natural desires. Hence he is unfree when he is locked up, or chained, or when someone forces him at the point of a gun to do what otherwise he would not do. This is quite clear, and everyone will admit that the everyday or legal notion of the lack of freedom is thus correctly interpreted, and that a man will be considered quite free and responsible if no such external compulsion is exerted upon him. There are certain cases which lie between these clearly described ones, as say, when someone acts under the influence of alcohol or a narcotic. In such cases we consider the man to be more or less unfree, and hold him less accountable, because we rightly view the influence of the drug as 'external', even though it is found within the body; it prevents him from taking decisions in the manner peculiar to his nature. . . . In the case also of a person who is mentally ill we do not consider him free with respect to those acts in which the disease expresses itself, because we view the illness as a disturbing factor which hinders the normal functioning of his natural tendencies. We make not him but his disease responsible.[10]

To say a man decided freely, we are told here, is to say he was not constrained or compelled in his decision. That in turn means that *he decided as he wanted, unhindered by external or internal forces, and that he decided in a manner peculiar to his nature.* It seems evident that one may make such a decision even if determinism is true, even if all decisions are necessary consequents of antecedents. There are many ways in which this last analysis might be improved without fundamentally changing its character. Were I going to suggest in the argument to come that decisions which we ordinarily take to be free do not fall under some such characterization, rather more precision would be desirable. My different claim will be that while all of what we take to be free decisions are indeed unconstrained in something like the suggested sense, we do not take them to be only this. Nothing but a radical addition to such a characterization, one which moves away from its central idea, would make it adequate.

This would, of course, be disputed by a supporter of the compatibility theory. The main argument advanced on behalf of the theory, as in the quoted passage, is that its conception of freedom is *the relevant because the ordinary* one. All we need do is reflect on what people have in mind in their talk of free decisions. We will see it to be nothing other than an absence of compulsion or constraint. Imagine, we may be told, a trial before a jury. The jurors come to believe on the basis of evidence presented that the defendant was robbed of money owned by his employer. An assailant threatened him and knocked him down in the street. The jurors believe that the defendant's subsequent action in giving up the money was anything but a free one. Surely, we are exhorted, it is obvious that their belief is simply that he was compelled to do as he did. What else is or could be in question?

Suppose now that the jury, on the basis of further and different evidence, comes to believe that there was collusion between defendant and seeming assailant, that the gun wasn't loaded, and that the defendant did not act in fear. Clearly enough, the jury now regard the action of giving up the money as a free one. It is clear, we are told, that their belief is simply that the defendant was not compelled to do as he did. What else could be in question?

That there is something else in question, if rarely in the forefront of reflection, can be brought out quite easily. Let us add the more extraordinary supposition that the jurors are convinced, by a third presentation of evidence, that each of the defendant's decisions relevant to the offence was the necessary consequent of preceding causes. None of his decisions could have been otherwise than it was, given the circumstance that obtained. No decision was constrained but none could have been different. If the jurors believe this, certainly, they will again regard the action as an unfree one. We ordinarily do intend to convey, when we assert that a man decided freely, that he was not constrained, but this intention is to be understood against the background assumption that decisions are normally *not* causally necessary consequents. We take this as given. If we were to accept that a decision *was* such a consequent, then, whether or not constrained, we would not regard it as free.

Assertions of free decision thus normally involve something explicit and something implicit. What is explicit is that someone was not constrained; what is implicit is that his or her decision was not a causally necessary consequent. It is false to suppose, then, that the compatibilist conception of a free decision is the whole of our ordinary conception.

This reply seems to me adequate, if too much on the level of the initial argument. Both argument and reply too readily assume that there is some single ordinary sense of 'free' and the many other terms in question. What seems indisputable is that there is *an* ordinary use of the terms, perhaps the most ordinary use, which is as I have described it. That it is an ordinary and perhaps the central use, however, is not sufficient to establish that it is that one relevant to the present discussion. This is another assumption of the argument which requires qualification. Relevance is dictated by particular concerns and interests, and what is relevant for one party to a dispute may not be so for another. We can give up the supposition that there is but one test of relevance. Most people who reflect on human freedom are concerned above all with what may be called, if opaquely, a question of responsibility. They are given to an extremely common conception of persons as agents and originators rather than causal phases, a conception sufficiently fundamental as to make full analysis difficult. For people who have this concern, the question at issue is *whether we are free in such a sense as to be responsible*. It happens to be the case, predictably, that this question makes use of an ordinary sense of the word 'free'. That it does so is not important.

The conception at which I have gestured is one that has often been misconceived, usually in the interest of argument. To wish to know if we are responsible is not to wish to know if we may profitably be punished, blamed, rewarded, praised, or treated in related ways. It is simply false that the question of a man's personal responsibility, as usually conceived, is the question of whether punishing him, or whatever, will have good effects.[11] It is, in good part, a question of whether or not he could have acted otherwise than he did. I shall consider this element more closely in a moment. For the present, what I wish to suggest is that if we are asked to reflect on what people ordinarily have in mind with respect to questions and judgements of freedom, the best answer is that they are concerned with a freedom which involves responsibility. This would be true of our imagined jurors. What they have in mind, then, cannot be presented as merely a matter of constraint or its absence.

A second argument for the compatibility theory is of a similar character. When we ordinarily speak of actions as free or unfree, it is said, our judgements have certain implications. If we say of a man's action that it was free, we imply that he may be treated in certain ways. If his action is taken to have been unfree, we imply that he may not be treated in these ways. Precisely such implications are had by the assertion that a man's action was unconstrained. This is indirect evidence that in our ordinary usage a free action is an unconstrained one and an unfree action a constrained one. The implication of a judgement that Green's action was a free one is that he may be praised, rewarded, blamed, or punished for it. The implication of a judgement that it was not free is that he cannot with justification be treated in any of these ways. There are the same implications with respect to judgements of absence of constraint and judgements of constraint.[12]

For the reason already given, that ordinariness is not the relevant final test of a definition, let us recast this argument. The concern of some people with human freedom, we may say, is rooted in a concern about the justification of such responses and practices as blame, punishment, praise, and reward. They wish to know if we are free in such a way that these things are in place. The given answer is that these things are indeed in place with respect to actions that are unconstrained. Since absence of constraint is consistent with determinism, they may put their worries aside. This answer requires, however, that we accept a particular justification for punishment and the rest. It requires that we accept that punishment's justification does not presuppose any freedom on the part of offenders other than absence of constraint. For those who think otherwise, that the justification of punishment is wholly or partly retributivist, the fact that men's actions are often free in the sense of being unconstrained will not be sufficient.

There is a third argument, closely related to the first one, for the claim that the freedom compatible with determinism is the relevant one. Reformulated, it runs as follows. There are those who are concerned with the question of whether actions are free in such a sense that they *could have been otherwise than they were*. Their concern is with whether we can ever act otherwise than we do. They too can be reassured. The conception of free action as unconstrained *is* a conception of action that could have been otherwise. This argument depends on a particular analysis of what it means to say that something could have been otherwise than it was. The statement that a man could have acted otherwise than he did, it is claimed, means simply that he *would* have acted otherwise *if* he had so decided. To say that a man could have decided otherwise than he did is to say that he would have decided differently if sometime earlier he had made a different decision than he did. To say Brown could have decided not to malign his brother today, when he did so, is to say that he would not have done so if he had made some decision earlier – if, perhaps, he had decided years ago to stick to the strict truth in such matters.

Given this view of 'could have' statements, obviously they do follow from statements about absence of constraint. If my action

was unconstrained, although the necessary consequent of antecedents, it could have been otherwise in the given sense. Those
who wish to know if we have a freedom to act or decide otherwise,
then, need not think that determinism makes it impossible. The
rejoinder to this argument, clearly, is that the recipients will reject
the given analysis of their interest. They do not want to know if
we are free in some sense such that we could act otherwise than we
do, *in a particular and peculiar sense of the latter words*. They do
not want to know if we *would* act otherwise *if* things had previously been other than they were. No doubt they believe this to
be true.

We do on occasion use 'could have' in the conditional way
suggested by the argument, although perhaps not in conjunction
with 'acted' or 'decided'. However, we also have a non-conditional use of 'could have' where to say that a man could have done
otherwise means simply that he was then in a position to do it.[13]
He did not in fact do whatever it was, as we imply, but he might
have done it given things just as they were. He might have done
it, given his past as it was. To come to the final point, it is *this*
sense of 'could have' which occurs in the intended question about
freedom. We wish to know if we are free in such a sense that we
could act in ways other than we do, *in the non-conditional sense of
the latter words just indicated*. It is not true that the conception of
a free action as an unconstrained but determined one is a conception of an action that could have been otherwise in this sense.
There is no reason for thinking that free actions, in this sense,
remain possible if determinism is true.

There is one more argument advanced by those who hold the
compatibility theory. Hobbes, Hume, and most of their successors
have been at pains to maintain that no coherent or satisfactory
account can be given of our decisions and choices if they are *not*
presented as the necessary consequents of antecedent causes.
Briskly put, the claim is that interpretations of such terms as 'free
decision', if not deterministic, are incoherent or unclear to the
point of uselessness. It has usually been maintained, simply, that
if decisions are not causally related to antecedents they must be
random events. But, it is said, this makes for an absurd conception

of decisions. If they were this, no man could ever be in any sense responsible for his conduct. Quite as obviously, it is said, it is simply false that decisions are of a random character, that they bear no relation to their makers' characters, personalities, desires, motives, perceptions, and so on.

'Random', by implication at least, is here used ambiguously. It either may mean 'not caused', which perhaps is its correct sense, or it may mean something like 'unrelated in any significant way to antecedents'. It must be granted, obviously, that any account of free choices which makes them random events in the second sense is nonsense. No such account, one hopes, has ever been offered. Can it be that any account of choice incompatible with determinism must reduce to some such thing? It has sometimes seemed that those who hold the compatibility theory have half supposed in this connection that a truth of logic supports their case. However, while it is necessarily true that decisions are either caused or random, where 'random' means 'uncaused', it is not at all necessary that if they are uncaused they stand in no significant relation to antecedents.

That is, it does not follow from the fact, if it is one, that decisions are not caused, that they are in no significant way related to antecedents. Indeed, if decisions are *either* caused or quite unrelated to antecedents, we are all of us given to a mistake. We do not ordinarily think, and we do not act as if we think, that decisions are caused, that for causal reasons they cannot be other than they are. But neither do we think that they have nothing to do with perceptions, feelings, and personal dispositions. On the contrary, we think there are intimate connections. It must be admitted, certainly, that no adequate account of these connections has ever been given, which is to say that no adequate analysis of decision has ever been given. There have been metaphors and there have been attempts to account for decision in terms of its supposed machinery. There are the notions of the Will and the Self, neither of them enlightening.

It seems to me that there is no reason here for abandoning the question of whether free decisions as ordinarily conceived are a reality. We need not turn to the doubtful reassurance of the compatibility theory. It is not as if we must choose either to describe free decisions in the compatibilist way or to talk nonsense. We do, and it is no surprise, have a working idea of free decisions. They are those which were unconstrained and which, in the unconditional sense, could have been otherwise. We may explain that to say they could have been otherwise is to say that they were not causally necessary consequents. We may add that they were related in significant ways to their makers' perceptions, dispositions, and so on. This description, in so far as it goes beyond the notion of absence of constraint, is alarmingly negative and vague. It is none the less intelligible. It is worth remembering, of course, that the alternative account of decision, which makes it a matter of causal sequence, goes no way at all toward explaining what must still be regarded as its unique character. Decision, supposing it to be causal sequence, is very unlike other causal sequences. Here there is as much left unclear or unsaid.

4. Other Reconciliations

The compatibility theory, while it still has defenders, has for a time been paid rather less attention than certain related contentions. One of these is advanced as a denial of mechanism, that kind of determinism which involves a rejection of consciousness and so regards men as machines. Mechanism, it is said, is a matter of physical events and states and so has no relevance to what is quite different, human choice and action. It is no more than a bogy.

The fear that theoretically minded persons have felt lest everything should turn out to be explicable by mechanical laws is a baseless fear. And it is baseless not because the contingency which they dread happens not to be impending, but because it makes no sense to speak of such a contingency. Physicists may one day have found the answer to all physical questions, but not all questions are physical questions.[14]

Moves in a game of chess, as the writer goes on to say, are governed both by the rules of the game and in quite another sense by the players: by their choices, deliberations, intentions, intelligence, stupidity, and so on. The writing of good prose is governed by both rules of grammar and an awareness of style. There is no possibility of reducing the choices and deliberations of the chess players to the rules of chess. They are not this sort of thing. There is no possibility of reducing considerations of style to the rules of grammar. They are not that sort of thing. Questions about chess moves in terms of rules must not be confused with questions about them in terms of the players. Questions about prose with respect to grammar must not be confused with questions about prose with respect to style. It may be true that human behaviour, in some wide sense of that term, is governed both by physical laws and, on the other hand, by choice, intelligence, purpose, and the like. There is no contradiction or inconsistency in supposing this, and there is no question of supposing that truths about choice, intelligence, and so on may be reduced to truths about physical laws. Two kinds of question may be asked, not only one.

Taken literally this is an argument specifically aimed at mechanism. What we are told is that one thing, an action for example, may be 'in accordance with two principles of completely different types and such that neither is "reducible" to the other.'[15] An action may be 'explained' by causal laws which make no mention of consciousness. It remains consistent to explain it also by such notions as choice and intelligence. I have no wish to discuss mechanism or materialism, which is quite separable from our thesis of determinism. However, the claims put forward may also be taken in a wider way, such that they do refer to determinism as we have conceived it. So taken, they are that such things as human actions may be subject to causal laws and yet free or responsible. Two kinds of question may be asked about them, and that they are caused does not exclude their being free and responsible.

This is of the nature of Johnsonian declaration rather than argument. *Why* is there no inconsistency in saying of a man that his signing of a petition was both a matter of causal laws and also a matter of free choice or judgement in an ordinary sense? This must be true, of course, if there truly are separate questions about human behaviour, such that an answer to one has no bearing on answers to the other. It is not enough to turn to the compatible but irreducibly dual governance of chess moves and the writing of good prose. *If* there is no inconsistency in saying of the man that his signing was a matter of causation and also a matter of free choice, *then* his signing is in a way analogous to a move in chess and the writing of good prose. But what ground do we have for thinking that there is no inconsistency? The traditional compatibility theory supplies a particular analysis of free choice at this point. Certainly something is required.

(We may notice in passing that it is sometimes thought that since human choices, decisions, and actions are not merely physical events they cannot be explained by events and states that are entirely physical in nature. There seems no reason to suppose this. Certainly determinism as we have conceived it cannot be a purely physical theory.[16] It takes in both physical and mental events and states. In this, it is hardly unique. We commonly make particular causal judgements where the cause is physical and the effect of a non-physical nature. A determinism which involved a thorough-going materialism would be simpler, in the sense of containing terms of only one category. The determinism we have been discussing is in the related sense complex, but this in itself cannot be a serious objection. If we can in fact distinguish the terms of the causal relation, that they are of different categories is not an obstacle.)

Another contemporary view related to the traditional compatibility theory appears to turn on a distinction between an action and a motion. It is a mistake, we are told, to regard the physical or physiological causes of bodily movements as also the causes of actions.

No doubt a comprehension of the details of the bodily mechanism will enable us to provide a causal explanation of the fact that arms and legs get moved in such-and-such ways given such-and-such excitations of the sense organs. No doubt, too, a being who lacks the developed bodily mechanism with which intelligent human beings are endowed is incapable of performing various actions including the action of raising one's arm at will. But if we distinguish, as we must, between the rising of one's arm and the action of raising one's arm, it is not at all clear that if we offer a causal explanation of the former in terms of events within the bodily mechanism we are *eo ipso* offering a causal explanation of the latter.[17]

We are told, indeed, that 'absolutely nothing about any matter of human conduct follows logically from any account of the physiological conditions of bodily movement'. These propositions are asserted, it appears, on the odd assumption that determinism is the contention that neuro-physiological events cause movements of the body and limbs *and that therefore* certain specified actions are caused. If we suppose this, we face the difficulty that there is not a one-to-one correlation between bodily movements, however defined, and actions. When a man's arm goes up, he may be signalling a turn, or waving to a friend, or bidding at an auction. One sees which from the context – it does not follow logically from a description of the mere movement. Equally a man can perform the action of warning somebody by gesturing, writing a note, speaking, or merely glancing in some direction.

Even given this eccentric depiction of determinism, the argument cannot establish the desired conclusion. It cannot establish the proposition that even if body and limb movements are the consequents of antecedent causes, this has no importance whatever for actions. It cannot establish this because there *are* logical connections between statements describing bodily movements and statements about actions. If both my hands are rising above my head during a certain time it follows logically that I am not. digging my garden in the usual way. In fact, a moment's reflection indicates that *any* sequence of bodily movements is inconsistent with very considerable numbers of actions. If all my bodily movements are caused, then my freedom of action is very severely restricted indeed. As I have implied, however, there is a more fundamental objection to the view we are considering.

Determinism can without logical fault be the thesis that physical events and states cause such things as decisions and actions. There is no need to suppose that it must be the indirect thesis that neuro-physiological events and states cause large-scale bodily movements and that these in turn are connected in some way with actions.

Why should we think that physical events and states cannot be regarded as the causes of actions? It is a fact that while we are perfectly able to use the notion of an action, we are not clear about its analysis.[18] Such states of affairs are familiar enough. Are we to say, perhaps, that actions are those movements of a person which are purposive? Does this mean they are movements for which he can give a reason, some reason or other? We do not have to come to a decision on these questions and many like them for our present purposes. We successfully discriminate between actions and other things, notably mere motions. If we can do this, we can consider whether actions are causally necessary consequents. No reason has been given for thinking that we cannot. We need not know everything of a class of events, or arrive at a correct philosophical analysis of the covering concept, in order to judge of them whether they are caused. Indeed, if we had to do this, we should know very few causal connections indeed.

There is one other attempt[19] to dissolve the problem of freedom and determinism at which I should like to look more closely. It is worth attention both as original and because it provides a different view of some familiarities. Its stated object is more adequately to defend the compatibility theory, and if it is successful it provides a new defence of the theory.

Most of our relationships with other people are said to consist in or to be governed by two different sorts of attitudes, *reactive* and *objective*. The first sort includes resentment, certain attitudes of love, gratitude, forgiveness. Such reactive attitudes are to a great extent dependent upon our beliefs about the attitudes of others toward us and reflect a kind of demand for goodwill or regard. They are at the root of a multitude of kinds of relation-ships, of which some are those between members of a family, col-leagues, sharers of a common interest, friends, lovers, people who meet briefly in various situations of life.

Consider occasions when resentment, for example, is a possi-bility, occasions when we have been injured by someone's action or manifestation of attitude. We in fact do not feel resentment, or feel it less than we might, when we accept that the action was not intended or that the person could not help it. What is also true, on these occasions, is that we do not respond with a suspension of *all* our reactive attitudes. We do not respond by coming to regard the agent as an inappropriate object of such attitudes.

On other occasions when resentment is a possibility, the injurious action may be explained (1) by pleas that the agent isn't himself or is under a great strain or, extraordinarily, that he is acting according to post-hypnotic suggestion. Alternatively the action may be explained (2) by pleas that he is only a child, or is schizophrenic, or subject to some known compulsion. On occasions of these kinds, of which the second group is more important, our resentment again is modified or disappears. Also, we are told, our *other* reactive attitudes to the agent are suspended or changed for a time or thereafter. When we see someone as warped or deranged, gravely neurotic or a child, *all* our reactive attitudes tend to be profoundly modified or to disappear. We move away from involvement or participation in a human relationship and towards an *objective* attitude.

To adopt the objective attitude to another human being is to see him, perhaps, as an object of social policy; as a subject for what, in a wide range of senses, might be called treatment; as something certainly to be taken account, perhaps precautionary account, of; to be managed or handled or cured or trained; perhaps simply to be avoided. ... The objective attitude may be emotionally toned in many ways, but not in all ways: it may include repulsion or fear, it may include pity or even love, though not all kinds of love. But it cannot include the range of reactive feelings and attitudes which belong to involvement or participation with others in inter-personal human relationships; it cannot include resentment, gratitude, forgiveness, anger, or the sort of love which two adults can sometimes be said to feel reciprocally for each other.[20]

If we take up this attitude mainly to persons who are abnormal in something like the mentioned ways, or whose situations are abnormal, we can also adopt it with respect to those who are normal. We can retreat from ordinary reactive attitudes in order to avoid involvement with others, or for reasons of policy, or out of a kind of curiosity.

One of the questions to which these reflections are an introduction is this: Would our accepting that determinism is true lead to the general decay of our reactive attitudes? Would it mean the end of gratitude and resentment, reciprocated adult loves, the essentially personal antagonisms? The answer given is that it would not, essentially for the following reason.

The human commitment to participation in ordinary inter-personal relationships is . . . too thoroughgoing and deeply rooted for us to take seriously the thought that a general theoretical conviction might so change our world that, in it, there were no longer any such things as inter-personal relationships as we normally understand them; and being involved in inter-personal relationships . . . is being exposed to the range of reactive attitudes and feelings that is in question.[21]

A second question is this one: what would it be rational to do if we came to believe determinism to be true? That is, putting aside the question of what we in fact would do, would it be rational to attempt to retreat from reactive attitudes? This, it is said, could be 'a real question' only for someone who fails to understand the depth of our commitment to such attitudes. This commitment is integral to the framework of human life, not something that can come up for review. Furthermore:

if we could imagine what we cannot have, viz. a choice in this matter, then we could choose rationally only in the light of an assessment of the gains and losses to human life, its enrichment or impoverishment; and the truth or falsity of a general thesis of determinism would not bear on the rationality of *this* choice.[22]

If we came to believe in determinism it would not be rational to be governed by what we took to be a true belief. If a belief in determinism were to lead us to suppose reactive attitudes out of place, in rationality we should persist in them.

Two propositions that are advanced, then, are that we would not and should not retreat from our normal human relationships if we came to accept determinism. A third one is that all our speculation so far is in a way otiose. The doctrine of determinism is itself unclear, we are told, but this much is evident: it is a doctrine which is thought by some to have a certain consequence. It would lead, if accepted, to our giving up reactive attitudes. If the doctrine in question does have this feature, it becomes somewhat clearer what it is, since we do know what ordinarily leads us to give up reactive attitudes to a particular individual. It is that he is incapacitated, seriously abnormal. But if the doctrine is clearer now, it is also obvious that it is incoherent. It is the incoherent doctrine that *everybody* is abnormal. This is a nonsense.

Let us, before turning to some related arguments that are advanced, examine what has already been said. The specific beliefs thought to lead to a shift toward objectivity in ordinary life are that the person in question is deranged or deluded, morally or intellectually underdeveloped, neurotically compulsive in an extraordinary way, systematically perverted in some way. This account, as may be anticipated, seems to me crucially misleading. It is true, no doubt, that considerations of this kind almost always precipitate our withdrawals toward objectivity in the given sense. That these considerations are in the forefront of our experience, however, is so for the reason that we generally assume that something else is true. We assume that human choices and actions are *not causally necessary*, that individuals can choose and act in ways other than they do. If we believed otherwise of someone, this would as surely give rise to a departure from reactive attitudes.

Consider resentment at a hurtful action. We may cease to feel it if we believe (1) that the agent is schizophrenic or in some other way incapacitated. We would as readily come to cease to feel it, however, if we believed (2) that he could not have acted in any other way than he did. The truth of this may be obscured in several ways. One may be inclined to doubt that resentment *would* disappear in the second case. Strong feelings, one may say, would persist. How, exactly, are they to be distinguished from resentment? But precisely the same difficulty arises in the first case. Given this, what may be put in question is the general distinction between reactive and objective attitudes, and any general claim about their genesis and persistence. We do not seem to have anything that suggests a distinction between our response to the given abnormal behaviour and what would be our response to behaviour believed to be determined.

In the second case *as much as in the first*, surely, involvement and participation in a human situation would give way to taking account of the agent as someone to be handled, treated, or at least in certain ways avoided. Consider the reactive attitude of adult love. One may be inclined to say that we might not cease to feel love for someone whose behaviour was taken to be determined. It can at least be replied, though, that our response would be similar if we came to believe the person to be in particular ways incapacitated or abnormal. Again, what is in question is the general doctrine about kinds of attitude and their persistence. What can reasonably be maintained is that a shift would take place as certainly if behaviour came to be regarded as determined as it would if the agent came to be regarded as incapacitated in one of the given ways. With respect to the reactive attitudes of gratitude and forgiveness, the contention can hardly be denied. These responses would not persist as they now are, certainly, in the face of a realization that determinism was true of the person in question. We would feel that questions of forgiveness and gratitude did not arise.

Given this, little needs to be said about the supposed incoherence of determinism. If one accepts that it might be true of everyone and also that to be subject to it is to be abnormal or incapacitated, there obviously is a certain difficulty. Not all members of a group can be abnormal, certainly, by the test of norms derived from behaviour of the group. But there is no reason whatever for accepting the conception of determinism as universal abnormality. The suggestion is that we must because (1) only beliefs as to abnormality could have the consequences in terms of attitudes claimed by some for determinism and (2) no other intelligible account of determinism is available. Both propositions, partly for reasons already given, are false.

To turn to the remaining contentions, would our acceptance of a general thesis of determinism lead to the decay of our reactive attitudes? The answer that it might do so seems as arguable as a denial.[23] In this area, clearly enough, one can do no more than engage in entirely vulnerable speculation. It would be absurd to maintain that in some relatively brief space of time, as a consequence of some limited corpus of evidence, we might depart from reactive attitudes. The possibility of an evolution of outlook, as a consequence of constantly improving evidence, is another matter. This would not be the *end* of inter-personal relationships but their radical alteration.

Would it be *rational* to attempt to retreat from reactive attitudes if we came to believe a general thesis of determinism? If we succeeded, it was implied, our existence would cease in some sense of the word to be human. Given this, if we had a choice, the rational course would not be to attempt to change our attitudes. As was rightly maintained, the question at issue is an entirely hypothetical one. Our attitudes might or might not change, but that they might change or persist as a consequence of *decision* is impossible. What is also true is that a continuation in reactive attitudes as we have conceived them would be inconsistent with our new view of persons. Such attitudes would imply that they could choose and act in ways they could not.

All of what we have been considering is an exercise in philosophical strategy. It is an attempt to get clearer about freedom and determinism by turning one's attention from a field where vision is obscured by habitual doctrine to a neighbouring one. As we have seen (pp. 117–18), it has always been maintained by those who hold the compatibility theory that even if determinism is true, we can continue in certain of our *moral* responses. We can, for example, continue to regard punishment as justified. We cannot regard offenders as in a certain sense responsible for their actions, but this is not necessary. Punishment is wholly a matter of prevention, of securing certain effects. So with acts of blaming, and responses of other kinds. The propositions we have been considering bear on these matters. We have turned to the subject of determinism and *non-moral* attitudes, reactive attitudes, in order to see more clearly what is true with respect to determinism and certain moral attitudes. We now return to that question.

Reactive attitudes are those that can be had by a person only because of the actions or attitudes of others *toward him*. They have analogues which are attitudes that may be felt by a person on account of the actions of others *toward others*. These may seem to be seen as disinterested, vicarious, impersonal, or generalized, and are said to be moral attitudes. They are attitudes to agents, rather than judgements about the rightness or wrongness of actions, and they centrally involve regarding persons as in a way responsible. There are also attitudes of a third category. These are those that a person may have to himself because of his actions toward others. If we begin with resentment as an example of a reactive attitude in the original sense, its moral analogue in the second category is moral indignation or moral disapprobation. It is also related to the third-category feelings of being responsible, of shame, and of guilt.

Predictable claims are made. If a man acts toward another in a certain way we may feel moral indignation. If we come to believe, say, that he acted out of a certain kind of ignorance, our attitude changes. If we come to believe he is in certain ways abnormal, perhaps someone whose picture of the world is a complete delusion, it is again true that our moral indignation changes or disappears. More important, however, we tend to cease to regard him as a fitting object of *any* moral attitude. He is not seen 'as a morally responsible agent, as a term of moral relationships, as a member of the moral community'.[24] He is not someone of whom one can say in a certain way that he ought to have done this, was responsible for that, or deserves moral condemnation for something else. Would acceptance of some general thesis of determinism lead to the decay of these attitudes? Would it be rational to attempt to inhibit such attitudes if we came to believe such a thesis? Do we ever retreat from such attitudes with respect to a particular person, in ordinary life, for reasons of determinism? In each case the answer given is no. The reasons are exactly parallel to those given in connection with the attitudes discussed earlier and are open to the same rebuttals.

I said a moment ago that these reflections on moral attitudes were intended to give a kind of support to the traditional compatibility theory. In order to defend that theory, its supporters conceive punishment and indeed ordinary moral judgements about individuals as no more than instruments of policy, treatment, or control. It is only by so conceiving them, it is supposed, that they remain a possibility in the face of determinism. In effect, supporters of the theory reconcile these things with determinism by assigning to them what we have been calling an *objective* character. They make them the expressions of objective attitudes.

If the whole enterprise of the argument we have been considering had been successful, we would have the satisfaction of also reconciling determinism with moral responses of a different character, those which I take to involve imputations of responsibility. The argument is not successful and that conclusion cannot be drawn.

One final remark. In considering free will and determinism, one is likely to overstate the importance of moral implications of one kind and another. There is very nearly as much reason, I think, to consider the problem in the light of other than moral attitudes. We wish to know, surely, if we are free in such a sense that what have been called the reactive attitudes are in place. This is an important interest in itself, and like other such interests dictates a criterion of relevance. We have the conclusion, given all the above argument, that it is mistaken to think that *if* determinism is true there is no large consequence having to do with our reactive attitudes. There *is* the consequence that they are, in their present form, out of place.[25]

5. Believing Determinism

If determinism is true, to bring together all that has been said, we are not free in such a way that we are responsible agents, or can ever decide or act otherwise than we do, or can take certain non-moral attitudes to be beyond question. Nor are we free in such a sense that we may consistently persist in certain moral responses. These consequences of determinism are in several ways related one to another, but I shall say no more about them. What I wish to suggest instead is that there is one more incompatibility, more fundamental than these. It is unusual in that it itself may be thought to have a curious consequence with respect to determinism. I shall first summarize the argument.

If determinism is true, then *judgement*, in a certain sense, is impossible. Determinism is inconsistent with our most rooted conception of judgement and so, I shall suggest, if determinism is taken to be true there is no possibility of confident belief. It follows, further, given that our claims to knowledge presuppose belief, that if determinism is taken to be true we cannot claim knowledge. In particular, we cannot persist in the belief that determinism is true. We cannot continue to claim that we know it to be true. Any attempt to prove it to be true, then, will be self-defeating. All that we can possibly do, if we choose to reflect on the matter, is to come to believe it false. It may be suggested at this point, mistakenly, that if we cannot claim knowledge of the truth of determinism, we might none the less persist in regarding it as probable or likely. The answer, of course, is that if determinism is claimed to be probably true, then that very claim to knowledge of a probability is put in question.[26]

The argument consists fundamentally in the claims that inasmuch as judgement of a certain kind is inconsistent with determinism, so is the possibility of confident belief and claims to knowledge. In considering this, let us admit first that *thinking* is not inconsistent with determinism. One would not hesitate to say, at any rate, that a man might *have the thought that* something or other was the case even if the events of his thinking it were causally necessary consequents. We regard the having of thoughts as something passive, as it was once common to say, and perhaps for this reason we are not opposed to the idea that having thoughts may be something subject to causation. Is this an attitude of absolutely general scope? It seems so. It seems true of the having of thoughts which are close reports of sense experience and it seems equally true with regard to, say, idle reflections, thoughts that certain things are relevant evidence for something, thoughts that conclusions are logically necessary or inductively well established. This is also related to, or perhaps identical with, the point sometimes made in the assertion that 'belief is involuntary'. Against this, however, we must put some other facts. They concern what may be called concepts of judgement: those of judging, assessing, inquiring, investigating, appraising evidence, and a great many others. To do any of these things is, to say no more, not merely to have thoughts.

Assuredly there are possible but not actual uses of these terms of judgement, with respect to persons, that do not have the consequence in which I am interested. Suppose we imagine someone, *of whom determinism is true*, reflecting on some scientific law. He wonders if it is vacuous, thinks it isn't, reflects on the kinds of evidence for it. We might say of him that he is engaged in an inquiry in the same sense that we might say it of a computer. We might evaluate his procedure in a number of ways. Centrally, we might evaluate it as to the correctness or truth of particular beliefs to which he comes. One distinguishing feature of this situation we imagine, however, would be the absence on our part of a quite different evaluative attitude. As in the case of a computer, we would not in a certain familiar sense commend the thinker for his performance, give him credit for it. It would not be that we would give it to someone else, or something else, but rather that the question would not arise at all. This would be explained by our supposition that each of the thinker's reflections was a causally necessary consequent. Whatever answer or speculation he came to, or indeed whatever question, his coming to it was a matter of causal determination.

We might say of a thinker of whom we imagined this to be true that he was in a sense making judgements, testing hypotheses, considering propositions for consistency. Nevertheless, there is another use of such descriptions which we would take to be out of place. We certainly would not be surprised if someone said something like this: 'If what is true is that he couldn't at any moment think anything other than he does, given causal antecedents, it's absurd to say that he's really judging or carrying out an inquiry at all. He's not *doing* anything. All that's to be said is that things are happening to him.' It would not come as a surprise to be reminded that there is a use of descriptions of intellectual sequences that involves the assumption that they are not matters of causal necessity. Indeed, this may be said to be the central ordinary use of such descriptions.

What I wish to suggest is that if we could judge only in the first sense and not judge in this second sense, the ordinary one, we could not have confident belief and make claims to knowledge. It is requisite of my coming to such beliefs that I take them to be the product of a kind of process which is impossible if determinism is true. It is easy here and elsewhere to succumb to one of the persistent temptations of this discussion. It is easy to assert that we take ourselves to know that something is so because the evidence *is* this or that and *does* support the conclusion. This is no more than a concealing abbreviation. The evidence does not announce the conclusion. It is nowhere near a sufficient condition for my claiming to know that I am here that in fact I am here.

Let us consider several possible objections to the thesis I am advancing. 'Perhaps,' someone suggests, 'you are reluctant to say that we would claim to know something under the supposed conditions because you are impressed or worried by what is essentially an irrelevant consideration. As you have implied, if we could be said to know anything under conditions of determinism we could not, in a certain sense, *take credit for it*. I suppose there is some sense of the words in which this is true. We could not take credit or be commended, because none of our beliefs would seem to be related to our doing. It could be said, if the language fits, that our beliefs happened to us. But none of this goes any way toward explaining why we couldn't have confident beliefs and claim knowledge if determinism was true.' This supposed explanation of error seems to me ineffective. People may find determinism, in so far as it has consequences for certain fundamental attitudes to themselves and others, a consequential doctrine indeed. It is, in a way, diminishing. It will be in place to consider such a diagnostic explanation of the thesis that is being advanced only after the reason for it has been examined.

Alternatively, another attempt might be made to explain the supposed mistake. 'Perhaps what is bothering you,' it might be said, 'is that in ordinary life we do sometimes explain what we take to be errors by what seem to be causal explanations. Take the case where a man is called upon to judge the probable results of two possible courses of action. One of these is an orthodox course, the other a revolutionary one. He himself is a man of strikingly traditional and circumscribed outlook. We believe, when he finishes his investigation, that he has judged the likely consequences of the two courses of action very badly. We may say that he has done so because, given his outlook, he is incapable of an impartial and generally perceptive analysis of what is in question. It may seem, that is, that we connect mistaken judgements with their being caused. Perhaps this is what moves you to feel that determinism and confident belief are incompatible. But, if you reflect a bit more, you will see that just the kind of explanation given of the man we have just imagined can be given of someone we take to have made a perfectly correct estimate of something or other. In this case, what we say is that he came to the right answer because he is a man of certain character, one such that his inclinations do not distort his judgement.' This supposed explanation of error may be an explanation of the attitudes of some people. There is no reason for supposing that the claim I intend must rest on any such misconception. Nor do I accept, of course, any implication of the objection that we *normally* take judgement to be causally necessary.

Suppose now, to forget about objectors for a moment, that we ourselves are asked to make some such investigation as the one just imagined. In the past we have carried out such investigations and then been forced to the realization that we made mistakes. Someone now says, of our present conclusions, that they seem to him mistaken. He does not show how. He says only that our having made what he takes to be mistakes comes as no surprise, because he considers us incapable of surmounting the effects of prejudice. If we are moved by this at all, I contend, it will be impossible to avoid doubt about our conclusions. What we may say or do, of course, is another matter.

The ground of our doubt will be that we are impressed by the claim that *we could not have decided otherwise than we did*. It may be objected at this point that we might indeed have doubts, but only for the good inductive reasons of our already proven fallibility. It may be replied that while there are such situations, it is also a familiar fact that there are situations of just the sort suggested. In any case, precisely the same argument can be made out with respect to a man who has a splendid record of getting things right. If I am him, and *if* somebody produces a convincing argument to the effect that because of a cause inherent in a certain situation I was incapable of concluding in any other way than I did, I shall fall into doubt. I shall take more convincing of the alleged incapability than in the previous situation, but that is not really important. What is important is my response *if* I do come to believe I could not have concluded in any other way.

A particular distinction is worth reiterating at this point. That what we take to be true *is* true is a matter of the way things are. That it *is* true or false is a matter of the facts as they are. In the usual case, the truth or falsity of what we believe does not depend on how we came to believe it. I may come to believe what is true by an absurdly irrelevant process of reflection. I am not at present interested in the conditions of truth, but rather the assurances we require in order to take our beliefs to be true. Under what conditions can we have confidence in what we believe? The examples indicate that a necessary condition of having confidence in a belief p is the further belief *that one could have come to some belief other than p*. That is, a necessary condition is that the belief was not a causally necessary consequent. It is no good saying that we have confidence in our beliefs when we think they reflect the way things are. Certainly it is a necessary condition of my believing something that I take my belief to correspond to the facts. There is a prior question, however. It is this one: Under what conditions can I be confident that my beliefs *do* correspond to the facts?

What is it that leads us, or leads some of us, to resist the claim that we might have confidence in a belief while thinking that we could not have come to any other? The explanation, I think, is that having confidence in a belief requires us to think that we have good reasons for it. We must think, that is, that the thoughts which led to the belief were in fact good reasons for it. Certainly they *might* have been just this. It is not that we believe they could not have been.[27] The difficulty is that *whether or not* they were good reasons for the belief, the belief was a necessary consequent of something. We may suppose, for simplicity, although it is not essential to the argument, that the thoughts constituted the causal circumstance which had the belief as their necessary effect.

Is there some confusion here? Is it open to someone to say that we might have good reasons for the belief whether or not the thoughts which produced it were such? It is true, of course, that there might *be good reasons for the belief*, where that means simply that the belief may be true. What we are after, however, is something in consciousness that gives support to the belief, reasons in the sense of thoughts. These, however, give rise to beliefs as effects.[28] That they are, as we say, *good* reasons or *bad* reasons, is immaterial. Their causal properties, to put the matter one way, are not their logical properties. The belief that p may be an excellent reason for the belief that q and a reason against the belief that r. But why should we think that the first belief *causes* the second and does not cause the third?

It may seem, at this point, that what is demanded is that we *only* move from beliefs which are good reasons for certain propositions to beliefs in those propositions. That is, it may seem that the demand amounts to the requirement that we never fall into error. This is an absurd demand and, it may be said, it is similarly absurd to argue against determinism on the ground that it does not exclude the possibility of error. This is misunderstanding. What is being claimed is that if we are to stay confident in a belief we must believe we have good reasons for it. Its seeming correctness for us depends, as it must, on the thoughts we have had. If we accept determinism we must take it that these reflections would have produced the belief whether or not they were good reasons for it.

I have, I am afraid, already said about as much as I am able to bring into literalness and clarity in support of my contention. That confident belief requires judgement, in the ordinary sense, is to some people a very nearly irresistible claim. To some others, perhaps few in number, it is resistible. One's reaction presumably has to do with self-images that are out of clear view, in a way beyond adequate conceptualization. It is notoriously true that we lack enlightening or satisfying descriptions, of a positive nature, of judgement in the ordinary sense. We would like to have something specific and tangible about the supposed relationships between one's evidence-beliefs or premiss-beliefs and one's beliefs that certain conclusions are true. We should like to have useful concepts much less crude than those which have been pressed into service in this discussion. It does not help to declare that conclusions must be derived from 'active reflection'. Nor is there help to be found in recourse to such phrases as 'the faculty of judgement', or in recourse to the elusive notion of rationality. There is also the embarrassment that one cannot give an effective explanation of why better descriptions of ordinary judgement are not forthcoming. All that one has is the feeling that there is some sense in the irritating utterance that thought cannot take itself as its object.

These are excellent reasons for a certain hesitancy of argument. They are not good reasons, it seems to me, for abandoning the point of view. The alternative conception of judgement, as something of which determinism is true, is as far from being a paradigm of completeness and clarity.

6. Implications

Let us review what has been said. Determinism is not to be put aside as insufficiently intelligible to allow for useful discussion. That state of our understanding of the causal relationship does not give us this conclusion. Nor, although I have not paid them much attention, do certain difficulties in the philosophy of mind. Determinism, secondly, is not to be reconciled with our notions of freedom in the traditional way of the empiricists. That there is a conflict is not to be evaded either by the familiar stratagem having to do with constraint or the several successors to that doctrine. If determinism is true, our conception of persons as responsible agents is false, we cannot decide or act otherwise than we do, and our reactive attitudes and some of our moral responses are in question. Furthermore, as I have just suggested, if determinism is true we cannot persist in confident belief or advance claims to knowledge. At this point, however, I wish to correct a certain impression.

There seems to me no point in refusing to recognize the extent of the conflict between determinism and other things. It is greater than many philosophers have supposed. At the same time what has been said about belief and knowledge-claims should not be misconstrued. It seems to me true that we could never come to accept determinism in the way that we now accept many things. We can never, with respect to determinism, have a part of what we now regard as necessary to confident belief. It is not too much to say that we can never have about it what we now describe as confident belief. This is not to say that we can never come to *accept* it. If we were to do this, our concepts both of belief and its grounds would necessarily change. We would not have what we presently count as beliefs and grounds. These changes in themselves, putting aside other consequences of the acceptance of determinism, would amount to a transformation in outlook. That it would be a deeply fundamental one is not a reason for thinking that it could not occur. It seems possible that there have been others in the course of human development.

Through all this there persists the question of the truth of determinism. A long discussion of the evidence, given the evidence that seems to exist, would give rise only to an answer that is already familiar. The issue is not in fact decidable.[29] I am inclined to add that this description of the state of affairs is at least misleading. It seems true that there is a considerable difference between the way in which we come to decide particular propositions about the world or ourselves and the way in which we come to change more inclusive conceptions which underlie and govern large areas of belief. It cannot be false or misleading to say, however, that there remains a question about human freedom and responsibility.

A justification of punishment in terms of retribution, then, makes what must be regarded as an assumption. We may then add a question to the evaluative criticism already made of the traditional retribution theory. The same question arises with respect to those attempted justifications which are in part retributivist. A related question faces those critics of the retribution theory who begin from an assumption of the truth of determinism. It also faces those who regard criminality in a certain way as a consequence of some quite general doctrine of determinism. To anticipate what I shall suggest is the best defence of a practice of punishment, it does *not* require an assumption of freedom in the way of retributivist theories. That possible justification of punishment does not depend on the assumption that men can act otherwise than they do. However, given our present attitudes the acceptance of that justification, like any other belief, does require that we are able to judge differently from the way we do.

1. This ordinary sense of 'cause' is closely related to the legal sense, which is carefully discussed in H. L. A. Hart and A. M. Honoré, *Causation in the Law* (Oxford, 1959).

2. The remark is by Moritz Schlick, 'Causality in Everyday Life and Recent Science', *Readings in Philosophical Analysis* (New York, 1949), edited by Herbert Feigl and Wilfrid Sellars, p. 517.

3. Cf. John Watling, 'Propositions Asserting Causal Connection', *Analysis*, 1953, and Peter Downing, 'Levels of Discourse', Ph.D. dissertation, University of London, 1959. This view is fully developed in chapter one of my *A Theory of Determinism: The Mind, Neuroscience, and Life-Hopes*.

4. I do not mean to imply that there are no useful senses of 'cause' other than the two mentioned or that only a determinism based on the sense just set out poses a problem for human freedom.

5. A useful layman's summary of recent research of the kind mentioned in this paragraph, together with bibliographies, can be found in *The Machinery of the Brain* (New York, 1963), by Dean E. Wooldridge. See also chapter five of my *A Theory of Determinism: The Mind, Neuroscience, and Life-Hopes*.

6. Moritz Schlick, *Problems of Ethics* (New York, 1939), translated by David Rynin, p. 143.

7. See, in addition to Schlick, op. cit., and works to be discussed: A. J. Ayer, 'Freedom and Necessity', *Philosophical Essays* (London, 1954); C. L. Stevenson, *Ethics and Language* (New Haven, 1944), chapter fourteen; Philippa Foot, 'Freewill as Involving Determinism', *Philosophical Review*, 1957; Paul Edwards, 'Hard and Soft Determinism', in *Determinism and Freedom* (New York, 1958), edited by Sidney Hook; John Hospers, 'What Means This Freedom?', in Hook, op. cit. The, or one, genesis of the doctrine is to be found in Aristotle, *Nicomachean Ethics*, Book Three.

8. Hobbes, 'Of Liberty and Necessity', *English Works*, volume four.

9. Hume, An *Enquiry Concerning Human Understanding* (Selby-Bigge edition), p. 95.

10. Schlick, op. cit., pp. 150–51.

11. Schlick, loc. cit. For the best known detailed reply see C. A. Campbell, 'Is Freewill a Pseudo-Problem?', *Mind*, 1951.

12. Cf. R. M. Hare, *Freedom and Reason* (Oxford, 1963), chapter four.

13. The compatibilist analysis of 'could have done otherwise' is advanced by G. E. Moore, *Ethics* (London, 1912), chapter six. The criticism is due to J. L. Austin, 'Ifs and Cans', *Philosophical Papers* (Oxford, 1961).

14. Gilbert Ryle, *The Concept of Mind* (London, 1949), p. 76.

15. Ryle, op. cit., p. 78.

142 *Freedom*

16. Cf. Bernard Williams, 'Postscript', in *Freedom and the Will* (London, 1963), edited by D. F. Pears, p. 141. (Also, New York, 1963.)

17. A. I. Melden, *Free Action* (London, 1961), p. 72. See also R. S. Peters, *The Concept of Motivation* (London, 1958). (Also, New York, 1965.)

18. The distinction between understanding and being able to give a correct philosophical analysis of a term or proposition is perhaps due to G. E. Moore, 'A Defence of Common Sense', *Philosophical Papers* (London, 1959). See especially p. 37.

19. P. F. Strawson, 'Freedom and Resentment', *Proceedings of the British Academy*, 1962.

20. ibid., pp. 194–5.

21. ibid., p. 197.

22. ibid., p. 199.

23. Cf. Isaiah Berlin, 'Historical Inevitability', in *Four Essays on Liberty* (Oxford, 1969).

24. Strawson, op. cit., p. 202.

25. This is not to say that *all* that is involved in, say, gratitude or resentment is out of place. I discuss this issue further in one of the *Essays on Freedom of Action* (London, 1973) edited by myself.

26. I have, since the original edition of this book was published, come to change my mind about the general argument of this section. It no longer seems to me at all correct to say, as it does to others, perhaps even a majority of philosophers, that determinism is inconsistent with judgement and knowledge. If determinism is a tenable doctrine, we also have the further argument against the retribution theory of punishment mentioned at the beginning of this chapter.

I have chosen, for the usual reason, to let the section stand as it is. For an account of why its conclusion seems to me mistaken, see my *A Theory of Determinism: The Mind, Neuroscience, and Free-Hopes*.

27. As is suggested by A. J. Ayer, 'Fatalism', *The Concept of a Person and Other Essays* (London, 1963), p. 266.

28. That reasons, in this sense, can be causes seems to me true but should, no doubt, have been argued. See Alasdair MacIntyre, 'Determinism', *Mind*, 1957; Donald Davidson, 'Actions, Reasons and Causes', *Journal of Philosophy*, 1963; David Pears, 'Are Reasons for Actions Causes?', in *Epistemology* (New York, 1967), edited by Avrum Stroll.

29. About this too, since the original edition of this book, I have changed my mind. See chapters five and six of my *A Theory of Determinism: The Mind, Neuroscience, and Life-Hopes*.

CHAPTER SIX: COMPROMISES

1. Retrospect and Prospect

There no longer are defenders of the traditional retribution theory, or at least of the version that we are obliged rather than permitted to punish offenders because they deserve it. At any rate, there are no defenders writing in the usual places. That the theory *as clarified* should find defenders is pretty well unthinkable: the causing of distress or suffering to offenders, mainly to give relatively small grievance-satisfactions to others, would no longer be regarded as morally permissible, much less obligatory, if ever it was. The traditional deterrence view is also in decline,[1] for different reasons, if not so abandoned as the view that punishment is justified by reformative effects. On the other hand, the related theory that treatment rather than punishment is or would be justified by its effects alone is very much a part of the outlook of many people concerned in practical ways with criminality and other social problems. Whatever the popularity of these four views, it seems to me established that none of them is defensible.

The argument about victimization, to mention only that, applies to both the traditional deterrence theory and to reformist doctrines. Hence no combination of deterrence and reform is sufficient to justify either punishment or a system under which some offenders are punished and others treated. This remains true although the combination has a recommendation that may come to mind. Let us recall that one other argument against the traditional deterrence theory or at any rate its application was that a considerable number of individuals are either unlikely to be influenced or quite certainly not to be influenced by the prospect of punishment. One obvious way of avoiding *this* objection is to recommend a selective system of punishment and treatment. Nonetheless, if such a system were given over to only the aims of reducing offences and rehabilitating offenders it still would face the victimization objection. Also, it might well involve unacceptable indoctrination. If it did not have possible consequences of victimization, it could not be that it was governed only by the aims of deterrence and reform.

The retribution theory mainly fails because it pays attention only to certain desires, or at least pays them too much attention. These, of course, are grievance-desires. In effect, the retribution theory ignores the welfare both of offenders and of those individuals who may be harmed by future offences. It has the recommendation, on the other hand, that since it treats offenders and others as they deserve, it prohibits unacceptable victimizations. The forward-looking theories, those of deterrence and reform, are quite given over to the pursuit of welfare. They fail, in the view of a number of contemporary philosophers who have considered them, because they ignore desert, somehow understood. Given this, it has seemed possible that a solution to the problem of punishment can be found in a compromise. Punishing a man is justified, it is supposed, if *two* conditions are satisfied. The punishment must be deserved and it must prevent offences in the future. What remains of the traditional retribution theory is but one part of the supposed obligation, that part which limits or prohibits punishment rather than demands it (see p. 24). We are said never to be obliged to punish because it is deserved but rather to be obliged *not* to punish if it is not deserved.

I should like to look at some accounts of this kind although, as will be seen, we have already anticipated some questions that will arise and settled others. Let us take stock of our position. In the second chapter we arrived at a certain account of the meaning of desert claims as used by retributivists. To say a man deserves a penalty may be to say (1) that he has behaved culpably, (2) that his penalty would satisfy a grievance caused by his action, (3) that his envisaged treatment would be like the treatment of similar offenders, (4) that freely and responsibly he acted in such a way as to fall under a known penalty system, and (5) that unlike non-offenders he has gained satisfactions through the commission of an offence.

In the next chapter we saw that in certain circumstances which allow for choice, a punishment would be preferable to a victimization (chapter three, section five). This preference could be defended by elements of the claim that the punishment would be deserved. However, on further analysis, this claim amounted to just this: the punishment would be (i) in accord with a consideration of equality and (ii) more economical of distress than the victimization. We also concluded, earlier in the third chapter, that in a certain circumstance doing nothing at all would be preferable to a possible very unfair victimization (chapter three, section four). Again, the preference could be defended by the claim that the victimization would be undeserved. Here, however, this could be understood only as the proposition that the victimization would make for gross inequality of treatment.

Thus, to sum up, we came to regard desert claims as consisting in appeals to equality and essentially utilitarian appeals for the minimization of distress. The compromise theories of punishment, to which we are now coming, attempt to justify it partly by the argument that it is deserved. It is not seen or granted, however, that this argument can be no more than an appeal to one or both of equality and economy of distress. If it can be no more than this, these theories are unclear or confusedly claim a defence of punishment that does not exist. I shall amplify this in discussing them.

There is another preliminary point to be noticed. I have said that to support a man's penalty as deserved is ordinarily to say, partly, that his action was free and responsible. This is inherent in the contained propositions that he behaved culpably and in contravention of a known penalty system. It is undeniable that this is a part of what is intended by the usual talk of desert. It is part of what is intended, certainly, in the arguments of the traditional retribution theory and all or almost all compromise theories. It would be mistaken, therefore, to suppose that human freedom is not a direct presupposition of these views.

We may, however, produce radical variants of them in which the argument from desert is specified as having only the force of an appeal to equality and economy, and everything else is renounced. I shall consider a compromise theory of this kind. Here, that a man acted freely and responsibly will *not* be a presupposition. Here the argument from desert, still reasonably so called, will be that punishment may be in accord with principles of equality and involve a lesser distress than victimization. The latter depends in part on the fact we have noticed that offenders and possible victims have different expectations (chapter three, section five). That they have these expectations does not depend on their having in fact acted freely and responsibly. That they have them depends on their having knowingly acted in accordance with, or in contravention of, the law.

2. Logical Retributivism, Separate Questions

Two things need to be cleared away before we come to consider several compromise theories. The first is a quite different 'reconciliation' of the traditional accounts of the justification of punishment.[2] Desert, we are told, is not a moral but rather a logical condition of punishment. That is, to say a man was punished although he did not deserve it, or, as it is usually expressed, was not guilty, is to say something self-contradictory. It is to say something self-contradictory in virtue of the meaning of the term 'punishment'.

. . . the necessity of not punishing the innocent is not moral but logical. It is not, as some retributivists think, that we *may* not punish the innocent and *ought* only to punish the guilty, but that we *cannot* punish the innocent and *must* only punish the guilty. Of course, the suffering or harm in which punishment consists can be and is inflicted on innocent people, but this is not punishment, it is judicial error or terrorism or, in Bradley's characteristically repellent phrase, 'social surgery'. The infliction of suffering on a person is only properly described as punishment if that person is guilty.[3]

To adopt the recommended definition of punishment, which does reproduce some ordinary understanding of the term, *is* to adopt the view that guilt or desert is a logically necessary condition of punishment. It is now argued, quite unconvincingly, that precisely this view has been the essential thesis of retribution. It is claimed that retributivists have been merely concerned to assert that punishment *can* be of the guilty only, where this is an assertion not about what is morally allowable but rather about the meaning of the term 'punishment'. It will be evident that I take this to be false.

The traditional retribution theory maintains that we are morally obliged or at least permitted to punish those who deserve penalties and prohibited from punishing anyone else. It is not the view that we are not to *describe* imprisonments or fines as punishment if those who are imprisoned or fined are not guilty. The compromise theories which we shall examine may be described as partly retributivist in that they involve some moral prohibition on punishing those who do not deserve penalties. They are not partly claims to the effect that we must, if we are to be self-consistent, describe as punishment only what is done to persons who are guilty of offences.

Of course, if one does use the term 'retributivist' to describe the logical or terminological claim, it will be possible to name diverse accounts of punishment as retributivist. This will depend entirely on how the term 'punishment' is used in these accounts. One such account, if we make it explicit, is just that punishments are morally justified if they deter economically and that only those impositions of distress that are deserved can correctly be called punishments. This is the deterrence theory, with a morally irrelevant addition.

We have already considered precisely this account, and also rejected the supposition that the terminological addition is a barrier against victimization-criticisms (chapter three, section two). Defenders of this account, as we saw, wish to maintain two things. (1) The given moral justification of punishment is in terms of economical deterrence alone. (2) Undeserved impositions of distress, victimizations, are not permissible even if they serve to deter economically. Either (1) or (2) must be given up. If the envisaged victimizations are not permissible, then it cannot be true that punishments are justified solely in virtue of being deterrents. It must be that they are thought to have some other justification, which must be made explicit. What needs to be produced is not a definition. If, on the other hand, punishments *are* justified *solely* because they are deterrents, then certain victimizations would be similarly justified. There is one obvious line of retreat if it is thought that these victimizations would not be acceptable. One may depart from the deterrence account and take up an explicit view of the kind we are about to examine. On the straightforward one already mentioned, punishments are said to be justified when they are both deserved and also preventive of offences.

The second preliminary matter has to do with a way in which discussions of compromise views of punishment are commonly introduced. It will be worth looking at it briefly for several reasons. One is that it sometimes appears to be intended as something like an argument for the conclusion that punishment must be justified by several principles. Another is that it is regarded as a preferred or indeed essential mode of procedure. My own procedure has been, and mostly will be, to consider the single question, 'What, if anything, can morally justify the practice of punishment?' A number of philosophers would regard this as an error, one with considerable consequences.

It has been said that in our inherited ways of talking about punishment we persistently over-simplify separate issues. What we must notice, if we are to avoid confusion, is that there is more than one question to be considered.[4] The institution or practice of punishment has several features. Only certain persons are punished and only certain penalties are imposed. It therefore raises several quite separate questions of justification.

There is the overall question, 'What justifies the general practice of punishment?' or 'What is the good of maintaining this institution?' This has been named the question of the *General Justifying Aim* of the institution. Secondly, there is the question of *Liability*. It is this: 'To whom may punishment be applied?' Finally, there is the question of *Amount*. 'How severely may we punish?' We are invited to see that there are these three distinct questions, and also to see that different answers are in place with respect to them. Surely the General Justifying Aim of punishment must be the prevention of crime. The answer to the question of who may be punished, surely, is that only those who deserve it or are guilty may be. A partly retributivist answer is in place, it may be urged, with respect to the third question. A man should not be given a larger penalty than he deserves. In some such way as this one is led toward the view that punishment is justified only by several different considerations. Let us consider this supposed persuasion of the truth of compromise theories before deciding on the supposed necessity of asking separate questions.

One is led toward a compromise view, we are told, by the fact that the first question is rightly answered in terms of prevention, the second rightly answered in terms of desert, and the third in terms of both. Whether these things are true, of course, depends on how each of the three questions is understood. As so far expressed, they are vague and ambiguous.

Consider the second question, 'To whom may punishment be applied?' It is a long step in the direction of irrelevance to see this as peculiarly a question for a judge.[5] If one answers as if one were a judge, of course, there is a temptation to give the answer that punishment may be applied only to those who have broken the law. This may be to regard the question in a way which makes it irrelevant to our inquiry. A judge may indeed be said to be justified in singling out for punishment those who have broken the law. This is to say, ordinarily, that his action is in accord with his powers and duties, as defined by law. But we are not inquiring into *legality*, into legal powers and obligations. We wish to know what can be said in moral justification of what is done by judges in accordance with their legal powers and obligations.

Let us try to understand the given question, 'To whom may punishment be applied?', in another way – a way such that it might have the answer toward which we are being urged. It may be taken as this question: What, if anything, morally justifies our punishing only those who have broken the law? Could the fact that it is only these individuals who may be said to deserve punishment provide a *sufficient* answer to the question? Obviously not, since desert is not a sufficient justification for punishing any individual. This is the retribution theory, which has been rejected. It is rejected, indeed, by the philosophers whose compromise views we are considering.

One might (skipping some other possibilities) take the question to be this: What justification is there for having as a feature of the practice of punishment a total prohibition against punishing those who are not offenders? As we have seen it is in general but *not always* true that we must not victimize, penalize non-offenders, if prevention is to be economical. This final version of the question, then, *can* be answered in terms of desert alone. We have a certain bar or prohibition because only offenders can be said to deserve penalties. This is to say, if my reductive argument about ordinary desert claims is correct, that we have the bar because it serves economy and equality.

One can give similar interpretations, with similar results, to the third question, 'How severely may we punish?' As for the first one, about the General Justifying Aim of punishment, it is ambiguous in a way peculiar to itself. It may be taken to be about the *aim* of punishment, which is certainly to be distinguished from its justification. It is sometimes true that to mention the aim of a particular line of action is to mention an accepted justification. On other occasions this is not so. My aim in badgering a man may be to get back a book he has borrowed; my justification may be that he promised to return it in a week without fail. It does seem true to say that one aim of punishment is prevention. A goal we want to achieve is a state of affairs where there are fewer offences committed. But it is clear that if the question about the practice or institution of punishment is to specify a part of our present inquiry, which is a moral one, it cannot be taken to be about only the aim or goal of the practice.

If we are asking what adequate moral justification can be given of the practice, it is quite mistaken to think that one can be given in terms of the prevention of offences alone. This is established by the argument about victimization. Some such argument is accepted by those who espouse compromise theories. How then can they suppose that the moral justification of the practice can be prevention alone when they also require another different reason, in terms of desert? That this second reason may be related to a particular feature of the practice, the sentencing procedure, is immaterial. Something the same may be said, not that it matters much, for the reason having to do with prevention. One might mention the publicity of punishment.

It is not at all clear, then, why anyone who feels that a compromise or two-value justification is necessary should also think the practice as a whole justified by only one of them. There is some explanation, no doubt, in the confusion of aim with justification. This confusion may be made easier, incidentally, by an assumption similar to one noticed above. That is, it is sometimes supposed that the question about the justification of the practice is peculiarly one for legislators. Legislators are concerned with a society's larger intentions, including the prevention of offences, although not exclusively so concerned. Even if they were concerned solely with aims, nothing would follow about the answer to our question. Of course one *can* contrive a moral question, in some sense about the practice, whose answer will be in terms of prevention alone. It is: What is to be said for the practice of punishment other than that it is governed in certain ways by rules of desert?

Let us sum up our progress so far. It seems that it is *possible* to produce specific questions about punishment such that they may have different kinds of answer. These appear not to be the questions had in mind by the philosophers who have favoured this procedure. But, and this is the most important point, that we can ask particular questions that *may* have the desired answers does not in itself establish anything about the answers. The mere fact that we can ask these particular questions is consistent with *all* the answers being solely in terms of prevention, or solely in terms of desert. There is no reason for thinking that some separate-questions procedure inevitably or logically leads one to a compromise theory. The existence of separate questions does not constitute an *argument* for the conclusion that punishment must be justified by several principles.

Is it nevertheless true that one is likely to fall into confusion if one does not ask these questions, or some other set of separate questions? This seems to me mainly the claim that philosophers who have given single-reason answers about punishment, inadequate ones, would have done otherwise if they had asked separate questions. This is less than convincing. Utilitarians did not ignore the fact that there are prohibitions with respect to who can be punished and to what extent. In effect they isolated the question about the basis of these prohibitions and gave, as we have seen, partly mistaken answers. One can say of the traditional retributivists, similarly, that they were not unaware of the claim that the practice of punishment does have certain preventive effects. Following Kant, they commonly introduced this fact into discussion in order to deny its moral relevance.

Are *we* likely to fall into confusion if we do not ask separate questions? We shall not fall into the confusion of thinking that a single-reason answer to the moral question about punishment will do. Nor does it seem likely that we will risk other confusions. Certainly we must keep in mind the different features of the practice of punishment, and not only those having to do with certain prohibitions. We must consider what contribution may be made to the justification of the practice by particular features. But this we can do without a mechanical separation of questions. One question will do.

Our fundamental and final concern, obviously, must be with the question of what justification can be given for the practice of punishment taken as a whole. It seems to me clear that this is a satisfactory formulation of the problem which all theories of punishment attempt to answer.

3. Punishment and Rights

So much for preliminaries. I should like now to look at the intricacies of four accounts of punishment which involve claims about both prevention and desert. They are expressions, in different ways, of persisting attitudes and errors.

The first one is announced, quite mistakenly, as a view to the effect that while the justification of punishment is not to be found simply in terms of preventive effects, no part of the justification has to do with the desert of offenders. Rather, we are told, it is partly a matter of *rights*.[6]

The state is said to have a '*prima facie* obligation' to protect the rights of individuals, rights which may be infringed by criminal acts. It has a *prima facie* obligation to try in some way to prevent offences before they occur. However, there are certain principles which govern the measures it may take. All individuals, including those accused of offences, start with rights to life, liberty, property and other things. These are rights against the state as well as against other individuals. In virtue of having these rights, however, each man has obligations to others. He has obligations to respect *their* rights. If he does respect them his own rights remain intact. If he does not, he loses them, and the state can act against him.

All of these propositions must be taken to be about moral rather than legal rights. It is not always true that a state is under any kind of moral obligation (even a *prima facie* one, the nature of which will be explained in a moment) to maintain legal rights. This is not the case if the rights in question lack moral justification, as many have. Given even that all of the legal rights of citizens *do* have a moral justification, they can give rise to the moral obligation in question only in virtue of their moral acceptability and not merely their legality. They can give rise to the moral obligation, that is, only in virtue of their status as *moral* rights. I do not wish to maintain, of course, that the existence of expectations which are founded on rights fixed in law does not give rise to *any* special moral obligations. What I wish to maintain and what is hardly controvertible is that there is no overriding moral obligation to maintain a *status quo* simply because it is supported by legal rights.

Suppose an offence has been committed. The state has a *prima facie* duty to try to prevent more offences of this kind, violations of the rights of individuals, and punishment may seem to be a means to this end. However, the state is under another *prima facie* obligation not itself to violate rights. Such obligations, incidentally, are merely reasons counting in favour of a course of action. To be under such an obligation, it must be stressed, is not to be under an obligation in one ordinary sense. One can act in a way not in accord with a particular *prima facie* obligation and yet not be open to moral censure or reprobation. To be under conflicting *prima facie* obligations with respect to a particular situation is to be in a position such that there are reasons for and against a particular action. A consideration of *prima facie* obligations, however, at least in some cases, gives rise to an obligation in another sense, an obligation whose breaking *does* involve moral blame. This we may call an absolute obligation.

To return to our imagined offence, consider the possibility of imprisoning Brown, who is *not* the offender. The state is under a *prima facie* obligation to Brown to respect his rights, and a *prima facie* obligation to all citizens to try to prevent the recurrence of offences of the kind in question. Unless circumstances are extremely unusual, such that society will be in extreme danger unless Brown is imprisoned, the emerging absolute obligation of the state is not to imprison him. On the other hand, consider the possibility of imprisoning Green, who *is* the offender. In this case the state is not under a *prima facie* obligation to respect his rights since he, in committing an offence, has not respected the rights of others. What is true here is that under certain conditions it is morally permissible for the state to imprison Green. It need not do so; it may if this is thought likely to prevent further offences.

We are told that this is *not* a justification of punishment partly on the basis of desert. It is urged in this connection that it is not possible to assess an individual's culpability. In any case, 'for the state to make such an attempt would seriously interfere with its proper work. Its proper work is that of protecting rights'.[7] But why, exactly, on the given account, does Green lose his rights? Why does it become morally permissible to punish him but not Brown, assuming that the punishment will have a preventive effect? The reason given is that he has violated the rights of others. Clearly enough, though, if he had violated them in a completely accidental way, or involuntarily, it would not be thought permissible to punish him. One cannot but think, then, that the given reason really amounts to the claim that he deserves punishment. To say that he has violated a *right* is also to imply that his victim can make a certain claim. This is of secondary importance in the present context. What we appear to have is a partly retributivist justification of punishment. That this is mistakenly denied, or unseen, is partly to be explained in the following way.

The retribution theory is characterized as the doctrine that we are justified in punishing for the reason that there should be a proportion between moral goodness and happiness. '... a state of affairs in which the good are happy and the bad unhappy is better than one in which the good are unhappy and the bad happy.'[8] But, it is said, it is impossible to assess the moral goodness or badness and the happiness or unhappiness of individuals. Judges would have to take into account their whole lives in order to do so, which is but one difficulty. What we actually do is different, and something which has a different justification. Legislators make certain actions offences and fix penalties for them. They are governed in this by the need to prevent such actions and also, with respect to the penalties, by the principle among others that 'the punishment should be proportional to the offence'.[9] A judge merely enforces the existing law, 'except when the law has allowed a scale of penalties within which he can choose'. In this case he chooses in accordance with the same kind of considerations that guide legislators.

To present these two accounts of procedure and justification in this way is slightly to disguise the feature that they share. In the second account, the legislators are governed by a principle of proportion, which cannot be other than a principle of desert. That this is done at a certain level of generality, not with respect to individual men and their acts, does not alter the fact. Judges also proceed partly on the basis of such a principle with respect to particular defendants. This is the standard case. It is not true, as the second account of the practice of punishment implies, that there is only a limited place for judicial choice between penalties. In short, there seems no good reason for denying that we here have a justification of punishment partly in terms of desert. The second account is, in effect, fundamentally similar to the first account.

Is there anything to be gained by the terminology of rights? I think not. To say that the state has a *prima facie* obligation to protect the moral rights of citizens is to say that it has a *prima facie* obligation to prevent certain harmful acts. Any further implications are not at present important. To talk of rights is to secure no significant advantage and to run the risk of mistakenly thinking that we are concerned merely with legality. Is there anything to be gained by the terminology of *prima facie* obligations? The answer again seems to be no. *Prima facie* obligations are moral reasons for action, claims to which situations give rise, and they are correctly and adequately described as such.

4. '*Because he broke the law*'

In contrast to the one we have considered, there are a number of views advanced which pay attention to the need and value of preventing offences and yet claim to justify punishment *solely* on retributivist grounds. In one[10] of these we are told that our having laws and a legal system (if these can be separated) *is* partly justified by reasons of prevention. However, no part of the justification of punishing a man has to do with prevention. The justification, one that leads the author rightly to regard what he puts forward as other than 'orthodox' retributivism, is *simply that the man has broken the law*. His punishment, we are told, has nothing to do with desert. In this latter respect the view is rather like the one we have just considered. In its attempt to exclude considerations of prevention from the justification of the man's punishment, it is quite different. This view derives from a disinclination to deal in men's deserts and perhaps a kind of reverence for law.

Societies are said to be justified in having laws at all, rather than advice-systems or something of the sort, by the better effects. They are also justified in having particular laws rather than others partly by the effects.[11] The behaviour of citizens becomes to some considerable extent 'reliable and predictable'; the good citizen enjoys a certain security in his life. We may say for short that a part of the justification of law and a legal system is that it prevents certain kinds of behaviour. The other part has to do with the fact that the laws we have are such that offences and penalties are arranged in scales and the heaviest penalties are reserved for the most serious offences. It is explicitly said that this particular feature of the legal system is not to be explained, or not only to be explained, by the fact that because some offences are more harmful we are more anxious to prevent them and so provide heavier penalties.

There remains the independent question of what justifies the punishment of a particular man who breaks one of society's laws. '. . . one fact and one fact only can justify the punishment of this man, and that is a past fact, that he has committed a crime.'[12] For a number of reasons, which I shall consider in a moment, it is maintained that *no part of the justification* has to do with preventing offences. It is also maintained, for several reasons I shall consider, that the justification of punishing the man *has nothing to do with* the fact that he has performed an act of certain desert. We are told that 'No punishment is morally retributive or reformative or deterrent. Any criminal punished for any one of these reasons is certainly unjustly punished. The only justification for punishing any man is that he has broken a law.'[13]

What we have before us, then, amounts essentially to two propositions. (1) The existence of law and the legal system is justified partly by utilitarian effects, partly by desert. (2) Individual punishments, in contrast, are justified by the fact alone that offenders broke the law. These propositions, in my view, have their origins in a number of elisions and mistakes. Let us consider the second one first.

1. As is so often the case in such discussions, two questions which there *is* every reason to distinguish seem to be run together. We begin as usual by asking: 'Under what circumstances is the punishment of some particular person justified?' The answer, in effect, is that the circumstances are those in which a person has broken the law, and in these circumstances a judge is morally obliged to act. He is under a certain personal obligation since he has given an understanding. Perhaps there is intended the further suggestion that he is under a legal obligation. However, it is clearly mistaken to think that an action is morally justified simply because someone has promised to perform it or is under a legal obligation to do so. The question of justification has become confused with others. It is certainly true that we cannot explain a judge's legal obligations by pointing to preventive effects of his action in punishing an offender. It is also true that we cannot explain a certain moral claim upon him, which in fact derives from a personal undertaking. This goes no way toward showing that we cannot give a moral justification of his action which refers to its effects or is based on the offender's desert.

2. There seems also to be a related confusion. We begin with the question of justification and then come to deal, as the lines quoted a page back show, with this: 'When is a punishment *just*?' There is all the difference in the world between these questions. A

punishment may be just in the sense of being strictly in accord with law or in the sense of being the deserved punishment. It may not be in either case, that it is justified. The traditional retribution theory gives as the reason for punishment that it is just in the second sense. Our response to that theory is that punishment's being just is not enough to justify it. With respect to the present point, it is perfectly true that the fact that a punishment has preventive effects does not make it just. It is just, to state one part of the requirement, only if the person penalized has broken the law. However, this is to go no way toward the desired conclusion that it is not possible that particular punishments are at all *justified* by preventive effects.

3. We are told that preventive effects do not result from particular punishment but rather from related things. Publicity is given to punishments and it is through publicity that we secure deterrence. Punishments are accompanied by reformative measures and it is through these that we may secure reformation. In general, particular punishments cannot have as part of their justification that they are preventive since they are not directly preventive themselves. To confine a reply to the question of deterrence, it simply is not true that the effect on the offender himself is not direct. Also, with respect to others, the contention ignores the unsurprising supposition that the public threat of punishment generally depends for its effectiveness on punishments actually being imposed.

4. Another argument may also be intended, one that is thought to have application to things other than punishment. It is taken to be established, for example, that the general rule that one ought to keep one's promises is justified in a utilitarian way by its good effects. It is then maintained that there are occasions when keeping a promise will not have good effects and yet is the right thing to do. It then cannot be the case, we are told, that the justification of the particular action is to be found in its effects. The justification must be that the action is according to the rule that one ought to keep one's promises. In fact the justification of *any* particular action of promise-keeping is that it is according to the rule. This is, it is opaquely said, acting on principle.

I do not wish to discuss these assertions in detail but simply to notice one thing. *If* one does accept that sometimes one ought to keep promises despite bad effects, one still does not have to conclude that the justification of any act of promise-keeping is merely that it is according to the rule. It is difficult to see, of course, how this is a justification at all in the relevant sense. One may rather conclude (i) that the rule is derived from, or based on, both a utilitarian principle of effects and also some other principle, and (ii) that the same is true of individual acts of promise-keeping. A similar, and similarly failing, attempt may be made to maintain that the practice of punishment is justified in the main by its effects but particular impositions of punishment can be justified only by being in accordance with the rules that define the practice.

5. Finally, with special reference to the submission that desert plays no part in the justification of particular impositions of punishment, it is maintained that no human individual has the 'status' to judge the immorality of another. That, one is to suppose, is God's business. We have already considered and dismissed the problems having to do with assessments of harm and responsibility. They have seemed to some to be insuperable problems, partly because of the fact that standards for acceptable assessments have been set far too high (see chapter two, section three). However, even if they were insuperable, and men's ways absolutely inscrutable to men, there would be nothing to be gained by recourse to the argument which is being urged upon us. It cannot be that the justification of any particular punishment is merely to be found in the fact that a man has broken the law. Facts of legality and illegality must be seen for what they are, and no more. No one can maintain the rightness of punishments that have been imposed for offences against morally appalling laws. More important, it is clear that the bare fact that a law has been enacted making an admittedly wrongful act also an illegality is not the justification of the resulting punishments.

We must at least amend the proposition before us to this: the punishment of particular men is justified only by desert. Let us now consider this together with the other proposition, that law and the legal system are in part justified in a utilitarian way, by their effects. The resulting doctrine is mystifying because of a problem about the logical relations of the notions of law and punishment.[14] We are at least willing to consider the idea that for there to be law, anything that would count as law, there must be punishment. We are ready to consider the possibility that to say there is a law is to say that there is punishment for a certain kind of behaviour. If we take up something like this account of law, then the pair of propositions we are considering becomes nonsensical, based on a supposed distinction that does not exist. We cannot have law justified partly by prevention and particular punishments justified wholly by desert. Things are not improved, however, if we take up an account of law which makes it logically independent of punishment. The doctrine is then that punishment is justified by desert and laws justified in the main by their effects. This leaves open the possibility that if the having of laws ceased to be justified by the effects, punishments would remain as justified as before. This is the ordinary retribution theory, rightly discarded.

Our conclusions, or some of them, must be these. No sufficient argument has been given to show that a man's punishment is justified solely by the fact that he has broken a law, and cannot be justified by prevention or desert. If we radically amend the view in question, so that individual punishments are said to be justified by desert, then the combining of this proposition with the one about law and the legal system calls up the obvious replies which have been made.

5. A Right to Punish

One other theory announced as retributivist appears to be really two theories, one of which gives a large place to the preventive value of punishment.[15] It begins by distinguishing particular questions. There is the question of the definition of punishment, with which we are not at present concerned, and two others. (1) What, if anything, justifies punishment as such? or What, if anything, is the justification of the practice of punishment? (2) What method or system of determining penalties is best? We are intended to take the first of these questions, despite its different expressions, as amounting to this: What moral justification is there for inflicting *some punishment or other* on people who break the law? That is, the question does not single out for inquiry any particular practice of punishment, one with a particular penalty-system. The second question *does* have to do with particular penalty-systems.

In answer to the first question we are told that we have some practice or other of punishment because we want to secure a number of ends or aims. We wish to protect society, reform criminals, deter others. These ends or purposes are 'morally and socially desirable' but they should not be confused with the moral justification of punishment. The moral justification of the practice is that it is deserved. (The argument given for this exclusion of the mentioned utilitarian values involves the confusion between just and justified punishment mentioned above.) However, we are not *obliged* to punish because of desert. It is rather the case that because men deserve it *we have a right* to punish them. We vest this right in a judiciary. It is a right to punish up to a certain limit, up to what a man deserves for his offence. To what extent we exercise this right is a question that may be decided by reflection on the given aims of punishment. Given that we want to prevent offences and to reform men, it may sometimes be 'foolish or mean' to exercise the right.

Two things may be said about this. The first is that despite a certain ambivalence what has been said is plainly retributivist. We would, it seems, be justified in punishing even if there were no preventive effects. What else can be meant by the claim that we have the right to punish because men deserve it? As a consequence, this is as unacceptable as the traditional retribution theory. The other thing to be said about this answer to the first question is that it determines an answer to the second, the question concerning the justification of penalty-systems. We have not been given an argument for a practice of punishment of no particular penalty-system. Rather, we have been told we have a right to a practice such that men get penalties as severe as, but no more severe than, they deserve.

It seems then that the second question is already answered. It is answered again, however, and differently. A justified penalty-system is indeed one in which there are certain limits on penalties.

No man is punished more than he deserves. However, we may be guided in the construction of such a system, and also in its application to particular men, by considerations of deterrence and reform. Consider this passage:

> When the problem is to find the best system of penalty-fixing there is no doubt that a purely retributive theory would have serious weaknesses, both practically, because it may be very difficult to decide which of two crimes is the more serious and thus deserving of severer punishment, and morally, because if deterrent and reformatory considerations are altogether ignored when the list of penalties is drawn up a great social good might be sacrificed in order to achieve a small improvement in the accuracy of a punishment from the retributive standpoint. ... a modified retributive theory is perfectly possible, one which only uses retributive considerations to fix some sort of upper limit to penalties and then looks to other factors to decide how much and what sort of pain shall be inflicted.[16]

It is suggested here that particular penalties are justified in virtue both of being deserved and being preventive. Some, although deserved, may *not* be justified. This is inconsistent with what has gone before. Also, it makes it impossible to regard the theory as retributivist. If one takes the quoted passage in the way that seems to be intended, and disregards what has gone before, what we have is clearly an attempt to justify punishment in terms of several principles.

6. Explicit Compromise

It should now be clear that any successful attempt at justification must give a real place both to considerations of prevention and, in some sense, desert. It is futile to try with one hand to let in prevention as part of the justification of punishment and with the other hand to exclude it. If it is let in, of course, there is nothing to be achieved but misdirection from describing the resulting view as entirely or essentially a retributivist one.

In my criticisms of the three theories in the past three sections of this chapter, I have not touched on two essential points. One, mentioned at the beginning of the chapter, is that *any* compromise theory must include some attempt to explain the meaning and assess the force of arguments which mention desert. The theories discussed are also wanting in this respect. Secondly, at least the last two theories are wanting in that they are, or must be taken to be, claims that justified punishments are *always* both deserved and preventive. This is at least in question. In the third chapter above we noticed that there are already within the law many cases of what are regarded by many as being justified victimization. Convictions under statutes of strict and vicarious liability may be such. Impositions of what I have called 'exemplary penalties' are also defended. Any adequate attempt to justify punishment, whatever its final conclusion, must deal with this question. It must consider the possibility that it is *not* always necessary to observe considerations of desert.

(The question, incidentally, may be put in different ways. The definition of punishment we have mainly used does not require that anything correctly described as a punishment must be deserved. We can then ask: Must all justified punishments be deserved? One can require, of course, that anything that counts as punishment *be* deserved. One must then ask: Are *only* punishments justified?)

The most influential recent account of punishment[17] fulfils both these requirements: it at least attempts to explain the nature of desert-arguments, and it does not assume that desert in some sense is a necessary condition of every justified punishment. Further, it is an account which makes no attempt to avoid the conclusion that punishment requires for its justification an explicit recourse to arguments of different kinds. If it misdescribes this conclusion in a certain way, as we shall see, it is open to simple amendment.

The practice of punishment, in this account, is said to involve a prohibition, perhaps justifiably overridden in certain cases, against penalizing individuals who have not freely and responsibly performed an act which is an offence. This is explained and justified, firstly, by the consideration that they have responded in a particular way to a choice offered to them. The choice was between obeying the law and being left to themselves, or breaking the law and paying a price if found out. To defend the prohibition in this way, clearly, is to defend it by a part of our argument from desert (Item (4), p. 144). Also, secondly, the prohibition secures that penalties are returns for harm done. In general, offenders have gained satisfactions in their offences; penalties are prices to be paid. This may seem a reiteration of the defence just given. I shall regard it as the claim that imposing penalties on offenders is a move toward equalization of welfare and distress. So construed, this is again a part of our argument from desert (Item (5), p. 144).

Punishment also involves a restriction, perhaps sometimes not observed for good reason, on the particular penalties that can be imposed. This is a feature explained and justified by a number of rules. (1) Penalties must not cause more distress than would occur if they were not imposed. (2) A penalty must not be imposed if a man's action falls under a rule of justification, such as the rule having to do with injuring in self-defence. One of the aims of punishment is the protection of individuals from attack; it would be inconsistent, then, to punish a man for defending himself from attack. These two rules, clearly enough, explain and defend penalties by way of the principle of economical deterrence. The principle excludes judicial actions in opposition to the desired end of prevention and also requires that the end be secured at a certain distress-cost.

There are also other rules for penalties. (3) A man is to be excused a penalty if his act, although of a kind the law seeks to prevent, was unintentional, involuntary, or something of the sort. (4) He is to receive a mitigated penalty if he faced special difficulty in keeping the law, perhaps because of provocation. In both cases penalties are explained and defended by an element of our argument from desert (Item (4), p. 144). (5) Finally, a man is to be treated as others in his situation are treated. Similar offenders are to be similarly treated. This is also to explain and defend particular penalties by a part of our argument.

What remains to be said in brief exposition of the present doctrine is that it takes the practice of punishment *as a whole* to be justified *only* by its beneficial effect in preventing offences. I have already argued that it is impossible to maintain that the practice of punishment can be defended simply by reference to prevention. To attempt to do so is to attempt, in effect, to defend the traditional deterrence theory. Furthermore, it is inconsistent to claim that the practice as a whole, taking into account all its features, does not have as part of its justification what is said on behalf of particular features. (Perhaps some ambiguity explains the fact that this claim is made. Can it be that when it is said that the practice or institution is justified only by its effects, what is oddly meant is that its *public* existence or character is justified only by the likely effects? Perhaps one could not justify this by an argument from desert. Such a point is not to be confused with a proposition about the justification of the practice as a whole.)

We can, of course, make an amendment to what has been said in order to exclude this misconception. Also, in order to preserve a certain continuity in our own inquiry, we can state the view we are considering at the level of generality of the previous chapters. What I have in mind here is the rules of justification, excuse, and mitigation. To defend punishment partly by observing that it involves a rule of justification, as I have said, is to defend it by mentioning one way in which it pursues the prevention of certain actions as against others. This is implicit in the defence of the practice as an economical deterrent. To defend punishment partly by observing that it involves rules of excuse and mitigation is, as I said, to defend it by mentioning particular ways in which it is governed by considerations of desert. Deserved punishments, according to our analysis, have among other features this one: they are punishments of individuals who have, by actions for which they were responsible, contravened a known system of offences and penalties. Implicit in this are notions of degrees of responsibility, notions which may be summarized in terms of the rules of excuse and mitigation. The system itself may be regarded as incorporating these rules.

We lose nothing, given the purposes of the present discussion, if we describe the proposal before us in this way: A practice of punishment may in general be justified by the considerations that (1) it prevents offences economically, (2) those who are punished have performed actions for which they were responsible and which

contravened a known system of offences and penalties, (3) similar
offenders are treated in similar ways, and (4) imposing penalties on
offenders is a way of equalizing welfare and distress, since offenders have gained satisfactions through their offences. The words 'in
general' have this importance: we are not given a final answer to
the question of whether punishment may sometimes be justified
even when those punished were not responsible for the offences in
question. That is, we have not got a final answer to such questions
as whether there is a justification for certain penalties imposed as
a consequence of strict and vicarious liability.

I have already commented on the nature and force of the elements of such an argument for punishment. I should like once
more to consider the question since we are offered certain suggestions as to its answer. What justificatory importance has the fact,
taken by itself, that an offender has freely and responsibly, at least
to some degree, acted in a way prohibited by a known system of
offences and penalties? It is not, we are rightly told, that the fact is
important because it entails that the offender has behaved culpably. But the reason given for this truth is that in systems of
criminal law

there are necessarily many actions (quite apart from the cases of 'strict
liability') that if voluntarily done are criminally punishable, although
our moral code may be either silent as to their moral quality, or divided.
Very many offences are created by legislation designed to give effect to
a particular economic scheme (e.g. a state monopoly of road or rail
transport), the utility or moral character of which may be genuinely in
dispute.[18]

A possible reply to this is that it may be true that not all offenders
are morally culpable, but if this is so then perhaps the systems of
law in question are partly unjustified. There is a better reason for
resisting the idea that the justificatory importance of a free act
against a penalty system is that such acts are immoral. Even if they
are, why should this fact give us even part of a licence to punish?
As we have seen (p. 80), it appears to be impossible to extract
anything like a moral reason for action from the mere fact that
a man has behaved in a culpable way. This does not give one a

justification, or a part of a justification. One may have a certain response which has its origins in defensive reactions but that is another matter entirely.

One offered explanation of why we require a free act known to be an offence is that by so doing we secure two advantages.[19] Members of society are able to determine by their choices, at least to a considerable extent, what their futures will be. They are able, that is, to opt for law-abidance and its consequences or disobedience to law and its possible consequences. Thus there are considerable satisfactions to be gained: individuals can *enjoy a particular security*, one that would be denied them under some system which did not make their own choices the determinants of their futures. The satisfactions of security are, essentially, satisfactions which accrue from confidence in prediction. I can rule out the possibility of at least certain unpleasant surprises if I feel capable of keeping the law. There are also gains of another kind. That *I* choose what will happen to me, to some considerable extent, is itself a source of satisfaction. In order to see this clearly, one need simply compare the experience of choosing with the experience of, say, being coerced.

It seems undeniable that we have here one recommendation of a punishment system which requires that those punished have performed free actions known to be offences. It is not the only recommendation of such a system, however. There is, as we have noticed (p. 81), an argument to be had from reflection on the experience of apprehended offenders as against victims. There can hardly be any question but that a man who chose not to offend will be more distressed by victimization than an offender who has done just that. One's being victimized would in no way be a matter of one's own prediction and could not but produce a unique shock, anxiety, and indeed suffering. And so it may be thought that this is an argument against victimization stronger than the arguments having to do with the satisfactions of choosing and prediction.

Both arguments, it should be noticed, defend the requirement of a more or less deliberate offence as something that helps to secure prevention *at an economical rate*.[20] Sticking to the requirement makes for economy of distress. Is there anything else to be said for the requirement? It is usually thought that it has some recommendation which has nothing to do with any of the consequences just mentioned.

Consider again a choice between a punishment and a victimization, where each would have the same preventive effect and no more distress would be caused to the victim than to the offender. Suppose, furthermore, that the victimization would have no effect on future satisfactions deriving from prediction and choosing. Clearly enough, there is never likely to be such a case, but it is certainly conceivable. Would there, in this instance, be anything to be said for punishment rather than victimization in virtue of the fact that only the offender had freely and responsibly chosen to offend? There is a tendency to answer yes. I take it, however, that in so far as one can find 'reasons' for one's inclination, they consist in a refusal to accept the case as specified. That is, one has in mind some respect in which the consequences of the punishment would be preferable to the consequences of the victimization. There seems nothing to be said for the bare fact in itself that the offender voluntarily offended.

It may be that this is denied as a part of the doctrine we have been considering. There is said to be a moral principle to the effect that 'no one should be punished who could not help doing what he did.'[21] It seems to be implied that a voluntary act, taken by itself and with no regard for consequences, is of moral importance. It is also observed that

Human society is a society of persons; and persons do not view themselves or each other merely as so many bodies moving in ways which are sometimes harmful and have to be prevented or altered. Instead persons interpret each other's movements as manifestations of intentions and choices, and these subjective factors are often more important to their social relations than the movements by which they are manifested or their effects. If one person hits another, the person struck does not think of the other as *just* a cause of pain to him; for it is of crucial importance to him whether the blow was deliberate or involuntary. . . . If you strike me, the judgement that the blow was deliberate will elicit fear, indignation, anger, resentment: these are not voluntary responses; but the same judgement will enter into deliberations about my future voluntary conduct towards you and will colour all my social relations with you. Shall I be your friend or enemy? Offer soothing words? Or return the blow? All this will be different if the blow is not voluntary. This is how human nature in human society actually is and as yet we have no power to alter it. The bearing of this fundamental fact on the law is this. If as our legal moralists maintain it is important for the law to reflect common judgement of morality, it is surely even more important that it should in general reflect in its judgements on human conduct distinctions which not only underlie morality, but pervade the whole of our social life. This it would fail to do if it treated men merely as alterable, predictable, curable, or manipulable things.[22]

We certainly do distinguish between those who injure us deliberately, those who injure us involuntarily, and, one may add, those who do not injure us at all. We act differently in response. In so far as we are *justified* in so doing, however, this may be explained by something other than the mere fact that some injuries are the consequences of voluntary actions. What can be said for acts of blaming may be what can be said for certain punishments. The fact taken by itself that an act was voluntary may not in itself be morally important in either case.

Let us grant that in ordinary life we do react differently, and quite spontaneously, simply and solely because an act was voluntary. That is, let us admit that we have distinctive emotional responses. Is it suggested, on the basis of these facts, that the bare consideration that a man has freely offended gives us a moral reason for punishment? Such a suggestion, in my view, would be mistaken. We may be able to give a partial *explanation* of a feature of our practice of punishment by reference to these facts. Nothing is more likely than that there will be a connection between that practice and our ordinary attitudes and behaviour. To concede that is not to concede the point at issue.

It is not to concede that the fact, taken by itself, that a man has freely and responsibly acted in a certain way is of moral relevance to the question of our further action. Certain responses which we ordinarily have to a person we regard as responsible for his behaviour, responses described in the preceding chapter as moral ones, are not of importance to the determination of our subsequent conduct. A conclusion of a related kind is espoused by some as a consequence of an acceptance of determinism. This is a very different route. We have come to our conclusion by reflection on moral attitudes as they are, not as a result of commitment to doctrine.

7. Strict Liability

Before drawing our own final conclusion about all that may be said in justification of punishment, we must consider the other large controversy: strict liability and related procedures. Are we sometimes justified in punishing individuals who do not deserve it, individuals who did *not* deliberately or negligently contravene a system of offences and penalties? The question arises in connection with strict and vicarious liability and in a slightly different way with exemplary penalties. It arises, too, as a consequence of the judicial doctrine of objective liability, which I shall not consider.[23]

The extension of rules of strict liability to cover more and more offences has given rise to a considerable controversy, as indeed it should have. Few things can be said briefly and safely on the subject, and it may be that for a philosopher to venture into it is foolhardy. Still, something is required. What I shall say will be for the most part derivative. One certainty is that it is very nearly impossible to define even the present limits of strict liability. In almost every case a court rather than a legislature has decided that a particular offence is to be tried under rules of strict liability. This itself, in democratic societies, raises a considerable and difficult question. It appears to be possible that almost any statute which does not actually mention the necessity of intention or negligence in connection with the prohibited act may be construed by a court as allowing for conviction where such things are absent. A study of the law of the state of Wisconsin suggested that of 1,113 statutes creating criminal offences, 660 were so written as to allow courts to convict in the absence of intentionality or negligence if they so desired.[24] This would require only further use of increasingly familiar principles of statute interpretation.

Offences where strict liability *may* be the rule, some of which have been mentioned already, include these:

(1) selling adulterated food, selling whisky to a man already drunk, labelling food products in a misleading way, giving short weight of certain commodities,

(2) driving dangerously, not having adequate accident insurance, having an unsafe vehicle, disobeying traffic regulations,

(3) contraventions of factory safety acts and of wages acts,

(4) sexual offences having to do with girls under the age of sixteen, and the offence of bigamy,

(5) possessing an altered passport, infringing building regulations, acting in contempt of court, transporting gambling equipment, engaging in certain kinds of banking and financial transactions, possessing drugs.

It is sometimes said, not merely in defence of strict liability as we have it but in support of an extension of strict liability to cover *all* offences, that this is the logical consequence of a rejection of the retribution theory. If the rightful function of the courts is not to 'punish the wicked' but to prevent offences, there can be no objection to the multiplication of offences of strict liability.

If the law says that certain things are not to be done, it is illogical to confine this prohibition to occasions on which they are done from malice aforethought; for at least the material consequences of an action, and the reasons for prohibiting it, are the same whether it is the result of sinister malicious plotting, of negligence, or of sheer accident.[25]

This can hardly be acceptable. The rightful function of the courts is not merely to prevent offences, but to do so in an acceptable way. As I have suggested already, and will again, one way of achieving economy of distress in the prevention of offences is by taking into account the responsibility of defendants. One need not, in order to oppose strict liability or its extension, advocate the traditional or indeed any retribution theory.

A more common argument for strict liability has a number of premisses. It is said to be difficult to prove responsibility with respect to the offences in question. Can one *establish* that a motorist was negligent, that a barman did know the man buying whisky was already drunk, that the seducer did know the girl to be under sixteen? Sometimes the difficulty is located, so to speak, in the nature of things. Sometimes it is maintained that it is extremely difficult or impossible to prove responsibility given our present machinery of justice and the resources which we allot to it. A second premiss must be that it is very necessary that we prevent offences of the kinds in question. There are very extensive dangers to be avoided. Thirdly, it is often maintained that the penalties imposed as a consequence of strict-liability convictions are light ones, at least if one takes into account the resources of offenders. It is said that penalties for motorists under strict-liability rules are manageable ones; larger penalties for prohibited financial transactions can be afforded by those who engage in them. The conclusion is that we are sometimes justified in punishing those who may not have voluntarily offended.

Each of these premisses may be called into question. Can it be shown with respect to all strict-liability offences that it is *more* difficult to prove negligence or intention than with offences where strict liability does not obtain? In some of the latter cases, where proof of negligence *is* required, it is often a relatively easy task. Presumably there is not great difficulty in establishing the negligence of a workman who throws something from the roof of a building into a busy street. But what of proving that a man knew he was receiving stolen goods? There are many cases, surely, where proof is difficult indeed. (An advocate of the extension of strict liability to *all* offences may maintain that proof is *in general* difficult or even not possible at all by rational means. The argument for this conclusion appears to me to consist in an unwarranted extrapolation from cases whose difficulty cannot be denied. There are motoring offences, certainly, where the establishment of negligence is or would be a very considerable undertaking. It may well be, to mention another group of cases, extremely difficult to deal adequately with claims having to do with insanity and mental abnormality.[26] This seems an insufficient ground for the general conclusion that is drawn.)

Secondly, is it true that all strict-liability offences, against others where there are the normal requirements of proof, are *peculiarly* dangerous, *peculiarly* in need of deterrence? Can this be made out with respect to the mentioned sexual offences, or action in contempt of court, or possessing an altered passport? One suspects that there is a better argument, despite some curious attitudes to them, with respect to certain motoring offences.

Finally, to pass on to the third premiss, is it at all obvious that all the strict-liability penalties are relatively light ones? There presumably are men who would suffer very considerably as a consequence of being convicted of going to bed with a girl under sixteen. There are also small shopkeepers whose trade may be seriously affected by a conviction in connection with adulterated food. *Some* motorists whose penalties include suspension of their driving licences can hardly be regarded as having been lightly penalized. In almost all of these cases, further, it will be thought that convictions must really be deserved, and the usual opprobrium will attach to them. It may sometimes be made clear by the sentencing judge that it is possible or probable, or even something like established, that the defendant did not intend the offence and was not negligent. This will not prevent people in general from supposing otherwise when they hear of a conviction in a criminal court. (Such facts as this, incidentally, have led to suggestions that offences under strict-liability rules should not be called crimes but rather 'quasi-crimes' or 'administrative misdemeanours' or 'violations'.)

Against such considerations, the supporter of strict liability might put the following argument. It is not the case that the penalties in question are unfair since, in effect, those who are penalized are selected by something like a random method. They are selected, if in fact they did not intend to offend and were not negligent, on the basis of accident. If there is a need for deterring punishments and if we cannot satisfy it by punishing those who deserve it, what fairer method than this? The argument is not one to be found in legal writing, I think, for understandable reasons, but it is a coherent one for all of that. Its weakness is obviously that it depends on assumptions about which there can be considerable doubt. *Is* there such a need for deterring penalties? *Is* it true that we cannot deter as much as we need by punishing those who voluntarily offend? It is only if these things are positively established that we should approve of the suggested method.

It is patently impossible, on the basis of what can be said here, to draw any firm conclusions about all of the offences where strict liability is in question. My own inclination is that with respect to *most* of them, neither the dangers to be avoided nor the difficulties in proving responsibility are so great as to warrant treating individuals in the given way. It is difficult to resist the supposition that strict liability is a fact not so much as a consequence of the given arguments but because of some retributivist determination that none of the guilty should escape. With respect to *some* of the offences in question, where there is a larger danger to be avoided, there may be a justification for a recommended alteration in judicial procedure.[27]

We might, with respect to these, distinguish penalties in some way as to their weight. This would be a difficult but neither an impossible nor an unfamiliar task. In the case of heavy penalties there should be a strict adherence to the principle that the responsibility of defendants be proved by the prosecution. In the case of relatively light penalties, the procedure would be different. It would not be necessary for the prosecution to prove the accused acted with intention or negligence. However, it would be possible for a man to escape conviction by his showing, perhaps on balance of probabilities, that he did not intend the offence and was not negligent. Such a practice would decrease very considerably the incidence of undeserved punishments. It would not rule them out. The argument is that the relatively few undeserved penalties which would be imposed would be justified by the gain in the prevention of dangerous offences. It seems possible that a similar system would be defensible for offences now governed by vicarious liability.

There remains the question of exemplary penalties. Here there is usually no question of punishing a man who was in no way responsible for the action in question. Exemplary penalties may none the less be regarded as penalties which are in a particular sense not deserved. They are penalties greater than those imposed on other similar offenders. The matter presents difficulties because of the vagueness of the requirement that similar offenders be treated in similar ways. Certainly it is the case that judges ought not to depart from the penalty limitations laid down by statute for particular kinds of offence. A penalty not within the specified range is certainly unjustified. There is room within the range, however, for a good deal of choice, and there has often been a wide variance in sentencing from court to court. Some penalties *permitted* by statute may be undeserved, it seems, in that the offenders in question are more severely penalized than others. They are more severely penalized than others who have committed offences of similar harmfulness and responsibility. Is there a justification for sometimes departing from the rule that offenders similar in this respect are to be treated similarly? The argument advanced is that sometimes there is a need for an unusual deterrent. It seems to me impossible to assert that we should *never* be influenced by this consideration. At the same time, it seems more than arguable that many exemplary penalties are not open to justification in this way.

8. Conclusions

Implicit in what has been said in this chapter and before is a conclusion about (1) the justification of a possible practice of punishment or, better, a practice of punishment in a possible society. I should like to make this conclusion explicit, to clarify it in several ways, and also to examine certain implications. There will remain other questions, including (2) that of the justification of our practices in our societies as they are, and (3) that of what principles must govern the assessment of these practices. These are more important questions and their answers are also implicit in the foregoing.

The answer to the first question can be summarized in this way. Punishments may be justified when they are economically preventive of offences and in a certain sense deserved. They may sometimes be justified when they are *not* deserved. Let us for the moment ignore cases of the second kind, which may be regarded as rare.

What we have then, more usefully, is that punishments may be justified when

(1) they are economically preventive of offences,
(2) those individuals punished have voluntarily acted in ways which contravene a known system of offences and penalties,
(3) they are punished as other similar offenders are punished,
(4) their penalties serve to equalize welfare and distress with regard to offenders and non-offenders, and
(5) their penalties do not produce situations of gross inequality of distress.

The last requirement was omitted, or not specifically mentioned, in the doctrine considered at the beginning of the preceding section. It is included here because we would not regard as justified an economical punishment which avoided small amounts of distress for each of very many people at the cost of a great deal of distress for a single individual. The propositions of this claim that have to do with desert, (2) to (5), of course do not include any we have discarded in chapters two and three. Nor do they include the proposition that justified punishments satisfy grievances. This is a recommendation of punishment but we may take it as written into our first proposition. That is, grievance-satisfactions are to be taken into account in calculating whether a punishment is an *economical* deterrent: one, in a phrase, that costs less dissatisfaction than would occur without the punishment. We *could* use the proposition about grievance-satisfactions, satisfactions that do *no more than* satisfy existing grievance, in order to limit the severity of punishments and rule out certain victimizations. Our fifth proposition, about the avoidance of inequality, and the first, about economy, will do the job.

Nonetheless, the five-part claim as we have it is still misleadingly and inefficiently formulated. We have accepted that to argue for a punishment by the consideration that an offender responsibly and knowingly offended is to argue for it as in a way economical. For one thing, it is productive of less distress than would be caused to someone who was penalized although he had not responsibly and knowingly offended. The second stated requirement for a justified punishment, then, is no more than a repetition of something implicit in the first. What of the third, fourth, and fifth requirements?

The fourth is that penalties imposed must re-establish an equal sharing of welfare and distress with respect to offenders and non-offenders. What I wish to suggest is that the third and fifth requirements are in a way consequences of the fourth. Let us suppose that we have a society where there exists very considerable equality of welfare and distress. This equality is disrupted by the commission of offences. Penalties can be imposed which will indeed have the feature that they deal with the disruption. That is, they at least tend to re-establish the state of affairs that existed before the commission of offences. In their offences, it may be argued, offenders gained satisfactions and others were deprived. In the ensuing punishments the balance is righted.

Penalties which have this feature, of course, are necessarily penalties which fulfil the *fifth* requirement: they do not produce situations of gross inequality of distress. Further, given that the punishments are to re-establish equality, we have the consequence that offenders who are alike in a certain respect must be treated in like ways. We have the conclusion, more particularly, that offenders who have gained like satisfactions from their offences should receive like punishments. Only by doing this can we return to the society of equality. The *third* requirement, then, is also a consequence of the fourth.

(There is also the other consideration, discussed in chapter three section five, which seems to be implicit in the third requirement. It may be regarded as the necessity that offenders who have caused a similar harm, and by actions of a similar degree of responsibility, should be treated alike because they have similar anticipations. In this case, what we have is something that follows from the initial requirement of economical prevention.)

Given these considerations we can produce a simpler and clearer form of our conclusion about *the justification of a practice of punishment in a possible society. It would be an absolute requirement of such a practice that it prevented offences at an economical cost of distress. If this was achieved, it would at least in general be the case that punishment was of those individuals responsible for actions contravening a known system of offences and penalties. It would also be an absolute requirement that the penalties would re-establish equality of satisfactions and distress.*

In the supposed society of equality, it seems, certain penalties will satisfy both these requirements. If Green commits an offence, and gains certain satisfactions from it, the penalty suggested by considerations of economical deterrence will be one which makes for the re-establishment of equality. This, however, to pass on, is precisely what is *not* true of punishment in our societies *as they are*. Given that they are societies of extreme or considerable inequality, and that to some large extent offenders come from deprived classes or groups, punishing them will contribute to inequality rather than equality. That is, a large proportion of those punished have already been subjected to unequal treatment: even taking into account satisfactions got from offences they have already had a larger share of distress and a lesser share of welfare than other members of society. The penalties they are given will make a further contribution to this inequality. The conclusion to which we have come, then, is that there is a justification which a practice of punishment in a conceivable society might have, a justification suggested by several of the doctrines we have considered. It is *not* a justification which can be given for practices of punishment in our societies as they are.

To turn to that question, we might initially answer it this way. Our existing practices of punishment have this to be said for them:

(1) some punishments are economically preventive of offences,
(2) those punished have, in general, responsibly contravened a known system of offences and penalties,
(3) they are punished as other similar offenders are punished,
(4) their penalties do not produce situations of gross inequality of distress.

One thing to be said about this is that proposition (2), again, must be seen as reducing to a claim about economy of distress. Another thing to be said is that proposition (3), once again, also comes down to an argument based on the principle that we must act economically in attempting to prevent offences. The argument rests on the fact that like acts give rise to like anticipations (see pp. 81–2). We seem at this point to be left with the argument that our existing practices of punishment have to be said in their defence that they sometimes are economically preventive of offences and that they do not themselves produce situations of gross inequality of distress.

There is, however, one thing that may be added. I have kept it out of sight until now in order to reduce a bit the complexity of our reflections. If there is the way in which our practices contribute to *inequality*, by reinforcing existent social inequalities, there is also a way in which they contribute to *equality*. That is, it may be maintained that a society *very like ours*, except that it *lacked* the control of punishment, would involve *even greater inequality*. It is important that this contention be put in this way. It is important that we have in mind an alternative society which like our present ones involves very considerable inequality, aggressiveness, acquisitiveness, and weaker and stronger individuals and groups.

The point here is that we should not drift in the direction of a certain position of unreality. There is very little to be said for some such defence of our practice of punishment as this one: *any* society which lacked a practice of punishment would involve even more inequality than our present one. There is very little to be said either for or against such a claim. To dismiss or to embrace it, in any rational way, is an impossibility given our present state of knowledge.[28] We know too little, to mention but one large area of speculation, of the effect of possible social institutions on what is called human nature. Utopian conceptions of society and their dismissals, in their many forms, must be regarded as what they are: speculations and pointers to experiment, not premisses for practical argument of any general kind.

What we can now say, given this last addition, is that *our punishments have this defence. They sometimes deter economically. They do not involve treating single individuals, as against other members of our societies, in such a way as to produce gross inequality of distress. They contribute to the avoidance of even greater inequalities than we can now have in our societies.*

I have said that our punishments *sometimes* deter economically.
It is, to say the least, very arguable that many are not economical.
Some that come to mind are the very common short prison sentences for minor offences and particularly severe penalties for
certain dramatic crimes. One thinks also of penalties for certain
broad classes of offences. It has often been maintained with good
reason that offences against property, as distinct for example from
offences against the person, are penalized in an unacceptably
severe way. Again, there is some very considerable question about
repeated punishment of chronic offenders: the greater the number
of previous court appearances, the more likely it is that a man will
offend again.[29] Distress to more victims of offences is not avoided.
One cannot but suppose that a considerable number of penalties
are uneconomical, finally, simply because of the extremely un-
settling variation in sentences for the same offence between
different courts.[30] To *establish* that many of our penalties are uneconomical, however, would require a large and careful investigation of a particularity and kind that cannot be attempted here. To
establish that many of our penalties do have a sufficient deterrent
effect would also require such an investigation. This also is in
question in certain cases.

We are here in an area of uncertainties. For this reason it may
reasonably be objected that our conclusion about the justification
of punishment in our societies requires much more than has been
provided by way of factual argument. This is, alas, a thoroughly
reasonable objection. That punishment does in a considerable
number of cases have a deterring effect seems to me adequately
established. That it does so economically in many of the same
cases seems to me true but not established here. That it ensures a
lesser inequality seems also true and also not established here.
That our punishing should be governed by a vastly greater hesitancy seems true and less in need of establishment.[31]

Answers of a kind, then, have been given to two of the questions
mentioned at the beginning of this section. There remains this: By
what tests should we decide the moral acceptability of practices of
punishment in our societies? What principles should direct more
particular investigations of their justification? The answer, which

will be anticipated and which does seem to me established, is that *acceptable practices must prevent offences at the lowest possible cost of distress, and certainly not by causing more distress than would occur without them. Furthermore, they must not themselves give rise to excessive inequality, and must secure that more equality or less inequality obtains than would obtain in their absence.* It is not a *fundamental* requirement of the moral acceptability of a practice of punishment that those who are punished deserve it, where this is taken to mean essentially that they have freely and responsibly offended.

That men deserve punishment is not by itself a sufficient justification. The retribution theory is a mistake. It is not sufficient that punishment deters economically, or that it reforms men. Both the traditional deterrence theory and the theories of reform are mistaken. Finally, to turn to a typical compromise theory, it is not a sufficient justification that punishment is economically preventive and also deserved, where the latter refers only to the simple fact that it is imposed on individuals responsible for offences. What *can* justify punishment is the reduction of distress at an economical rate, *usually* to be obtained by imposing penalties on those responsible for offences, and the facts, if they are such, that the practice does not produce gross inequality of distress within a society and does avoid a society of even greater inequalities than those that now exist.

1. There remain defenders of the related claim that punishment, when it rather than treatment is in place, is to be justified by its deterrent effect alone. See T. L. S. Sprigge, 'A Utilitarian Reply to Dr McCloskey', *Inquiry*, 1965.
2. Anthony Quinton, 'On Punishment', *Analysis*, 1954; reprinted in Peter Laslett (editor), *Philosophy, Politics and Society*, First Series (Oxford, 1963); John Rawls, 'Two Concepts of Rules', *Philosophical Review*, 1955. See also S. I. Benn, 'An Approach to the Problems of Punishment', *Philosophy*, 1958; Benn and R. S. Peters, *Social Principles and the Democratic State* (London, 1959), pp. 182–3; Arnold Kaufman, 'Anthony Quinton on Punishment', *Analysis*, 1959.
3. Quinton, op. cit., p. 86.
4. H. L. A. Hart, 'Prolegomenon to the Principles of Punishment', *Proceedings of the Aristotelian Society*, 1959–60; other separations of the problems are to be found in W. D. Ross, *The Right and the Good* (Oxford, 1930), p. 56; J. D. Mabbott, 'Punishment', *Mind*, 1939: P. H. Nowell-Smith, *Ethics* (London, 1954), p. 272;

Antony Flew, 'The Justification of Punishment', *Philosophy*, 1954; Mabbott, 'Professor Flew on Punishment', *Philosophy*, 1955; S. I. Benn and R. S. Peters, *Social Principles and the Democratic State* (London, 1959), chapter eight; Benn, 'An Approach to the Problems of Punishment', *Philosophy*, 1958; John Rawls, 'Two Concepts of Rules', *Philosophical Review*, 1955; K. G. Armstrong, 'The Retributivist Hits Back', *Mind*, 1961.

5. See Nowell-Smith, op. cit., and Rawls, op. cit.

6. Ross, op. cit.

7. ibid., p. 60.

8. ibid., p. 58.

9. ibid., p. 62.

10. J. D. Mabbott, 'Punishment', *Mind*, 1939; 'Professor Flew on Punishment', *Philosophy*, 1955. A lecture entitled 'Moral Rules' (*Proceedings of the British Academy*, 1953) is also of relevance. Mr Mabbott, in a letter, has suggested that his original essay in particular has been misread. It seems to me that the interpretation I offer is reasonable but interested readers should consult his essays.

11. This is the original claim, rightly described as a utilitarian one. In the later articles it is said that laws and rules are justified by the fact that *if* they were universally observed the effect would be better than if there were no such laws or rules. This is a departure from utilitarianism. Suppose it turns out that a particular rule is not universally observed and is unlikely to be. Suppose, what is more, that partial observance of the rule has on balance a bad effect. A utilitarian would give up the rule. This is not necessarily true of anyone who accepts that the rule is justified by the fact that *if* it were universally observed, the effects would be good.

12. 'Punishment', p. 152.

13. ibid., p. 158.

14. See Hart, *The Concept of Law* (Oxford, 1961).

15. K. G. Armstrong, 'The Retributivist Hits Back', *Mind*, 1961.

16. Armstrong, op. cit., p. 489.

17. Given by Hart in a number of papers, all of them reprinted in *Punishment and Responsibility* (Oxford, 1968). In my account I have incorporated at least one of his later amendments to his original and best-known paper, 'Prolegomenon to the Principles of Punishment'.

18. Hart, *Punishment and Responsibility*, p. 37.

19. ibid., p. 44 ff.

20. Cf. Hart, op. cit., p. 48.

21. ibid., p. 39.

22. ibid., pp. 182–3. Cf. Nigel Walker, *The Aims of a Penal System* (James Seth Memorial Lecture, 1966).

23. See Hart, op. cit., pp. 38–40, etc.

24. Colin Howard, *Strict Responsibility* (London, 1963), p. 7; other discussions of strict liability are to be found in Glanville Williams, *Criminal Law, the General Part*, second edition (London, 1961), and Jerome Hall, *General Principles of Criminal Law*, second edition (New York, 1960).

25. Barbara Wootton, *Crime and the Criminal Law* (London, 1963), p. 51.

26. Wootton, op. cit., chapters two and three.

27. See Howard, *Strict Responsibility*. Cf. Hart, *Punishment and Responsibility*, chapter eight.

28. Crime, in our societies, is very largely the work of males. That females do not

offend anything like so much is to be explained in large part by cultural factors. Would a more pervasively 'feminine' society, if it lacked a practice of punishment, involve greater inequalities than ours?

29. W. H. Hammond and E. Chayen, *Persistent Criminals* (London, 1963).

30. Roger Hood, *Sentencing in Magistrates' Courts* (London, 1962).

31. I am now still less confident than when I wrote this, and indeed not confident at all, about a defence of our punishments. It has become more apparent to me, as it has to many, that our punishments entrench and enforce inequalities in our societies. Some relevant considerations are to be found in *Violence for Equality: Inquiries in Political Philosophy* (London, 1988).

CHAPTER SEVEN: LIBERTY AND PUNISHMENT

1. *Mill*

We have come to the conclusion about what may justify punishments in our societies. In so doing, we have given an answer of a kind to another question. If we assume, as seems reasonable, that only those actions should be crimes which may justifiably be punished, we have an answer to the question of what actions should be illegal or count as crimes. It is a familiar fact of political and social philosophy that a related question, about what actions should *not* be crimes, has long been a subject of controversy. Or, if that is not quite true, there has long been controversy about a slightly wider question. What limits should be set to the intervention of the State and society in the lives of individuals? What should be left to individuals, without fear of either criminal prosecution or coercion in any other form? This has long been discussed without reference to the problem of the justification of punishment. I should now like, by way of undeveloped postscript, to bring together these two areas of dispute. That they *are* connected is obvious.

Doctrines about State and social intervention, or those that are interesting given a prior commitment to democracy, can best be approached through Mill's essay, *On Liberty*. It remains true, oddly, that his central principle is still thought to be precisely enunciated in the following passage.

. . . the sole end for which mankind are warranted, either individually or collectively, in interfering with the liberty of action of any of their number, is self-protection . . . the only purpose for which power can be rightfully exercised over any member of a civilised community, against his will, is to prevent harm to others. His own good, either physical or moral, is not a sufficient warrant. He cannot rightfully be compelled to do or forbear because it will be better for him to do so, because it will make him happier, because, in the opinions of others, to do so would be wise, or even right.[1]

Mill has in mind the exercise of coercion by private members of society and groups, mainly but not only in the form of 'public opinion', and also punishment by the State. If we restrict ourselves to the latter, his claim here appears to be that punishment *may* be justified when a man harms others by his actions and can never be justified on the grounds merely that his actions are taken to be immoral or to be harmful to himself. That is, there is a possibility that punishment is justified in the one case, and none in the other.[2] Since *On Liberty* appeared, the most common criticism has been that Mill's doctrine rests on a simple mistake and thus is pointless. Its main intention is to exclude the State from a certain area of life, which may be more fully described as that one in which individuals do not harm anyone, even themselves, or harm only themselves, or harm certain others only with their full consent and agreement. The others in question, agreeing partners as I shall call them, must be 'of full age and not forced or deceived'.[3] The supposed mistake consists in thinking that there *are* any actions which harm only an individual or agreeing partners and nobody else.

The solitary drunkard or drug addict, consenting homosexuals, pimps and their customers, procurers of abortions, anyone who commits an act of euthanasia or attempts to commit suicide – all these individuals and many others who offend against customary morality are assumed by Mill's critics to be harming themselves or their agreeing partners. It is supposed that this is not something from which Mill would in any way dissent. However, it is argued, it is just a mistake to suppose that in any of these contraventions of morality, only agents and partners are harmed. The addict makes himself incapable of contributing to society and so harms others. Also, some may be influenced by him and so become addicts. Furthermore, there are indirect effects on other moral and social standards. In general, there are no merely self-harming actions: actions, that is, that harm only the agent and any agreeing partners. It appears to be supposed that Mill was oblivious of this supposed truth. When it is seen, we are told, his doctrine must be regarded as consummately self-defeating. Its intention is to exclude the State from a quite considerable part of individual life. It succeeds only in excluding the State from uncontroversial activities which harm nobody at all.[4]

This view of *On Liberty* must often have been the product of not having read it. In the third paragraph after that one which contains the passage quoted above, Mill reiterates that the State is to be excluded from 'all that portion of a person's life and conduct which affects only himself, or, if it also affects others, only with their free, voluntary and undeceived consent and participation'. He then adds: 'When I say only himself, I mean directly, and in the first instance, for whatever affects himself, may affect others through himself; and the objections which may be grounded on this contingency will receive consideration in the sequel.'[5] He does in a later section make good his promise and consider the objection that there are no merely self-harming actions, in the sense defined above. Furthermore, he chooses explicitly to admit it.[6]

What, then, *is* 'the one very simple principle' which he intends and which he too vaguely states in the earlier parts of his essay? The first[7] of three answers that I shall discuss is one which supposes that Mill intended to distinguish between two kinds of harm that may result from an individual's action, two kinds in addition to the harm caused to the agent himself and any agreeing partners. The distinction between these two kinds of harm is made by way of the idea of interests or rights.

To say a man has certain interests, in the relevant sense, is to say that if he is harmed in certain ways he has a right of redress. These interests, we are told in this interpretation of Mill, are those which 'depend for their existence on social recognition and are closely connected with prevailing standards about the sort of behaviour a man can legitimately expect from others'.[8] To take an obvious case, ownership of property gives rise to interests. If my property is damaged by others under certain circumstances, I can make some recovery under existing law. We have the distinction, then, between harm to individuals which involves injury to interests and harm to individuals which does not involve injury to their interests.

Harm of the first sort gives rise to a right of redress; harm of the second sort does not.

The suggestion is that Mill's intention was to advance this principle: The State may possibly be justified in intervening when a man harms another, who is not an agreeing partner, and in so doing injures his interests. Mill does write in one place that 'for such actions as are prejudicial to the interests of others, the individual is accountable, and may be subjected either to social or to legal punishment, if society is of the opinion that the one or the other is requisite for its protection.'⁹

This interpretation has a considerable advantage over its predecessors. Even given the assumptions about the harmfulness of all supposed immorality and the impossibility of actions harming only agents and partners, Mill's principle is not useless. For example, it does appear to exclude the State from interference with a drug addict, who might be said to harm others in indirect ways, perhaps through his failure to contribute to society, but cannot be said to injure any established interests of others. There is, I think, a tenable distinction between harming a man, simply, and harming him in such a way as to injure his interests. It should be noticed, however, that the two notions are not so different as may be supposed. The relevant notion of a man's being harmed is not purely a descriptive one. If I am harmed, I am deprived of something desirable to which I have *some* claim or reasonable expectation. (I am not harmed if I am deprived of something I have stolen.) I may be deprived of something to which I have *some* claim, however, without its being correct to say that interests of mine have been injured. That is, I may have nothing very like a right of redress. It might be said, if the words are in place, that the distinction between harm and harm involving injury to interests is one of degree rather than kind. My use of the word 'harm' at this point, obviously, is a wide one, considerably wider than the notion of harm within the law.

Nonetheless, if this version of Mill's principle does not have the disability of the traditional and mistaken one, there are other things to be said against it. The principle so construed, as has been argued,¹⁰ is essentially conservative, protective of the *status quo*, since the extent of State action in the controversial area is determined by what are actually established, legally or socially, as interests. Given this, it cannot reflect Mill's intention. It is not in accord with the tenor of his thought[11] or with specific recommendations in *On Liberty* that the State should not be barred from interference with behaviour simply because the behaviour in question does not endanger or damage interests of a recognized kind. There is also another related disability. Mill makes it clear that he regards whatever principle he intends as based on the Principle of Utility, albeit not in quite Jeremy Bentham's sense.[12] But the version of the intervention principle under discussion does not derive from the Principle of Utility. Indeed, it appears to be inconsistent with it. It could be consistent with it only if the all-important interests in question, those which were legally and socially recognized in Mill's time, were precisely those enjoined by the Principle of Utility. There was not this identity, and Mill did not suppose that there was.

What principle, then, should we take him to have intended? That question, perhaps, does not really express the necessary nature of our inquiry. Given the inconsistencies of *On Liberty*, it requires a certain piety to think that Mill did have clear in his mind some exact principle which he failed to formulate adequately. We might better ask, I think, to what Mill is committed, given several fixed points, most importantly his Principle of Utility.

Another answer[13] to one of these questions is the principle, briefly stated, that the State may not intervene with respect to actions which harm others than the agent and partners if this harm arises solely by way of the beliefs of those individuals. It is in general true that Mill did wish to exclude the State from interference in activities which may be said to cause harm only via beliefs, such as Sunday sport which offends the sensibilities of Sabbatarians. To make Mill's principle only this, however, would raise an obvious difficulty. It would not serve to exclude the State in such cases as that of the discreet drug addict. The supposed harm he causes to others, by failing to contribute to society, does not depend on their beliefs if any about the wrongfulness of taking drugs. An attempt is made to meet this difficulty in the following way. Mill's principle, whatever it is, depends on classifying actions in terms of their consequences. A preliminary question, then, is what things are to count at all as consequences of action. In particular, suppose I do A rather than B, and X would have followed had I done B. Is the non-occurrence of X to be regarded as a consequence of my doing A? It is suggested that Mill's answer to this preliminary question is that the non-occurrence of X counts as a consequence of my doing A if this non-occurrence occasions perceptible hurt to an assignable individual or is such that I may be said to have failed in a specific duty to the public.

I wish to suggest two of a number of difficulties involved in this interpretation of Mill. (1) What we have when more fully stated is the principle that the State may not intervene in a man's behaviour if some harm cannot rightly be counted as a consequence of his actions, or if a harm which is a consequence arises by way of the beliefs of the person harmed. The first part of the principle may be taken to exclude the State from interference with the addict. That is, he may not have failed in a specific duty to the public or caused perceptible hurt to an assignable individual. The second part of the principle excludes the State from interference in cases like that involving the offended Sabbatarian. (The State is also excluded, of course, by *this* part of the principle, from interference with the indiscreet addict who *is* said to cause harm by way of the beliefs of those harmed.) It is the first part of the principle that seems to me unacceptable. How are we to determine when a man has performed an action such that the ensuing harm is a consequence of the action? One *might* concede that whether or not perceptible hurt has been caused to an assignable individual is a question to be settled by consideration of the facts. One might concede, more precisely, that it is neither an evaluative question nor one concerned with prevailing norms and standards. Such a concession cannot be made with respect to the question of when a man has failed in a specific duty to the public. This question, under an ordinary interpretation, is one to be settled by consideration of prevailing norms and standards and, in particular, consideration of the law.[14] Given this, however, the principle which is being advanced is in one crucial part conservative in effect and quite likely inconsistent with the Principle of Utility. The principle in one important part shares the disability of the one previously considered.

(2) It can hardly be taken as the principle intended by Mill. It cannot be reconciled with his many formulations which do not mention belief-dependent harms or his failure explicitly to mention in *On Liberty* the essential definition of consequences.

2. *Reinterpretation*

I wish now to offer another view of the essay.[15] It is certainly true that it was a part of Mill's desire to state a principle incorporating the notion of interests in connection with harm caused to others than agents and agreeing partners. A reading of his fourth chapter, in which after an explicit discussion he agrees that self-harming actions also harm others, can leave no doubt of this.[16] What is *not* true, however, is that we must understand the interests in question simply as those actually recognized or established by society. At the beginning of the fourth chapter Mill very much gives the impression that he has come to the point of providing the canonical form of his principle. He writes that each citizen, if his liberty is not to be intruded upon by the State, must follow a certain line of conduct toward others.

> This conduct consists, first, in not injuring the interests of one another; or rather certain interests, which, either by express legal provision or tacit understanding, *ought to be* considered as rights; and secondly, in each person bearing his share (to be fixed on some equitable principle) of the labours and sacrifices incurred for defending the society or its members from injury and molestation.[17]

What I wish to point out, of course, is that the interests in question are here specifically *not* identified with those interests which 'depend for their existence on social recognition and are closely connected with prevailing standards about the sort of behaviour a man can legitimately expect from others.' Mill's principle as here stated is essentially this: the State may not interfere unless a man's actions injure what *ought to be* accepted as the interests or rights of others, whether or not they are accepted. (The second requirement mentioned in the quoted passage is not relevant for our purposes.) What is the test of whether there has been damage to what ought to be regarded as a man's interests, as harm which ought to give him a right of redress? For Mill the test must be the Principle of Utility. In short, what we have is that the State may not interfere with my behaviour if I do not violate interests of others – those interests they would have in a utilitarian society.

Three things can be said for this understanding. (1) It too escapes the traditional objection that Mill's principle allows interference with all behaviour other than the kind that causes harm to nobody at all. (2) The principle so understood is not conservative and, to say the least, is consistent with the Principle of Utility. It is evidently the principle to which Mill is committed. (3) It does not much matter, but it may also be regarded as what Mill often intended or had in mind. The passage I have quoted gives some support for this view. Of course, *On Liberty* falls short of being paralysed by rigour, and Mill's careless *largesse* in enunciations of his position makes it possible to find *some* passage that may be so read as to support any reasonable speculation. Two points about his many statements of position may be worth making. With respect to those that mention simply harm to others than the agent and agreeing partners,[18] it is not unreasonable to assume that he had in mind harm to interests. Secondly, it is likely that when he speaks as if his principle does turn on recognized or established interests, he had in mind those of them that he regarded as being in accord with Utility. But that the State may possibly intervene only when such interests are damaged is to be explained not by the fact that they are established but rather by the fact that they are in accord with Utility.

Unfortunately, when we take Mill's principle to be that the State may not intervene unless what I shall call utility interests of others than the agent and partners are injured or threatened, there is the following objection. The principle so understood certainly fails to fulfil Mill's main hope. It cannot do what he envisaged as its job. More important, *we* must regard it as failing in this respect.

Ultimately, Mill wishes to submit all actions, including those of the State, to the judgement of the Principle of Utility. In *On Liberty* his endeavour was to establish 'one very simple principle', of a subordinate nature, with respect to State intervention. This principle would in function be an analogue to the moral principles or rules having to do with truth-telling and promise-keeping. However, it may be objected, the principle we are taking him to have produced obviously *incorporates* the Principle of Utility. What we have is that the State may not intervene if my actions do not injure or endanger those interests of others which are in accord with the Principle of Utility. Any operation of the given principle of intervention, then, involves a use of the Principle of Utility. One must know or ask, in each case, if interests which may be claimed *are* in accord with Utility. One is no further ahead.

Perhaps this could do with fuller explanation. Mill writes in *Utilitarianism* that

> It is a strange notion that the acknowledgement of a first principle is inconsistent with the admission of secondary ones. . . . The proposition that happiness is the end and aim of morality does not mean that no road ought to be laid down to that goal, or that persons going thither should not be advised to take one direction rather than another. . . . Nobody argues that the art of navigation is not founded on astronomy, because sailors cannot wait to calculate the Nautical Almanack. Being rational creatures they go to sea with it already calculated . . .[19]

Mill attempts, with respect to the question of State intervention, to provide a useful principle of quite considerable generality but subordinate to the Principle of Utility. To do so, of course, would not simply be to devise a time-saver, but to give an answer to a difficult question about one of the consequences of the Principle of Utility. What we are taking him to have produced, however, is tantamount to the injunction that the State must not intervene when in so doing it would contravene the Principle of Utility.

This is the objection and it cannot be avoided. It will be worth while, however, from several points of view, to consider a possible rejoinder. It may be contended that it is not true that *every* operation of the principle of intervention involves an operation of the Principle of Utility. In many important instances, it may be said, this is not so. Let us approach this by way of another point. As we have seen, Mill's traditional critics suppose that (1) *all* acts generally considered to be immoral are also harmful acts. Individuals and their agreeing partners, if any, harm themselves by engaging in certain behaviour. (2) Furthermore, they harm others. It must be admitted that Mill in some places may appear to accept the first proposition. This is so when he gives his energies to dealing with the second one, and appears not to question the truth of the first. It is a fact, of course, but not to the point, that he does consider a good number of activities generally considered immoral to be harmful. It is an oversight to think that he accepts this of *all* the activities in question or is in any way committed to accepting it.

On Liberty is a work of reiterations, and not many things are more often repeated than the claim that orthodox or accepted doctrines and moralities are commonly mistaken. One of the things they may be mistaken about, obviously, is the question of whether or not certain actions and activities are harmful to the people involved. More to the point, Mill rightly believes that in many cases activities commonly taken to be immoral have not been harmful. More or less trivial examples can be had from the dietary rules of some societies. Today, it can certainly be argued that there are sexual actions and activities which are harmless and of which orthodox morality, if it can be located, disapproves. That Mill did distinguish what is ordinarily condemned from what is harmful is a contention that hardly needs support. If it is thought to be needed, it is provided by his hymn to individuality, the third chapter of the essay.

Given this, it may be said, it becomes apparent that the principle of intervention in question does not always, or in all important cases, bring in the Principle of Utility. The intervention principle, alternatively written, is (1) that the State may not intervene when an individual's actions are not harmful, and (2) it may not intervene when any harm to others than the agent and partners does not involve injury to utility interests. The second part, it may be said, does have the disability in question but the first part does not. We do then have a principle which does in certain important cases have the function that Mill had in mind.

Unfortunately, this will not work. The reason, which may be anticipated, is that it is not a factual question merely whether or not something constitutes a harm. The question calls for an evaluation. As I have said, if I am so affected by an action as to be harmed, my new state must by some standard be an undesirable one. The standard for Mill is obviously the Principle of Utility. What we then have is the conclusion that the principle of State intervention, in both of its parts, does involve the Principle of Utility. Of course it must not be supposed that *On Liberty*, even from what might be called a theoretical or doctrinal point of view, is without significance. If it fails to provide a useful and fairly general principle of State intervention, it does defend a position which can be clearly stated and also advances certain maxims of very considerable importance.[20] There is, given the Principle of Utility, to be no interference in freedom of thought and expression. There is to be no interference, at least in certain circumstances, when harm caused to an individual comes by way of his own beliefs and would not arise otherwise.

3. The Enforcement of Morality

We shall return to Mill's essay, and to what must be his position with respect to individual liberty, but I should like now to define and criticize two opposed, or seemingly opposed, doctrines and to consider a particular controversy. One is that a particular morality, a moral code thought to be shared by a society, is of such *intrinsic* value that the State may be justified in enforcing it on individuals by punishment. The State *may* be justified in interventions not only when individuals in some sense harm others than their agreeing partners, but also when they merely act in what are held to be immoral ways. These latter interventions are justified as means to the end of preserving the morality in question, which is important in itself.[21]

This is related to, if certainly not identical with, the traditional retribution theory of punishment. There is at least a possibility, indeed, that the doctrine of State intervention and the retribution theory of punishment would have different consequences in a particular case. It is at least a possibility that on occasion the punishment of a man who offends against accepted morality, in such a way as to break the law, would not be thought necessary for the preservation of morality. It is conceivable even that it be thought likely to have a harmful effect on that morality. In such a circumstance, presumably, the intervention doctrine and the retribution theory would not issue in compatible conclusions.

There are a number of quite obvious criticisms of this demand for the enforcement of morality and I shall do no more than mention them.[22] The argument presumably assumes a wide assent to the morality which punishment is to preserve. It seems not the case at least in contemporary societies that there is any such consensus. It must be remembered, of course, that we are dealing with such matters as sexual behaviour, abortion, attempted suicide, euthanasia, drunkenness, and drug-taking. Secondly, the argument contains at least one important ambiguity. Is the supposed end in question the securing of something like sincere belief in the accepted morality, a kind of willing commitment to it, or is it merely the end of securing behaviour in accordance with it? The former 'higher' end, I think, has usually been the goal. It is not at all obviously true, however, that the punishment of offenders is likely to secure this effect. One can at best have a number of hypotheses of a doubtful nature, hypotheses providing an indirect connection between the punishment of offenders and the supposed consequences of sincere commitment.

Thirdly, one might put aside both these difficulties and yet argue that the distress involved in the punishment of supposed immoralities, which may harm nobody, cannot be justified by attainment of the end in question, however construed. It is important to keep in mind at this point that the end in question is not the prevention of harm. The end is no more than commitment to a particular shared morality or else behaviour in accord with it. The argument is, if anything, less acceptable than the argument for the traditional retribution theory of punishment.

A distinct but related doctrine, which also is said to be opposed to Mill's liberalism, is advanced by one of his recent critics.[23] Its central contention is preserved in this passage:

... it is not possible to set theoretical limits to the power of the state to legislate against immorality. It is not possible to settle in advance exceptions to the general rule or to define inflexibly areas of morality into which the law is in no circumstances to be allowed to enter. Society is entitled by means of its laws to protect itself from dangers, whether from within or without. Here again I think that the political parallel is legitimate. The law of treason is directed against aiding the king's enemies and against sedition from within. The justification for this is that established government is necessary for the existence of society and therefore its safety against violent overthrow must be secured. But an established morality is as necessary as good government to the welfare of society. Societies disintegrate from within more frequently than they are broken up by external pressures. There is disintegration when no common morality is observed and history shows that the loosening of moral bonds is often the first stage of disintegration, so that society is justified in taking the same steps to preserve its moral code as it does to preserve its government and other essential institutions.[24]

The argument here is not that an established or shared morality is something which has such attractions in itself that punishment may be used to preserve it. The argument is rather that a shared morality is a necessary condition of the preservation of society. *That* is unquestionably a good thing, or perhaps it is the preservation of British or American or similar societies that is unquestionably a good thing. What may justify the punishment of certain acts, then, is that punishment may preserve the shared morality of the society, and preserving the morality preserves the society. It is the avoidance of harm on a grand scale that justifies intervention. There is one way, then, in which this doctrine is in agreement with Mill's intentions. In both cases we have an attempt to base a principle of intervention on considerations of harm. Although Mill did not envisage the catastrophic harm we are now asked to consider, the label 'utilitarian' may be applied to both doctrines.

We may here notice what is supposed to be the main distinction between the two doctrines. It is much insisted, in the one we are considering, not that we should at present punish this or that supposed immorality, but that there can be no 'theoretical limit' to the State's right of intervention. There may just now be no sufficient reason to legislate against some supposed sexual immorality, for example. However, should this immorality become widely practised, we might have sufficient reason. Given this possibility, there can be no acceptance of a doctrine which rules out legislation in advance. It is supposed[25] that there is in Mill a precise contrast to this, an attempt to set a theoretical limit of a certain kind, once and for all, to the State's activities.

This involves a confusion. Mill submits that if behaviour of individuals does threaten harm of a certain sort then interference is a possibility. He does not consider the proposition that some behaviour of individuals, generally considered immoral, may threaten the very existence of a society. He would no doubt have agreed, however, that *if* the supposed behaviour were to threaten the existence of a society, and *if* the continued existence of that society had a utilitarian justification, then interference might be justified. Nothing in his argument suggests otherwise. What is closed off is the possibility of intervention when there is *no* harm, in a certain sense, in question. But it appears that this theoretical limit is just as much a part of his critic's doctrine. However, the ultimate premisses of that doctrine are not made explicit. More to the point, perhaps, there can hardly be an argument to the effect that *no* proposals as to absolute limits on State intervention are acceptable. Could anyone object to the proposal that the State should be regarded as under an absolute prohibition with respect to the pointless degradation of its citizens?

Mill, although he does not consider the point explicitly, is clearly of the opinion that no significant probability attaches to the proposition that society will one day disintegrate or be endangered by the supposed immoralities in question. In this, he is surely right. The weakness of the supposition to the contrary, although on occasion misconstrued by critics, has been adequately indicated.[26] It is a significant probability that a society will *change*, in a number of different ways, if certain practices become widespread. There is more than a low probability, no doubt, that British or American society would eventually change very considerably as a consequence of a widespread practice of euthanasia. However, there is no reason whatever to confuse change in a society with the society's being destroyed or its being put in great danger. The vague proposition that the *existence* of a society may be threatened by departures from a shared moral code gains what little persuasion it has from confusion with a truth about change. There is another point to be noted. It is no doubt true that 'morality', where this means something quite other than a moral code about matters like sexual conduct, is an empirically or even logically necessary condition of the existence of a society. It is true that morality, where this has to do with acceptance of certain principles of mutual tolerance, is a condition of social existence. All societies satisfy some such condition. This is not to say that a particular moral code followed by a society at some point in time is a necessary condition of the society's continuance. There are, of course, still other difficulties in the doctrine we are considering. For example, it shares with its predecessor the supposition that there does exist in contemporary society an accepted or shared or established morality of the kind required.

4. *Consent, Culpability, Sincerity*

Although Mill does not succeed in producing a general principle of State intervention, one which does not incorporate the Principle of Utility, his position can be clearly stated. It is that there is to be no intervention unless (1) an individual causes harm, as determined by Utility, to someone other than an agreeing partner, and (2) the harm involves injury to interests sanctioned by Utility.

One may be puzzled, at this point, by the inclusion of the second requirement. Why should it not be thought sufficient, as a ground for intervention, simply that an individual causes harm, harm according to the Principle of Utility, to someone not an agreeing partner? I take the explanation to be that while an individual may indeed cause harm in the given sense to someone else, to allow the possibility of intervention by the State in *all* such cases would make for an even less acceptable state of affairs. To allow the possibility would so restrict individual freedom as to produce more distress or less satisfaction than the alternative course. The alternative course is to allow the possibility of intervention in essential cases. The limit is settled by way of the notion of interests. Intervention is a possibility when interests sanctioned by Utility and then actually established are injured. The doctrine excludes intervention on the ground simply that behaviour is thought to be immoral. It also excludes intervention when an individual harms another but not so severely as to damage interests established on the basis of the Principle of Utility.

We have considered two critical and highly dubious responses to a view of this kind. There are also several other criticisms which I should like to consider briefly before making my own, of a rather different kind. One recurring one is that the law, and in particular English and American law, has not followed Mill. It is not in general a defence to establish that a person harmed did in fact consent to the action in question. It is not a defence in cases of assault or euthanasia or suicide pact. The explanation, it is said, of this supposed refusal to countenance the fact of agreeing partners must be that in the law certain acts are punished simply because they are immoral.[27] There are a number of things to be said about this.

(1) It is fairly obvious that Mill, when he defended what he called 'the liberty . . . of combination among individuals',[28] did not intend to condemn wholesale the legal principle that the consent of an injured party is not in general a defence. His concern was in the main with 'combinations' of agreeing partners other than those involving such offences as assault and euthanasia.

(2) With respect to cases involving such offences, one can reasonably suppose he would have supported such legal rules as have the effect of ensuring that supposed agreements are indeed full agreements between knowledgeable and entirely uncoerced partners. One can also suppose he would have approved of rules whose effect is to ensure that supposed agreements are settled and persistent. Such rules, which do not amount to the prohibition of 'combinations', can hardly be displayed as attempts to punish

immorality on the ground alone that it is immorality. They are, rather, strategies to avoid abuse of the liberty of combination, abuse which would consist fundamentally in harm of one individual by another.

It must be admitted, despite what has been said, that the law has in the past often not been guided by Mill's principle. It has punished supposed immorality for itself, and still does so. What can be made of this? Where the given principle of intervention and the law diverge, one can take the law to be mistaken rather than the principle. It is at this point that critics of Mill are wont to have recourse to a supposition about the wisdom of the ages. It is, in one formulation, the supposition 'that there is a presumption that common and long-established institutions are likely to have merits not apparent to the rationalist philosopher.'[29] All that can be said here, since any consideration of what amounts to a considerable ideology is out of question, is that 'common and long-established institutions' come to be taken as indefensible with sufficient regularity to make the present argument less than overwhelming.

There is, it is said,[30] another principle of law which is not at all in accord with Mill's principle. It is clear, we are told, that the law as it stands *takes account of* moral culpability. Offenders are graded in the criminal calendar *partly* in accordance with this consideration; particular offenders are assessed with respect to moral culpability. The law as it stands is not an exemplification of the traditional deterrence theory. It is inconsistent, it is said, to find this morally tolerable and also to maintain that the law may not be used to enforce morality as such. One simple reply here is that even if everything prior to the given conclusion is true, there is no such inconsistency. I may with perfect logical respectability, to speak of nothing else, believe (1) that the justification of having a system of punishment and of particular acts of punishment *involves* moral culpability or desert, and (2) that there is no justification for either a system or particular punishments on the ground merely of the supposed immorality of certain behaviour. I shall have to grant, of course, that the law should be 'concerned with morality' where that is understood as a reiteration of the first proposition. This commits me in no way to the view that the law should be 'concerned with morality' where this means there is a justification for punishment in the mere fact of the existence of behaviour thought to be immoral.

We may also notice, finally, the objection that individuals who break the law and in so doing offend against accepted morality rarely do so with the conviction that they are right to do so.

Evidently what Mill visualises is a number of people doing things he himself would disapprove of, but doing them earnestly and openly and after thought and discussion in an endeavour to find the way of life best suited to them as individuals. This seems to me on the whole an idealistic picture. . . . If a free society is better than a disciplined one, it is because – and this certainly was Mill's view – it is better for a man himself that he should be free to seek his own good in his own way and better too for the society to which he belongs, since thereby a way may be found to greater good for all. But no good can come from a man doing what he acknowledges to be evil.[31]

It is easy, it seems, to suppose that a man whose behaviour diverges from one's own morality cannot but acknowledge that he errs. If speculations are to be made in this area, one as good as any is that among homosexuals, individuals who attempt suicide or euthanasia, those who secure abortions or choose to smoke marijuana, very considerable numbers are entirely willing to defend their actions. Of greater importance is the fact that it does not at all follow from a willingness to admit some behaviour is immoral that it is such. It is surely obvious that there does occur in social and moral development, between times when certain behaviour is widely considered immoral and is rare, and times when it is not so considered and is common, other times when it is to some extent engaged in but not widely defended. Finally, as is admitted, it may be argued that those who are sincere and of the opinion that their behaviour is defensible cannot be distinguished from the rest. Given this, it may be maintained that general arguments adduced by Mill for individual freedom should carry the day. In short, whatever evil attaches to insincere behaviour, it is outweighed by the benefits attaching to freedom.

5. *Equality*

As we have noticed, there is a similarity between the retribution theory of punishment and the view, stated at the beginning of the third section above, that an established moral code is of such good *in itself* that we may attempt to maintain it by punishment. They are both in a way anti-utilitarian. Their ends, giving a man what he deserves and maintaining a morality, are such that they pay a quite insufficient attention to welfare. Predictably, then, both doctrines can be rejected.

Mill's thesis, that there is a possibility of State intervention only when there is injury to utility interests, or a danger of it, is closely related to the deterrence theory. Taking only that part of his intervention policy which concerns punishment by the State, it is that a necessary condition of justified punishment is that there be harm of a certain kind, and that supposed immorality is by itself neither a sufficient nor a necessary condition. The latter part rules out the possibility of combination with most forms of the traditional retribution theory. Mill's doctrine does combine with the deterrence theory, in that the necessary condition of justified punishment is consistent with the sufficient condition proposed by the deterrence theory. Intervention by way of punishment is possible, one necessary condition has been satisfied, if behaviour does affect utility interests. Punishment *is* justified, according to the deterrence theory as we have construed it, if this condition is satisfied and it is also true that the punishment is economical.

Mill's doctrine, as we have seen, while it does not fulfil his central intention with respect to a kind of principle, has been the subject of mistaken criticism. It has mistakenly been found inferior to moralistic and legalistic views which are themselves unacceptable. However, there is at least some other criticism against which it cannot be defended.

At the end of his essay Mill turns from the subject of intervention in the lives of individuals *against their will* to a different matter: intervention in the form of help, presumably with the agreement of those concerned. He is opposed to it, on the grounds that help is better provided by individuals, that State intervention would here inhibit individual development, that the enlargement of government and bureaucracy, and its power, is a great danger. *A fortiori*, Mill would have been opposed to intervention in the lives of some citizens, against their will, for the purpose of helping others. Almost all contemporary ideologies, although to very differing extents, depart from this attitude. It is worth noticing incidentally that at least sometimes such interventions can be regarded as following from Mill's intervention principle. It can in many instances be argued that coercive intervention in the lives of some individuals, in order to make help for others possible, is not against utility interests. Mill departs from his principle.

What I mainly wish to suggest is that if the State may intervene only if actions harm or threaten utility interests, it will sometimes in its interventions not conform to principles of equality. This will be so, obviously, in several circumstances. Suppose A is claimed to have harmed B. Furthermore, interests of B sanctioned by the Principle of Utility have been injured. There will then be a possibility of intervention given Mill's principle. There is no reason for thinking, however, that the utility interests had by B must be in accordance with *equality*. The system of interests which includes the relevant interest of B may be such as to maximize utility or welfare. If it preserves unacceptable inequalities between individuals, however, and in particular involves a victimization of A, there may not be a case for action against A. At any rate, questions arise.

Consider this over-simplified model. R and S represent the consequences, in terms of quantity of welfare and its distribution, of two possible uses of resources in a society.

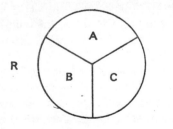
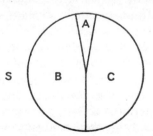

Thus, somewhat less welfare would be produced by the first possible use, but its distribution would be into equal shares for three parties concerned, A and B being two of them. The second use would produce more welfare, but its distribution necessarily would be into large shares for B and C and one very small share for A. His share would not only be greatly smaller than the other two, given the second possible use of resources, but would also be considerably smaller than the share he would receive given the first possible use.

The Principle of Utility requires that the society make the second use of the resources. Suppose now that the society acts on this principle and interests are established in accordance with it. In particular it adopts the second use of resources, which involves the unequal distribution and what amounts to victimization of A. Suppose that A attempts in a certain way to appropriate a part of B's share. In doing so, he endangers the utility interests of B. According to the intervention principle, there may then be action against him. This may be unacceptable, and clearly so in certain circumstances. There is the circumstance, for example, where each of the three parties requires a share of the sizes in R in order to come up to some agreed minimum standard of welfare.

I am aware that this is excessively schematic and that it avoids a great deal of complication and argument.[32] For obvious reasons, I shall not attempt to say more. My principal conclusion is that an acceptable principle of State intervention must accommodate not only utilitarian values but also equality. It seems clear, although not fully argued here, that it cannot be established that to accommodate the first is invariably to accommodate the second. The deterrence theory of punishment, and the associated doctrine of State intervention, fail in being merely utilitarian. We are left with only the possibilities of a certain compromise theory of punishment and an intervention policy that is similar in that it observes considerations of utility *and* equality.

One may have a certain amount of difficulty, at this point, in getting these several questions and their relation into focus. Mill set out to establish one necessary condition of justified intervention by the State or society in the lives of individuals against their wills. If we set aside part of his concern, having to do with coercion by other means than punishment, his question can be formulated as follows: (1) When is punishment *not* justified? or What is one necessary condition of justified punishment? His answer, as we have concluded, putting it in terms of the second formulation, is that a necessary but not sufficient condition of justified punishment is that an individual should have injured or endangered the utility interests of someone else, not an agreeing partner.

Our main question in the preceding chapters has been this: (2) What, if anything, constitutes a sufficient condition of justified punishment? One answer is that punishment's being economically deterrent, and that alone, is a sufficient condition. As I have said, these two answers to the questions, Mill's question and our own, are consistent. One can go further, I think, preferably on the basis of more detailed argument than I shall supply. It can be argued that to answer the second question by the deterrence theory commits one to answering the first question in Mill's way. One is committed, certainly, to giving as a necessary condition of justified punishment that it be deterrent. To maintain that punishment must be deterrent is ordinarily to maintain that it must prevent certain possible distress. This is the same distress, presumably, that is to be avoided by a respect of utility interests and if necessary by intervention to prevent their injury.

We have rejected Mill's intervention doctrine, and concluded instead that punishment must not be in question if there is no injury or danger to interests established on the basis of both utility *and* equality. Such injury or danger is a necessary condition of justified punishment. To the question of a sufficient condition of justified punishment, we have answered that punishment may be justified when it is both economically deterrent and in a certain accord with equality. Again, the second answer is consistent with the first. Also, I wish to suggest, the second answer entails certain answers to the first question. We must give as necessary conditions of justified punishment that it be deterrent and in accord with equality. This is, it seems, tantamount to the claim that punishment must not be in question if there is no danger or injury to interests established on the basis of utility and equality.

Given a certain concern we need never ask the lesser question. We need never ask it if our business is with the whole justification of the practice of punishment. We may find ourselves asking it if, in a way like Mill, we face a certain challenge. It is the challenge that one of what we take to be necessary conditions of justified punishment is not such. Such a challenge would be offered by someone who maintained, for example, that a justified punishment need not be economically deterrent but need only be for an offence against established morality.

It is worth noticing, finally, that it has been implicit in my argument in this chapter that desert or retributive justice, where it does not reduce to something else, does not enter into an acceptable account of the limits of State intervention. This rejection of retributive justice, when it is not a matter of utility or distributive justice, has of course been explicit in earlier chapters. A rejection of pure retribution, which centrally has to do with the supposed moral importance of responsible action in itself, has consequences for things other than punishment and State intervention. It has, evidently, consequences for moral, social and political practice generally.

1. *On Liberty*, in *Utilitarianism* (London, 1962), edited by Mary Warnock, p. 135.
2. ibid., p. 227.
3. ibid., p. 138.
4. That this has been what amounts to the orthodox view of Mill is shown, for example, by J. C. Rees, in 'A Rereading of Mill On Liberty', *Political Studies*, 1960, p. 113.
5. Mill, op. cit., p. 137.
6. ibid., p. 210 ff.
7. Rees, op. cit. A new postscript was added to the paper on republication in *Limits of Liberty* (Belmont, California, 1966), edited by Peter Radcliff.
8. ibid., p. 119.
9. ibid., p. 226.
10. By Richard Wollheim in a paper of which a reduced version appears in *Man and Society*, No. 6, 1963. Prof. Wollheim's own reading of Mill, which I consider below, is stated in this version. Cf. C. L. Ten, 'Mill on Self-Regarding Actions', *Philosophy*, 1968. Wollheim and Ten are considered further in my 'On Liberty and Morality-Dependent Harms', *Political Studies*, 1982.
11. Wollheim writes: '. . . it is an undoubted fact, clear from various sources such as the essays on Bentham and Coleridge, the *Autobiography* and the sixth book of the *System of Logic*, that Mill in his general thinking about politics was torn between the universalistic liberal approach typical of the 18th century and the

particularistic conservative approach typical of the 19th century. But in *On Liberty* he surely takes his stand unambiguously on the side of the tradition in which he was brought up rather than on that of the new thinking with which, as he tells us in the *Autobiography*, he tried to correct his own intellectual balance.'

12. Mill writes in *Utilitarianism* (op. cit., p. 257): 'The creed which accepts as the foundation of morals, Utility, or the Greatest Happiness Principle, holds that actions are right as they tend to promote happiness, wrong as they tend to produce the reverse of happiness. By happiness is intended pleasure, and the absence of pain; by unhappiness, pain, and the privation of pleasure.' Cf. my statement above, p. 85. Mill writes in *On Liberty* (op. cit., p. 136): 'I regard utility as the ultimate appeal on all ethical questions; but it must be utility in the largest sense, grounded on the permanent interests of man as a progressive being. Those interests, I contend, authorise the subjection of individual spontaneity to external control, only in respect to those actions of each which concern the interest of other people.'

13. Wollheim, op. cit.

14. Another answer, but not one suggested by Wollheim, is that the duties in question are those sanctioned by the Principle of Utility. Difficulties which attach to an answer of this kind are considered below in connection with what I take to be the most defensible reading of Mill's essay.

15. A part of what I have to say in this section, and of what I have said already, appears in my article, 'Mill on Liberty', *Inquiry*, 1967.

16. Perhaps this is too strong a claim. Cf. Ten, op. cit.

17. *On Liberty*, p. 205. My italics.

18. As suggested by Rees, op. cit., p. 135.

19. *Utilitarianism*, edited by Mary Warnock, p. 276.

20. For an enlargement of this important point, see my 'The Worth of *On Liberty*', *Political Studies*, 1974.

21. As pointed out by Hart (*Law, Liberty and Morality* [London, 1963], p. 55), James Fitzjames Stephen advances this doctrine among others in *Liberty, Equality, Fraternity* (London, 1873).

22. Some of those I include, as well as others, are advanced by Hart, op. cit.

23. Patrick Devlin, *The Enforcement of Morals* (London, 1965).

24. Devlin, op. cit., pp. 12–13.

25. ibid., p. 103, p. 113, p. 125.

26. See, on this and other points, Hart, *Law, Liberty and Morality*, and Wollheim, 'Crime, Sin and Mr. Justice Devlin', *Encounter*, 1959.

27. Devlin, op. cit., p. 132.

28. Mill, op. cit., p. 138.

29. Hart, *Law, Liberty and Morality*, p. 29.

30. Devlin, op. cit., p. 128.

31. ibid., pp. 107–8.

32. See, for some of it, Nicholas Rescher, *Distributive Justice* (New York, 1966).

POSTSCRIPT: THE NEW RETRIBUTIVISM
AND POLITICAL PHILOSOPHY

This postscript will in good part concern six arguments taken as making up what is called the New Retributivism.[1] It will also have to do with a seventh retributivist argument, and with the unexamined idea that reflection on punishment can lead a life of its own, independently of political philosophy. Both that idea and the arguments bear on the main question of whether punishment in out societies is right or wrong. It is a question not worn to a frazzle, as is the one of *how* it is that punishment is right, which piously presupposes that it is. My answer to the impious question gets very little wear in this reactionary and, as it sometimes seems, vengeful time. For a particular reason, it will in a way have to go undefended here.[2]

First a definition. An occasional contemporary philosopher sides with what seems to be the intent of the new California penal code, and thus *defines* punishment so as to make it morally justified at least in part by its being some sort of retribution.[3] Any such definition has the effect, among others, of making it conceptually impossible to ask if retribution is perhaps no part of the justification of punishment. The given definition thus impedes inquiry, and of course can settle no real moral question. No actual moral practice becomes right or wrong by act of definition. Anyone who supposes, to speak quickly, that retribution is rot, can accept such a definition and persist in his own moral view by maintaining that no actual practice, even in California, falls under the given definition.

Let us without further ado define punishment as *that practice whereby a social authority visits penalties on offenders, one of its deliberate aims being to do so.* Offenders are those found in good faith to have broken laws. Much more might be said of this conception of an offender, and of the conceptions of an authority and of penalties. To say but a word of penalties, they are measures that cause distress. A penalty is not well conceived *as an alteration in an individual's rights*, in the way of some elevated jurisprudential writing. A year's solitary confinement is not well described by a description which also covers a period of homeownership.

Philosophers and jurisprudents who have recently offered justifications of punishment clear the ground by getting rid of classical Utilitarianism, for good reason. The classical Utilitarian proposition is that punishment is justified since or when, compared with any alternative, it makes for a greater total balance of satisfaction over dissatisfaction, or a lesser total balance of dissatisfaction over satisfaction. There is the arguable idea, implicit in this view as in others, that punishment *prevents* offences, through incapacitation, deterrence, perhaps something called rehabilitation, and the formation and reinforcement of unreflective obedience to law.

The objection to the simple maximizing of classical Utilitarianism, which in several ways ignores individuals, is that it justifies certain punishments of offenders which stick in the throat. It is typically said in effect, rightly or wrongly, that the reason for this is that these are punishments which are greater than *deserved*. Further, what classical Utilitarianism gives as the whole justification of punishment could be had by awful official acts of prevention whose victims were not offenders – not individuals found in the requisite way to have broken laws – but rather were individuals known to be innocent. If these awful official acts are morally intolerable – again they are typically said in effect to be intolerable because *undeserved* – it must be that punishment if it is right has some recommendation other than the Utilitarian one.

It is not so easy to deal with Utilitarianisms other than the classical kind.[4] Indeed there are some doctrines occasionally *called* Utilitarian which at least come close to escaping the objections. It is also true that the latter doctrines are a very long way from those of Bentham and of his true successors, say J. J. C. Smart,[5] and are only wholly misleadingly called Utilitarian. They are not in an ordinary sense maximizing.

What follows in too much recent and contemporary reflection on punishment by philosophers and jurisprudents is an unanalysed or ill-analysed claim that punishment is partly or wholly justified because or when it is *deserved, a just desert, retributive, equivalent, proportional, commensurate, reciprocal, corresponding, fitting, merited, owed, according to the offence, according to our right or the offender's right.* The terms and constructions – they may be called *desert-locutions* – cannot properly be said to be synonymous since there is no single sense which they have. They can be, and often are, used interchangeably, with whatever reason or lack of it. It is in fact an understatement to say that locutions of the given kind have no single sense. They are hardly less than paradigms of multiple ambiguity and vagueness. To philosophers, and I suppose to some members of the reading classes in Wormwood Scrubs and those California penal farms, it must come as alarming that large books on criminal justice suppose that they can proceed on the basis of the declaration that punishment is deserved or whatever, where the declaration is multiply ambiguous and vague. Lawyers, or anyway some of you – you need us philosophers! Let us start with *A* for offender, *O* for offence, and *P* for penalty. What can be meant by saying that if or since *P* is deserved by *A*, the visiting of *P* on *A* is right or justified – or that *P*'s being deserved for *O* is an essential part of the justification?

Let us hastily put aside several answers drawn from what can be called the Old Retributivism. If *P is deserved for O* just *is* the proposition that it is right that *A* gets *P*, then we have no independent reason for its being right that *A* gets *P*. Here there is only circularity, the futility of *Circular Retributivism.*[6] Does it never happen that *P is deserved for O* is so used? On the contrary, a little attention to judicial pronouncements will establish that sometimes it is. More often *P is deserved for O* has as *one* part of its meaning that it is right that *P* be imposed.

Secondly, *P is deserved for O* has been taken as giving independent factual reason for the rightness of imposing *P*. The proposition has been taken to be that there exists an equality of fact between *A*'s culpability in his offence and the distress to be caused to him by *P*. This is *Culpability–Distress Retributivism*. One thing to be said of it, as it certainly has been before now, is that we need to have it explained how there can be such a fact, there seeming to be no *commensurability* in any factual sense with respect to culpability and distress. If there are common units of measurement, what are they?[7]

These two understandings of *P is deserved for O* will have to suffice as representative of the Old Retributivism.[8] Before turning to the New, it is necessary to try to clarify some usages. The term 'retributivism' can be used to refer to *theories* – certain views on punishment advanced by philosophers, jurisprudents and the like which involve desert-locutions. A bit more will be said of the character of these views later (footnote 34). Retributivism in this sense has as its two parts the Old Retributivism and the New Retributivism. The New Retributivism can be said, very loosely, to consist in attempts made to justify punishment since about 1970, bravely assumed to be new, and involving desert-locutions. The six arguments at which we shall look do have the virtue of attempting to make their use of desert-locutions clear.

So much for retributivism where it consists in arguments and doctrines of philosophers, jurisprudents and the like. In another sense of the word, retributivism is a practice and a tradition. A bit more precisely, it is a kind of punishment and a tradition of, and having to do with, such punishment. Retributivism in this sense consists in part in present and past punishment of a certain character – as distinct, say, from deterrent punishment or reformative punishment. It also consists in attitudes and ordinary talk, including the talk of judges, or judges when they are on their benches. The hallmark of the tradition, again, is desert-locutions.

The distinction between these two retributivisms – one consisting in philosophical and jurisprudential theory and the other in punishment of a certain kind and what goes with it – is perhaps clear enough for our purposes. It will be of importance. Very roughly, one of my claims will be that philosophical and jurisprudential retributivism, whatever else is to be said of it, is not a correct account of the practice and tradition of retributivism. That practice and tradition is informed by a quite different argument.

1. Intrinsic Retributivism

If we are after a reason for *It is right to impose P on A* it is point-less, as noticed several times already, to contemplate *A deserves P* if that is understood as *It is right to impose P on A*, or *There is good reason for imposing P on A*, or any relevantly like claim. One philosopher objects that this cautionary little thought involves error and confusion.[9] He further supposes, I take it, that what is standardly meant by those who use desert-locutions in connection with punishment is only this: that there is intrinsic good in pre-cisely the suffering of the guilty – as distinct from what causes it, the penalty. More generally, when people talk of deserved penalties or punishment, they are to be taken as really not talking of gaol sentences and the like, but of suffering itself, and they are saying that there is intrinsic good in the suffering of the guilty. The resulting view can be called *Intrinsic Retributivism*.

It is plainly false that desert-locutions in connection with punishment never have to do with the penalty, as distinct from the resulting distress. More often than not they do. Nevertheless, let us grant that people sometimes have in mind what is suggested, having to do with only the distress or suffering. In this case, as can certainly be granted, they do escape circularity. To support the rightness of a punishment, they say something about desert, and mean nothing about punishment itself, but that there is intrinsic good in its effect, the suffering of the guilty.

It is said that there is no good argument against the judgement that the suffering of the guilty is intrinsically good or good in itself, and that there is a widespread inclination to believe it 'among the people whose moral intuitions constitute the main data we have for settling questions of value'. Hence it is 'very likely' that the judgement is 'true'.[10] Still, it is allowed that this reason for punish-ment might be outweighed by others, that it is consistent with the judgement that we never ought to punish.

Intrinsic Retributivism raises several very general issues in moral philosophy. If these are not to be settled here, it is nonetheless possible to come to a view of the doctrine. First, it needs remember-ing that even if all mankind minus none were morally in favour of the suffering of the guilty, it would not follow that all or even any of them judged it to be good in itself, good without reference to anything else whatever, including what may come most quickly to mind, some consequential change in the minds, hearts, souls or whatever of the guilty. Secondly, it is mere bluff to announce the existence of a strong argument based on the claim that most or many of some group of people, a group whose intuitions somehow settle questions of value for us, have intuitions that the suffering of the guilty is good in itself. Supposing that the group can be conceived in any tolerable way, and of course in a way so as not to beg the question, it will undoubtedly include many who are morally opposed to or reluctant about the suffering of the guilty in itself, which they properly characterize as pointless or useless or irrational. How, they traditionally ask, can two bads make a good, two wrongs a right? Those who reject Intrinsic Retributivism include even retributivists.[11]

To put aside this head-counting, and the hard questions of its relevance, we evidently can consider directly the question of whether the judgement that there is intrinsic good in the suffering of the guilty is 'true'. Or rather, to avoid the wholly unexplained assumption of, as it seems, the objectivity of moral judgements – their having truth-values in the sense in which ordinary factual claims have them – we can consider whether the judgement is acceptable or what weight it has.

It will be useful to compare the judgement to two other judgements of intrinsic value. One is that there is intrinsic badness in suffering. If I contemplate the possibility of a person's suffering in itself, without introducing *any* further fact, I cannot but judge that it would be a bad thing, something I ought not to bring about. Consider someone who believes otherwise. He believes that if he presses a button in front of him, that will cause another to suffer. He has *no* further beliefs about the suffering. He has no beliefs as to the victim's previous actions, any deterrent effects of his suffering, any supposed repentance of his or any purifying or elevating effects, any relation of his suffering to the lives of others, and so on. Nonetheless, he judges that he ought to press the button. He appears to understand what he maintains, is inclined to act on it, and shows the ordinary moral emotions in connection with it. It comes to mind to say, if we suppose that he is not somehow dissembling, that he is *mad*. The judgement that there is intrinsic badness in suffering, then, is one whose denial carries such a corollary.

The second judgement as to intrinsic value, chosen more or less at random, is that there is intrinsic good in arranging straight lines of Norwegians. As with the judgement that there is intrinsic good in the suffering of the guilty, and the other judgement of intrinsic value at which we have just glanced, this judgement has to do with no further facts. Arranging Norwegians in straight lines is good in itself. To deny this judgement of intrinsic value is certainly not to be open to judgement oneself, or to be in danger of official action. It is the maker of the judgement of intrinsic good who is, at least, puzzling.

One point, then, is that while it may be open to anyone to judge anything whatever to have intrinsic value, it is only certain of these judgements that have weight. A second point is that if one actually succeeds in contemplating no more than *precisely* the suffering of the guilty, a judgement of its intrinsic value is perhaps *more* of the weight of the judgement about lining up Norwegians than the judgement about the badness of suffering itself. Certainly it is baffling, and not much like the latter judgement. The latter judgement evidently enters into resistance to the supposed intrinsic goodness of the suffering of the guilty.

Intrinsic Retributivism in its assertion of its peculiar intrinsic good is strongly reminiscent of what seemed to have been put to rest, the doctrine of Moral Intuitionism, to the effect that there are moral properties which are open to some kind of moral perception. It remains possible or anyway conceivable that it will be maintained that anyone who does not somehow see the intrinsic goodness of the suffering of the guilty is failing in moral perception, is a victim of moral blindness. (Presumably it will also be maintained that some other people who claim the existence of different intrinsic goods are in the grips of moral hallucination.) It will be necessary to maintain, incidentally, that those of us who are blind in the given way are not blind to one thing, but to a host of them.

Intrinsic Retributivism does not discover only one intrinsic good, but very many. It does not suppose, I trust, that there is intrinsic good in the rapist having just the suffering of a fine of £10, or of having his driver's licence endorsed. It does not suppose there is intrinsic good in the young bicycle thief having the distress of being imprisoned for life. This retributivism, presumably, discovers as many intrinsic goods, each involving a certain guilt and a certain suffering, as there are different guilts.

What is to be said briefly in reply to any supposition of the moral blindness of many of us is that there are great difficulties in any theory or account of moral perception or intuition, and hence of moral blindness, hallucination and so on.[12] It is important, of course that one feels no need of any such theory with respect to the judgement that suffering in itself is bad. Its foundation, whatever it is, does not bring in a curious faculty and its peculiar successes and failures.

Let us finish here, however, by retreating from what are areas of some difficulty in moral philosophy generally. Let us come to firmer ground. The best that can be said of Intrinsic Retributivism, to my mind, is that it might as a result of further thought come to provide an *insubstantial and obscure* reason for punishment. To come to a point to which I shall return several times, there surely is something solid in the retributivist tradition, something which can be made clear. It has in it an actual reason for action, one which moves ordinary men, men with an ordinary lack of what can be called moral sensitivity. It must be an axiom of inquiry, surely, that anything so persistent and effectual as talk and feeling about desert, and above all anything with such a history as the retributivist practice of punishment, has sense, clear sense, at bottom. We may not find a justification of punishment at the bottom of the retributivist tradition, but it cannot be that there is nothing substantial and clarifiable there. The view we have been considering, about the intrinsic goodness of the suffering of the guilty, is therefore not the truth about retributivism.

2. *Rights Retributivism, Indifference Retributivism*

The next doctrine at which we shall look[13] partly consists in
certain claims of a kind increasingly common in contemporary
moral and political philosophy, claims as to *rights*. All of us, it is
said, have rights – rights not to be injured, to keep possession of
our property, and so on. A condition of our having such rights is
that we respect the rights of others. In general, rights of mine
entail duties of mine to respect rights of others. When an offender
violates rights of someone else, he forfeits some of his own. As a
consequence, if his punishment were also to have a certain
recommendation having to do with the prevention of offences,
his punishment would be justified.[14] We can call this the argument of *Rights Retributivism*.

That is not to say that an offender loses all his rights. He keeps
all the rights which he has respected in others. He loses just those
of his rights which are the counterparts of the rights of another
which he has violated. Or rather, since it is said to be impracticable
to deprive him of exactly those rights – certainly it would be so, say,
in the case of the right not to be defrauded – the offender loses a
set of rights equivalent to those he has violated. Or, again, there
is not a prohibition on inflicting a harm on him equivalent to that
involved in his violation of the rights of another. Here we have the
long-running problem noticed above, of giving sense to talk of
equivalence. It is certainly a recommendation of this doctrine,
owed to Alan H. Goldman, that it provides a solution, which we
can call *Indifference Retributivism*. It gives us a third argument.
That is not to say that it discovers commensurability, a method of
common quantifying of culpability and distress. However, it can
be said to achieve much the same end as would be achieved by
commensurability.

The solution draws on the idea of preference scales, essentially
on the theoretically discoverable preferences of average or normal
persons, and above all on the theoretical discoverability of such
persons being *indifferent* between certain options. We have on the
one hand the loss or harm – say L_o – caused to the victim of an
offence by violation of certain of his rights. On the other hand we

have various losses or harms that may be caused to the offender by deprivation of certain of his rights, through punishment. One of these losses or harms – say L_p – is such that an average person would be indifferent between L_o and L_p, preferring neither to the other. We thus have a clear idea of equivalent rights, or equivalent harms or losses, or, as we can as well say, a penalty equivalent to an offence. Certainly there are difficulties of several kinds about this procedure, some of them in effect about the specification of an average person. As is said, however, they are difficulties common to all uses of preference scales. Let us take them as superable difficulties.

That is not to say that what we now have is persuasive. What it comes to is the proposition that there is a reason for punishment, a denial of rights, in the proposition that an offender has violated certain rights of another. There are two objections, the first having to do with what is meant by saying that the offender has violated certain rights of another. For several reasons, one being the con-clusion that is drawn, it is clear that *moral* rights are in question. To repeat, then, what is meant by saying that the offender has violated certain moral rights of another? It should be a matter of notoriety that so little attention is given to this question in a good deal of contemporary philosophy given over to talk and indeed declaration of rights.

To consider the matter by way of something else, the Old Retributivism includes something not mentioned above, the simple claim that the punishment of an offender is justified because of his culpability in his offence – at bottom, because he did what he ought not to have done, because he failed in an obligation. The simple claim has satisfied hardly any reflective person, whether or not of retributivist inclination. *Why* is the claim that a man has done what he ought not to have done in itself a reason for making him suffer? Why does it give us a per-mission or whatever? The question has taken several forms, and no satisfactory answer has ever been given.

What, exactly, is the difference between the claim that a man has done what he ought not to have done to another, failed in an obligation to another, and the claim that he has violated moral rights of another? The doctrine we are considering, like others, offers no explanation. Certainly there is a difference between the two claims, and there are several views as to what it is. One persuasive one is that the rights-claim, as against the ought-claim, makes reference to a supposedly established moral principle or to the existence of supposed support of another kind. Given some such analysis or another, there remains the question of how the. rights-claim can serve as an effective reason for punishment when the ought-claim cannot. That it is wholly unlikely to do so becomes clear, as it seems to me, as soon as the rights-claim is demystified by even the beginning of an analysis.

The second objection has to do with what needs to be allowed, as it has, the existence of what can be called an equivalence of fact between offence and punishment. Here too we have a question which needs answering. There is the fact, we are supposing, that an average preference scale would show indifference between being a victim of a certain offence and being an offender subjected to a certain punishment. Why is that fact in itself any reason for subjecting such an offender to such a punishment?

It needs to be granted, in line with what has been said already of the tradition of retributivism, that there is force in citing some sort of equivalence in defence of punishment. But how is the equivalence we have before us a reason? We can find innumerable equivalences of the given sort, between experiences of diverse kinds. There may be indifference, say, between getting a job and getting married, or getting a job as a result of a fair selection procedure and being married pretty unhappily. Such a fact supports no such claims as that my failing to give a man a job is a reason for someone's getting in the way of my marriage. Critics of retributivism in the past have objected to the want of clear sense in talk of equivalence, and failed to note what they might have, that the producing of certain factual equivalences would not in itself give a reason for action.

3. *Consensual Retributivism*

Another recent attempt to justify punishment[15] begins from what is presented as a single objection to classical Utilitarianism. In fact it is best regarded as two objections. One is that if the Utilitarian defence were the only justification of punishment, then all or a very great deal of punishment would be unjustified because it would involve an *unfair or inequitable or inegalitarian distribution of burdens* in a society. The rational aim of punishment is indeed the prevention or reduction of offences, or more precisely burdens of a certain kind, those borne by the victims of offences. The aim is pursued by imposing penalties, burdens of another kind, on offenders. But why can we use these persons, in particular, in pursuing our aim? The resulting distribution of burdens would on balance have to be judged unfair or the like to offenders if no more could be offered than the Utilitarian defence of punishment.

The other objection is that if only the Utilitarian defence could be given, then all of punishment would be unjustified, because it would involve treating all offenders merely as means and not also as ends. The Kantian maxim, I take it, is used in this objection in a commendably clear if not wholly explicit way. That is, not to treat men *as ends* is not to *recognize their own ends*.[16] Punishment considered merely as preventive does not consider the ends of offenders, presumably at least including their desires not to be punished. It treats them only as means to the end of the prevention of offences. It regards them only from the point of view of others' desires.

It transpires, if all goes well, that the view of punishment which meets the second objection also meets the first. If we satisfy the Kantian maxim, we also deal with the problem of distributive justice. What is required for a justification of punishment is an addition to a proposition about its preventing offences. What is required is Consensual Retributivism, which is the truth behind the historical absurdity that offenders want to be punished. It has to do essentially with what is called *fairness owed to consent*. Punishment must be fair in that it is among other things a product of the will of the person who suffers it, something which respects his own autonomy.

The matter is approached and clarified by way of five propositions about ordinary contracts in law. (1) Consent here can be shown or given by any voluntary act done with the knowledge that the act has as a consequence a certain duty or responsibility. I consent to pay the cab-driver merely by getting into his cab and giving an address. I do not need to say that I agree to pay. (2) Giving my consent, in so far as the law of contract is concerned, is not dependent on my attitudes then to what it is that I consent to do, or certain of my beliefs about it. I have consented even if I dislike the prospect of paying up, or am against it all things considered, or intend not to pay up, or believe that any obligation to do so can be avoided or will not be enforced. Nor is it true that I did not consent if, when the time comes to pay up, I do not want to do so, and so on. (3) However, in all cases of contractual consent, there is the requirement that the relevant laws be in some sense just: 'the justification of particular distributions based on the free choice of the parties presupposes the fairness of the legal framework within which those choices are made'.[17] (4) If I do give my consent, thereby entering into a contract, this gives others at least a *prima facie* moral justification for enforcing it. (5) Finally, if doing what I have consented to do will issue in an unfair or inequitable or inegalitarian distribution of burdens, it does not follow that I have not consented. It does not matter if the cab-driver is a secret millionaire, etc. Nor does it follow, therefore, that there cannot be the mentioned moral justification for enforcing the contract, despite the resulting distribution. This is the fairness owed to consent.

To come round to punishment, *an offence itself* constitutes a certain consent on the part of the offender. It is a consent *to give up his immunity to punishment*, which is to say to the gaining of a power by officers of the society. It is to consent to be used as a means to the prevention of offences. Here we have five counterpart propositions.

(1) The consent is owed to the fact that an offence is a voluntary act done with the knowledge that it has a certain *legal* con-

sequence, the loss of the offender's immunity to punishment. (2) The consent is unaffected by certain attitudes and beliefs of the offender. It does not matter that he is against his punishment and intends not to be punished. Moreover, his consent does not depend on any explicit or implicit acceptance by him of the criminal law to which his punishment is attached. (3) However, the law to which a punishment is attached, even if the offender need not accept it, must in fact *be* in some sense just – 'it should not be, for instance, discriminatory and should not proscribe actions that people have the moral right to do'.[18] Again, it must be that if keeping the law involves a burden, liability or obligation, these things are somehow justified. (4) Given the fact of the offender's consent, the authorities have at least a *prima facie* moral justification for exercising their legal power to punish him. (5) Finally, none of the foregoing propositions is put into question by the offender's punishment issuing in an unfair or inequitable or inegalitarian distribution of burdens in the society. There *is* fairness owed to consent.[19]

Consensual Retributivism, for the good reason that it could not, does not rest on the proposition that an offender consents to his *punishment*. The general idea of consent in question is the idea that a person, whatever his mixed feelings and disinclinations, is to be taken to consent to all the necessary consequences of his action of which he knows. In this sense he could not be said to consent to his punishment, since his punishment, unlike the loss of his legal liability to punishment, is not necessarily a consequence of his offence. There is no necessity about it. The fact of the matter may well be that he will not be punished. Moreover, if the theory did require its kind of consent to punishment itself, it could provide *no* reason for punishment where an offender actually does believe that he will not be punished. What the offender is said to consent to, then, is no more than the loss of his legal immunity. More precisely, what he consents to can be expressed as a certain conditional proposition: if he is caught, and if the authorities make no mistakes, he will not be regarded as having a legal immunity to punishment.

That leaves us with something further that it is essential to keep clearly in mind, the fact about virtually all offenders that they do *not* consent to being punished. They do not consent to it in the sense of believing it to be a necessary consequence of their action, and moreover they do not consent to it in a more standard sense. They do not consent to it in a sense, difficult to specify fully, where they can be said to desire all or more of what it is that they are said to consent to. On the contrary, they are wholly against their punishment, struggle to evade it, and so on. Rather than consent, they *refuse* or *dissent*.

But then the situation, to keep all of it in mind, includes the offender's consenting in the Consensual Theory's sense to a certain legal consequence, his losing his immunity to punishment, and his dissenting in every sense to his punishment. There is not much to be gained by asking if the first consent is 'really consent'. Let us rather ask what conclusions follow, given that the situation is as described.

First, to remember the two objections to Utilitarianism from which we began, does it follow from what we have, whatever else may be said for punishing the offender, that the resulting distribution of burdens in the society cannot be resisted as unfair, inequitable, or inegalitarian? Secondly, does it follow from what we have that his own end is being recognized if he is punished? Is his moral autonomy respected? Does it follow in turn, thirdly, that the authorities have *prima facie* moral justification for punishing him?

It seems to me impossible to accept the first two inferences, on which the third rests. It is not at all persuasive to say that the resulting distribution of burdens cannot be open to objections of the given kind since, to speak differently, we have on hand fairness owed to consent. What we have is the offender consenting in a secondary sense to a necessary condition of his punishment, and not consenting, in any sense, to his punishment. As for the second inference, how *can* it be said with any force that the offender's own end is being recognized? What we *do*, and what raises the entire problem, which is to say our punishing of him, is what he does not consent to, despite the fact that he has in a sense consented to a necessary condition of it. It is, with respect to what is important, quite false to say that the agent has 'consciously acquiesced'.[20]

As it seems to me, one can be much moved by this doctrine only by having something other than it before the mind's eye. If one is in fact supposing that all offenders consent to their punishments, or their situations, in some fuller way than specified, it is possible to think one has a strong reason for punishment. But such a proposition is not being maintained, and is in fact false.

It may be objected, against this, that consent in the specified sense is sufficient for an ordinary contract in law, and that there it gives rise to a moral justification for enforcing the contract. If such consent will work there, why will it not work with punishment? Much might be replied here, about the nature of the law in general and its safeguards, and in particular its safeguards with respect to persons who will lie about their past acceptances. Let me make only a remark on something else.

Suppose I get into a taxi-cab and give an address. I also tell the driver that I intend *not* to pay for the ride, and in the end succeed in overcoming his incredulity. He believes me. Still, for whatever reason, he delivers me to the right number in darkest Ritson Road. We need not take legal advice before concluding that it is far from certain that a contract was made. It is far from certain, too, whatever else is said, that *what happened at the beginning of the ride* issues in a moral justification for my paying a fare.

This suggests that while consent with respect to the law's contracts does not require proof of a certain intention, it is also true that a statement of the wrong intention, so to speak, gets in the way of consent and contract. What is of most relevance, however, is this: the commission of an offence is in closer analogy to this very odd taxi case than to the ordinary case where the passenger does not say he intends not to pay. The Consensual Retributivist points to a certain act, the offence, and claims it to be analogous to giving a cab-driver an address. But the offender will also give every evidence of not intending the upshot having to do with punishment. It follows that if we begin with an offence, and find a close analogy of it that might turn up in civil law, we do not find anything remotely like a clear case of consent and contract.

There are three other things to be remarked quickly about Consensual Retributivism. First, there is a certain amount of tension between parts of it. One of its propositions is that an offence is a certain consent to a punishment only if the law in question is somehow just, or if the burden of keeping to the law is a justified one. Another of its propositions, put one way, is that consent in the special sense can justify a distribution of burdens that is in a sense unfair or whatever. These two propositions, if they are not clear enough to be inconsistent, do not come together easily. Secondly, the view does indeed depend on the first proposition – the law's being just, its burdens being justified. Since this requirement is not clarified, and since it is not shown that it is met, the view is at least incomplete.[21] Thirdly, although it needs to be admitted, in line with a necessary realism about what can be done in moral and political philosophy, that Consensual Retributivism has not been *refuted* by me, it clearly does not provide a substantial and clear reason for punishment. It is unclear with respect to the requirement of justice just mentioned. The retributive tradition, above all its practices and institutions, has more in it. The consensual theory is not the truth about retributivism.

4. Contractarian Retributivism

A fifth and related line of thought about justifying punishment, Contractarian Retributivism,[22] begins rather as do the others. The Utilitarians, we may be told, are committed to using men as means to a social good, not treating them in accord with their dignity as persons, not recognizing that as persons they have rights. More particularly, the Utilitarians do not show what is necessary, that punishment treats a man as an end and in accord with his dignity and rights, where that is *respecting his own will or decision, having his own consent.* This is just as necessary with perfectly ordinary punishment as it would be with awful acts of victimization taken to have some preventive value. While the prevention of offences must evidently be a part of the justification of punishment, there is also something else that is absolutely essential.

One typical way in which others coerce us without infringing our rights, we are told, is by our own ordinary consent. If I consent to my neighbour's suggestion that he should keep the key to my wine store over the weekend, then he does not violate a right of mine later when I want it, but only thwart a desire. To come to the rights of offenders, it may be that they are not violated by punishment. This is so, we are told, despite the fact that they have not in the same ordinary way consented to be punished. They *have* in another way consented. It is not the way of Consensual Retributivism.

In considering this view, as becomes apparent even in its original presentation, there is no need to have things obscured by the several kinds of rhetoric, notably the rhetoric of *rights*. The essential claim is quite independent of it. It is that that justification of a punishment requires that the offender in some way consents to it, and offenders do in fact do this.

To continue, we can get some help in understanding how they do it from Kant, who writes that when a debtor is forced to pay up, 'this is entirely in accord with everyone's freedom, including the freedom of the debtor, in accordance with universal laws'.[23] What does this mean? Well, that in a certain conceivable but not actual situation the debtor 'would have been rational to adopt a Rule of Law'.[24] Kant is not much less explicit than his successors, notably John Rawls, in asserting that this is not the idea of any *actual* social contract, past or present, explicit or implicit. He writes that 'the contract is a mere idea of reason which has undoubted practical reality; namely to oblige every legislator to give us laws in such a manner that the laws *could* have originated from the united will of the entire people . . .'[25] To assert in the given way that an offender consents to his punishment is to assert that *if* he had been in a certain conceivable situation in which a social agreement was being made, and *if* he had been in a sense rational, he would have agreed to social arrangements which have the consequence that as an actual offender he is to be punished.

It is worthwhile distinguishing this claim about consent *by an offender* from something else, with which it is likely to be confused. That is the argument that a certain actual social arrangement, an actual society in accordance with some conception of justice, is right or justified because it would have been agreed upon *by certain imaginable contractors*, or by contractors in an imaginable situation. The situation, because it would exclude certain influences on the contractors' choices, would confer a recommendation on what was chosen. It is *not* part of this argument that the actual members of the actual society, influenced as they are, have ever made such an agreement, or indeed that they have in any diminished sense consented to anything. The actual members are not in any way identified with the contractors. Their obligation to support their society has to do with its goodness, which goodness is established by the proposition about imaginable contractors. Here too we have an argument for the rightness of punishment in a society, but not one that has to do with consent of actual members. Having had my say elsewhere[26] about what seems to me the particular futility of this form of hypothetical contract theory as a method of establishing substantive conclusions, I shall say nothing here.

The different claim we are considering is yet weaker. It is, to repeat, that an offender's punishment is justified, at least in part, by *his* consenting to it, in a special sense, which is to say in short that if he had earlier considered the matter of punishment, and if he had been rational, he would have agreed to the social arrangements under which he is now being punished. What is it to say that he would have made a contract *if he had been rational*? The short answer is this: he would have agreed if he had had the approving view of some given social arrangements had by a philosopher engaged in defending the institution of punishment.

Once Contractarian Retributivism is made clear, it is not easy to think of a weaker moral reason for imprisoning a man. The reason given is that he would, *if* he had had certain views, views which no doubt he does not now have, and may never have had, and may always have disagreed with or hated – *if* he had had such views, he would have consented to something. It is exactly as true that if he had had *other* views he would not have consented to the thing, and hence could *not* be said to consent to his punishment in the special sense. His punishment is being credited *to him* by way of an arbitrarily chosen counterfactual statement about him.

The difference between what is given as a reason for an offender's punishment, and my actual consent as a reason for my neighbour's keeping the key to my wine store, is immense. It is important not to drift into considering the supposition that the offender *did* have views of the requisite kind. If this were the supposition in question, Contractarian Retributivism could not hope to offer a satisfactorily *general* justification of punishment. It would leave quite unjustified the punishment of offenders without the requisite views.

Let me end here with the same remark as before. Retributivism as practice and tradition has not persisted because it has been this ineffectual line of thought. This is not the truth of retiributivism.

5. *Restorative Retributivism*

Finally, Restorative Retributivism, which is run together with consensual, contractarian and like ideas, but clearly can be separated from them, and, in my view, thereby improved.[27] We begin again with classical Utilitarianism. It is not only that it may issue in awful acts of victimization, but that it leaves out a consideration which is essential to the justification of ordinary punishment. Admittedly it is part of the justification of punishment that it is preventive, but it is also or as much a part that it involves a certain *equality, fairness, justice, rationality, equilibrium, balance, reciprocity, debt-payment,* or *order.*

To try to become clearer about this, we are invited to consider the nature or function of the law. It legitimates certain activities for an individual and proscribes other activities. I am permitted to inherit a car, but not to drive it while drunk; I can in general forbid entry to my house, but not to a policeman with a search warrant; I can buy food or medicines, but not steal them. The law, then, as well as allowing me to do things, to indulge myself in certain ways, places a vast array of what are called burdens on me, burdens of self-denial. It forbids to me certain choices, certain self-indulgences, certain exercises of my will, certain followings of my own inclinations. Each member of my society is subject to an array of burdens of self-denial. The general result is a distribution of the burdens of self-denial that is equal, fair, just, balanced, ordered or whatever.

What an offender does is to put down one of his burdens. As he should not, he chooses for himself, indulges himself, exercises his will, follows his inclination. This constitutes a departure or a further departure from the society's distribution of these burdens, a distribution that is equal, fair or the like. The essential recommendation of punishment, over and above its preventive recommendation, is that it *restores* equality, fairness or whatever, or is a move in that restorative direction. It does this, essentially, by *enforcing* a burden. The man who is punished is essentially a man whose desires, will or inclinations are restrained, not by himself but by others. The result is that the maldistribution of burdens which he has produced is corrected. Things are in a specific way put back to what they were. The punishment also encourages others to stick to the legitimate distribution.

It is important to be clear about the goods involved in the original distribution, in the ensuing maldistribution produced by offences, and in the distribution reasserted through punishment. Despite an uncertainty in some statements of Restorative Retributivism, these are not material goods, say cars, houses, food, or medicine. It is persistently asserted by one defender of Restorative Retributivism[28] that they are not, and of course they cannot be such. If the goods in question were material goods, we would be offered nothing like a *general* reason for punishment. We would have no reason for punishing attempted crimes which produce no material gain for offenders, because of failure or because no material gain was attempted, as in many offences of violence. Also, if the goods in question were material goods, it would be absurd to say the law produces an *equal* distribution of them, and any description of the distribution as *just* or the like would require further argument. Finally, it cannot be that material goods are what is in question since the unfairness of an offence is specifically said not to be an unfairness only to the victim – say the man who loses his car – but an unfairness to *all* the law-abiding members of the society.

Material goods, as I have been speaking of them, are certain things in the world. There are other things closely related to them which also cannot be the goods that are in question with Restorative Retributivism. I mean the satisfactions got from material goods. There are the same reasons for saying these are not the goods of Restorative Retributivism. It can be added that these goods also do not include the satisfactions of which one thinks in connection with offences not aimed at material gain, say certain offences of violence. The satisfactions of vengeance got by a murderer are not goods in the right class, it seems, since one can think of murders where they are missing but to which Restorative Retributivism must apply.

It becomes clear that the goods or benefits in question can perhaps be described as *satisfactions-in-acting*. They are the goods of indulging one's will, or, to speak informally, of *letting go*, whether legally or illegally. They are those goods which one does not have, precisely and only, as the product of obeying or forbearing, of denying or restraining oneself or reining oneself in. Instead, here, one may have the burden of *dissatisfactions-in-not-acting*. The car thief presumably enjoys satisfaction-in-acting above all at the moment when he breaks the quarter-light, although it makes sense to say he also enjoys it later, when he self-indulgently doesn't submit to the idea of returning the car or turning himself in. In sum, then, for present purposes, the law legitimates certain satisfactions-in-acting and it proscribes others, which is to say it enjoins certain dissatisfactions-in-not-acting. Offenders put down a burden, take a proscribed satisfaction-in-acting. Punishment puts such a burden on them, thereby reasserting a distribution of such burdens and benefits.

Various questions arise about the very nature of these burdens and benefits, and their relation to other dissatisfactions and satisfactions. These we must pass by. The first of two questions not to be passed by is this one: are the burdens which we now have more or less in view anything like *equally* distributed in our societies? That they are is suggested by a good deal of what is said in Restorative Retributivism. (It is perhaps suggested by that early New Retributivist, St Thomas Aquinas.[29] As implied earlier, the New Retributivism is not all absolutely novel.) To repeat, are the given burdens equally distributed? Well, one cannot avoid the thought that the burdens of self-restraint or dissatisfaction-in-not-acting defined by law are lighter for the man who has everything as against the man who has nothing. I refer to the having or not having of material goods and their satisfactions.

If the burdens of self-restraint are heavier for the man who has nothing, or – say instead – those in the bottom decile of income as against those in the highest decile, then if they offend they are moving the distribution *towards* equality, rather than away from it. Their punishment is moving the distribution *away from*, rather than towards, equality. Punishment lacks *exactly* the recommendation that is being claimed for it.

As I have already indicated, it is notable that one gets a veritable welter of descriptions of the distribution that is fundamental to Restorative Retributivism. If it is said to be or to involve equality, it is also said to be *just, balanced, reciprocal,* and so on. However, we are not much helped by abandoning equality for this justice, since this justice goes unexplained. The particular distribution in question goes undefended. It evidently needs to be defended if Restorative Retributivism is to be complete. The doctrine, if it is not taken as involving an *equal* distribution, is essentially vague. To glance back at the interpretation in terms of equality, incidentally, we would also need to know why *that* is a good thing. Is *any* equal distribution, at whatever level, a good thing, and better than any unequal distribution?

One final thought in connection with the nature of the distribution. What some Restorative Retributivists take the law to produce is perhaps not an ordering or order of burdens which has some *further* recommendation – equality or justice or some such. What the law is taken to produce, and what the offender disturbs, is order *simpliciter*: that is, a situation in which self-denials and self-indulgences are *subject to rule*, whether the rule is good, bad or indifferent. It is a popular idea among those who benefit from rules, as distinct from those who do not, that there is a great recommendation in any old rules. That needs arguing, and any argument this produces will be a small one.

A second question about Restorative Retributivism has to do

with the relative importance of specifically the goods with which it is concerned, and with the fact that the commitment of the doctrine is to distributive justice somehow conceived. To speak quickly, surely *having* money or food, and the satisfactions got from them, are of greater importance than specifically the benefits we have in view, satisfactions-in-acting. Surely *not having* money or food, and the ensuing dissatisfactions, are of greater importance than the burdens of self-denial with respect to them, dissatisfactions-in-not-acting. Thus, if one sets out to justify punishment by considerations of distributive justice, it is bizarre to leave out the former benefits and burdens – benefits of possession and burdens of lack or deprivation. It might well be, from the point of view of distribution, that a gain secured by punishment in terms of the distribution of self-indulgence and self-denial was outweighed by a loss secured by punishment in terms of what we can call the benefits and burdens of possession.

Restorative Retributivism, in my view, does little to justify punishment in our societies. It is necessary to say that this is a conclusion in a way shared and strongly defended by one Restorative Retributivist, Jeffrie G. Murphy.[30] He takes it that the injustice of our societies makes the doctrine inapplicable to them. He also maintains, to my mind mistakenly, that Restorative Retributivism, at least with Contractarian ideas added, is the best of doctrines of the justification of punishment, and that it would justify punishment in a just society. On the contrary, punishment there could not be justified simply by reference to burdens of the specified kind, with or without the addition of Contractarianism.

Of what else can be said against Restorative Retributivism, let me say only that at best it provides only an insubstantial and obscure ground for punishment. This sixth argument, like its predecessors, is not the truth of the tradition of retributivism.

6. The Truth of Retributivism

Most of these arguments, in one form or another, were also considered by the acute John Mackie. The particular verdicts we have reached differ somewhat from his, but there is no mistaking a similarity in general upshot. He concluded that no retributive principle of punishment can be 'explained or developed within a reasonable system of moral thought', that all the main lines of retributivist thought are signal failures, that we cannot make moral sense of them.[31] He also had another conviction, however. It was that a retributive principle 'cannot be eliminated from our moral thinking', that retributive ideas which in one way or another are unsatisfactory, from what can be called the point of view of reason, are deeply ingrained, a part of out lives.[32] The proposition that retributivism cannot be made decent sense of, and the proposition that it is inescapable – these comprise what Mackie calls the *paradox of retributivism*.

He offers what he calls a resolution of it, of which the first step is the Humean proposition that moral distinctions, such as the distinction between the deserved and the undeserved, are founded not on reason but on feeling or sentiment. What is in question with retributivism, fundamentally, is what he calls retributive emotion. Of this, Mackie offers a persuasive biological explanation, in terms of standard evolutionary theory. It begins with the advantage to species and individuals of retaliatory behaviour and feeling, and hence their natural selection; it proceeds by way of the socialization or moralizing of retributive emotion; and ends with such items as the consensual theory of punishment. I have no doubt that the explanation is at least in principle correct.

Nevertheless, this view of the tradition of retributivism seems to me not to deal with a main problem. It is not enough to grant that retributivism is entrenched. What must also be granted, as I have already argued, surely, is that somehow it *makes sense*. On reflection, surely, it is a remarkable supposition that a *tide* of ordinary moral thought and language over centuries, and, much more than that, a *tide* of institutions, should rest, as Mackie supposes, in so far as rational rather than causal grounds are concerned, on incoherence or on what is in fact without rational content. Certainly there are immense questions here, but it is surely impossible to suppose that in establishing, defending and developing retributivist institutions, punishment above all, men have not aimed at and secured something which is substantial and which is capable of clear description. There has been some profit in it all, profit which can be discerned and put into an argument. Further, it seems impossible that *no* decent argument attaches to a basic fact of this unremitting sequence of institutions: they rest on an array of connections between particular offences and particular penalties, and give these connections as an essential part of the justification of the penalties. It cannot be that all that can be said of the law's 'deserved' or 'fitting' penalties is that they derive from a confused image of factual equivalence between things that in fact are incommensurable, or from some other equally unacceptable notion, or that they derive from a clear notion of equivalence, but one which has no argumentative force.

It may be that there is no sufficient moral argument for punishment in the tradition of retributivism, and that what is said of equivalence in it does not provide one. To repeat, it cannot be that there is *nothing* that comes up to the level of argument, and that there is *no* force in talk of equivalence.

The truth of retributivism, as it still seems to me,[33] and in absolute brevity, is as follows. First, harmful actions give rise to what can be labelled grievances, which is to say certain desires for the distress of the agents, desires whose only and full satisfaction is in the belief that the agents are being distressed or made to suffer. Whatever else is to be said of grievances, one certainty is that they exist. A second proposition, no doubt disagreeable, is that the existence of these desires is an argument for their satisfaction. It cannot, as it seems to me, be left out. There cannot be an argument for dismissing certain desires from consideration which is nearly so overwhelming as the argument that their existence is reason for their satisfaction. There is a fundamental inconsistency in counting them as nothing. That is not to say, certainly, that the argument for their satisfaction cannot be outweighed by others. Thirdly, such desires can be *less than satisfied, more than satisfied,* or *just satisfied*. This again is a fact of life.

The truth of the retributivist tradition, more precisely, is that it seeks to justify punishment partly or wholly by the clear reason that it satisfies the grievances created by offences, through causing

distress to offenders, and that it takes penalties to be unsatisfactory if they do less than satisfy grievances or do more than that,
and satisfactory if they just satisfy it. Here, the sense of saying that
penalty P is deserved for A's offence O is that P will *just satisfy* the
grievance to which A has given rise by O. The requirement of an
equivalent penalty, in this sense, is a direct consequence of the
fundamental contention: that punishment is justified partly or
wholly by grievance-satisfaction. To do less than satisfy it would
simply conflict with the fundamental contention. To do more
would be to cause distress which would fail to have the given
justification.

Mackie had a view of the retributivist tradition which excluded
the possibility that this is its sense. Essentially, he took it to consist
in institutions such that we cannot look, for whatever value they
have, to the effects of the distress of penalties. There is no reason
to go along with this. The reason for doing so is essentially a
respect for what most apologists for the tradition, notably moral
philosophers and jurisprudents, have said of it.[34] What they have
said is that it depends on a reason for punishment that does not
mention the effects of the distress of offenders, notably the satisfaction it gives. There would be more call for respect if they were
successful in providing the supposed reason.

It is notable that what is said for punishment by those who are
engaged in it, the judiciary, is often of a very different character.
It is plain that when judges declare in one way and another that
the coming distress of offenders is *deserved*, they are not excluding
the satisfaction it gives to others. Consider the most entrenched of
judicial utterances, that offenders must *pay their debt*. What is to
pay a debt? Does somebody not *get* something? How very odd it
would be if no one did. Necessarily, someone does.

Various related objections have been made to this view. One is
that it is obviously false because it reduces to this: 'that a judge
ought to sentence because the people outside in the street are
baying for blood'.[35] It reduces to nothing of the sort. The fact
of punishment's being informed and defended by grievance-
satisfactions is a fact shaped by considerations of consistency,
precedent, the law's fundamental ideas of the reasonable, and so

on. (James Fitzjames Stephen, the Victorian judge, made the often-quoted remark that 'the criminal law stands to the passion of revenge in much the same relation as marriage to the sexual appetite'.[36] The remark, I take it, expresses my view of the truth of retributivism, and the consistent fact that retributive punishment is other than ungoverned vengeance.) It may be objected, again, that the view reduces the retributivist tradition to 'just a primitive bit of intuitive vindictiveness'.[37] Part of what can be said in reply is along the same lines: that the view in no way conflicts with the fact that the criminal law and punishment constitute a developed institution – authoritative and rule-governed. That the view finds a basis for punishment that can be characterized mistakenly as 'primitive' seems to me a recommendation of it. That it finds a basis which is 'intuitive', in one pejorative use of that word, which suggests want of clarity, is false.

To repeat, then, the sort of defence for punishment that is suggested by and indeed embodied in the retributivist tradition, at least in its more recent part, is that punishment is morally justified because it prevents offences and just satisfies grievance. That, at any rate, is the foundation of the defence. In the second part of that foundation we have what we have failed to find elsewhere, a retributive reason for punishment which is neither insubstantial nor obscure.

It is necessary to say, however, that what the retributivist tradition suggests is in fact a family of arguments based on prevention and grievance. They will differ, for example, in regarding prevention or grievance or both as giving rise to a moral permission to punish or to an obligation. Some of these arguments will have internal difficulties. For example, one cannot marry the grievance proposition in certain ways with the prevention proposition if the latter is construed in a classical Utilitarian way. It is so construed if, for example, it carries the Utilitarian idea that one must always choose the particular means to a given end which is least costly in terms of the distress it causes. There may be *no* penalty for a murder, say, which both satisfies the Utilitarian requirement having to do with the minimal effective distress to the offender, *and* the requirement of satisfying grievance.[38] Still, let us suppose that we can find members of this family of arguments that do not have such internal troubles.

On some of these views, we are both permitted and obliged to punish offenders when their punishments just satisfy grievance and also are in some defined sense preventive. If prevention seems an undeniable consideration with respect to the justification of punishment, and if the retributive part of these views is as it should be – clear and such as to specify an actual gain – that is not to say that any such view is defensible, that it *does* provide a moral justification of punishment. There are clear objections, of which I shall quickly mention but two.

Any such view gives weight to, and argues from, the existence of grievance-desires in a society. It gives weight to, and argues from, the possibility of certain satisfactions, satisfactions of grievances. As I have already said, it appears to me impossible to disregard the existence of such desires and their possible satisfaction. To do so is high-minded, certainly, but also confused. That is not the end of the story, however.

Consider an analogy. A man wants a whisky, and will be unhappy without it. That this is so is *a* reason for giving it to him. But of course there may be reasons against. They may be over-whelming reasons against his having a drop, or another drop. They may be such as to make it a good idea that he have only a well-watered whisky. They may be such as to make it a good idea to give him what he wants, but with an admonition. So with grievance-desires for the punishment of offenders. Clearly they cannot be taken just as they are, unreflectively, as automatic justifiers, or automatic part-justifiers.

How then do we judge them? Many things might be said, but, in the end, we shall come to one basis, which is a conception of the good or the fair or the right society. We shall necessarily regard the satisfaction of grievance-desires from the point of view of what we take to be the fundamental moral principle for the ordering of our lives together in society. Clearly it is impossible to embrace such a view of punishment as we are considering if it does not do this, and instead unreflectively takes grievance-desires as *given*.

A second objection to such a view, which takes us in the same direction, has been in a way anticipated.[39] Such a view takes only or mainly into account two categories of satisfactions. One is satisfactions of grievance-desires. The second is satisfactions of all our desires not to be victims of offences. But of course these are but *some* of the categories of desire which must and do often enter into our reflection on the good, just or right society. There are others. There are the ongoing dissatisfactions of offenders in being punished. There are also the dissatisfactions owed to a lack or deprivation of material and other goods, which dissatisfactions are not owed to offences but to the legal distribution of these goods within a society.

To make the point in question by way of an extreme example, suppose we consider the jusitfication of punishment within a truly racist society. There is an absurd incompleteness in supposing we can consider the justification of the society's punishments only in terms of the two categories of desire mentioned above. A view of the kind we are considering, then, is wholly inadequate because, at least, it is strikingly incomplete.

7. Political Philosophy and an Answer

Both the objections to such a view then bring us to the conclusion that it is necessarily bound up with political philosophy. More precisely, it is bound up with the question of the fundamental principle or principles for the judgement and guidance of societies. Views of punishment actually from the retributivist tradition are by no means unique in this respect. The same is true of all the theories of punishment which comprise the New Retributivism. The fact, far from being in the background, was forced upon us in consideration of Consensual, Contract and Restorative Retributivisms, as was noticed when we considered them. It is a fact too about the classical and other Utilitarian theories of punishment. Here, of course, the fact is also not in the background. The Utilitarian theories of punishment are presented, in the first instance, as deductions from a general principle, which principle is in fact a response to the fundamental question of political philosophy, that of how the various benefits and burdens are to be distributed.

It is one of my conclusions, then, that the question of the justification of punishment is immovably located within political philosophy, and, more precisely, that any answer to the question requires a prior answer to the fundamental question in political philosophy. Philosophical and jurisprudential reflection on punishment has in fact led a life of its own, for whatever reasons, and continues to do so. It cannot properly do so. For example, there is not the slightest possibility of dealing adequately or even pertinently with the question of its justification by attending only to the supposed intrinsic good of the suffering of the guilty, without reference to the rest of their lives and the lives around them.

This general conclusion is not, I think, a philosophical proposition of a certain somewhat boring kind. I have in mind propositions to the effect that solutions to certain problems presuppose solutions to others. The largest of these propositions are to the effect that moral philosophy depends on the philosophy of mind, ontology on epistemology, and so on. Consistently with that, one can respectably spend one's philosophical life concerned only with moral philosophy, or only with ontology.

The conclusion to which we have come is *not* that the problem of the justification of punishment is something which, although it presupposes or depends on something else, *can be considered independently*. The problem of the justification of punishment does not just presuppose in this way an answer to the fundamental question in political philosophy, essentially a question about the distribution of burdens and benefits in a wide sense. It is more proper to say, rather, since the satisfactions and dissatisfactions of punishment are *a part* of those burdens and benefits, *a part* of the very subject-matter of the distributive question, that to address the question of punishment necessarily *is* to address the distributive question. Further, it is simply *irrational* to address *part of* a single distributive question, where that is to ignore a part of what can be or in fact is distributed. No doubt punishment raises many questions, but there is nothing that can be called the question of its moral justification which is left to be considered if one puts aside the great question of the distribution of goods in society.

My second conclusion, already drawn, is that the New Retributivism is no success story. None of the views we have considered is effective, and no consistent combination of them is much better. The third, also already drawn, is that the clearer and *more* arguable justification of punishment which actually comes out of retributivist institutions is clearly inadequate.

What remains to be given, my fourth conclusion, can in some respects be anticipated. It is an answer to the question of whether punishment in our societies is right or wrong. My answer must be a part of a conclusion drawn from what I take to be the fundamental principle, certainly of a moral kind, by which societies are to be judged, and by which societies ought to be guided. Further, it can be anticipated that my answer to the question about our punishments must go undefended here, for the reason that the fundamental principle must go undefended. That is not something to be done quickly. It is not that punishment is a very large question, but that something else is.

The problem of classical Utilitarianism, in a word, is unfairness. This is so, as we know, with respect to punishment. The most common response to this, in connection with punishment, has been to go over to or attempt to add a principle of retributive justice. That is, philosophers and jurisprudents have advanced such doctrines as those we have considered: Culpability-Distress Retributivism, Intrinsic Retributivism, Right Retributivism, Indifference Retributivism, and the Consensual, Contractarian and Restorative varieties. It is a small virtue of some of the latter of these that they take a small step in the right direction – towards questions of distributive justice. They do not reach the subject, but give us a plethora of unexamined predicates instead: *equal, just, fair*, and so on. The correct response to the shortcoming of classical Utilitarianism, in my view, is not retributivism, but a clear principle of *distributive* justice, an answer to the question of how all benefits and burdens in society are to be distributed.

My own general answer is the Principle of Equality. It is not to the effect that we should have as our *main* aim the securing of an equality of anything. It is not a principle whose main aim is just some *relationship* between the well-being of individuals or classes. It is not fundamentally about getting everybody on a level. To see the mistake of such an aim, by way of one example of importance, suppose we are concerned not with wealth or a number of other things, but with *human satisfactions generally*, and in particular with all such satisfactions of two classes of people over their whole lifetimes. It must be mistaken to prefer an equality of satisfactions at a low level to an inequality at higher levels. The Principle of Equality, which can be argued actually to be the principle which has informed the tradition of egalitarianism, does *not* have the consequence that we should prefer the low-level equality.

The Principle of Equality is to the effect that our fundamental aim should be to make well-off those who are badly-off, and that we should use effective means. Its fuller statement, which has been attempted elsewhere,[40] does of course require adequate definitions of what it is to be badly-off and to be well-off. Further, its fuller statement requires a specification of the effective means to its end, particular policies which we should follow. Many of these, consistently with what was said above, *will be* policies having to do with the *equal* distribution of something, say political power.

A good, just or right society, then, is one directed by the Principle of Equality. Its institutions are in accord with it. Are our contemporary societies directed by the Principle of Equality? Is our punishment in accord with it? The answer is no, more so in this time than it has recently been. Does it follow that punishment in our societies lacks moral justification? That it is wrong? The short answer is yes.

The longer answer takes into account that our punishment is part of one of a certain set of possible alternatives. One is the alternative of our societies as they are but without punishment. One is the alternative of our societies just as they are, with punishment. A third is the alternative of societies in accord with the Principle of Equality and with punishment. A fourth is the alternative, to which there is no obstacle but ourselves, of such societies without punishment, or with very little of it. Our punishments now in our societies are wrong in the sense that they enter into what is at least the second worst alternative.

1. I am most grateful to the Royal Institute of Philosophy, and to Professor A. Phillips Griffiths, the editor of the Institute's lectures for 1983–4, *Philosophy and Practice* (Cambridge, 1984), from which this postscript comes. On the New Retributivism, see 'Symposium: The New Retributivism', *Journal of Philosophy*, 1978, containing articles by Hugo Adam Bedau, Richard Wasserstrom, and Andrew von Hirsch; D. J. Galligan, 'The Return to Retribution in Penal Theory', in C. Tapper (ed.), *Crime, Proof and Punishment* (London, 1981); articles discussed below, notably those by Davis, Finnis, Goldman, Morris, Murphy and Nino; Jean Floud and Warren Young, *Dangerousness and Criminal Justice* (London, 1981); Hyman Gross, 'Culpability and Desert', in R. A. Duff and N. E. Simmonds (eds.) *Philosophy and the Criminal Law* (Wiesbaden, 1984). The latter two are not discussed here but in my 'On Justifying Protective Punishment', *British Journal of Criminology*, 1982, and 'Culpability and Mystery', in Duff and Simmonds, op. cit.

2. My thanks to Nicola Lacey for criticism of an earlier draft of this postscript, and also to Peter Morriss and Carlos Nino – with whom my disagreement persists – and to critics who heard it at the Royal Institute of Philosophy, and at Birkbeck College, the City University and the universities of Aberystwyth and Edinburgh.

3. With respect to the code, see Galligan, op. cit., p. 144.

4. They are discussed in Nicholas Rescher, *Distributive Justice* (Indianapolis, 1966).

5. J. J. C. Smart and Bernard Williams, *Utilitarianism: For and Against* (Cambridge, 1973).

6. See above, p. 26; Anthony Kenny, *Freewill and Responsibility* (London 1978), pp. 69–76; and Hugo Adam Bedau, 'Retribution and the Theory of Punishment', *Journal of Philosophy*, 1978, pp. 611–15. Joel Feinberg, in an admirable analysis of the several settings in which we use desert-locutions, takes it as generally true that to say someone deserves something is to say he satisfies certain conditions of worthiness. *Doing and Deserving* (Princeton, 1970), chapter 4.

7. See above, pp. 27–8. The difficulty is not escaped, as some may suppose, by the idea that we can find rough or broad equivalences or correspondences or whatever. If there are no common units for quantifying tunes and buns, then a tune isn't equal or not equal to two buns – and it isn't roughly equal or not roughly equal to two buns either. Nor is the difficulty escaped by changing the subject: by supposing that we can *decide* or *judge* or *determine* that a particular penalty should go with a particular offence, as against *discover* or *perceive* a factual relation. This is a common form of lightly disguised Circular Retributivism. Galligan, op. cit., p. 166 f., and Andrew von Hirsch, 'Proportionality and Desert: a Reply to Bedau', *Journal of Philosophy*, 1978, pp. 622–4, may illustrate these futile hopes. For a good brief discussion of Circular Retributivism, see Feinberg, op. cit., p. 116 f.

8. Other understandings are considered above, pp. 26–33, et seq. I do not there take it, incidentally, as might be thought from a reading of J. G. Cottingham, 'Varieties of Retribution', *Philosophical Quarterly*, 1979, that retributivism can be *analysed* as the claim that offenders 'deserve' punishment. Nor, as might be thought, do I overlook the 'varieties of retribution' he distinguishes.

9. Lawrence H. Davis, in 'They Deserve to Suffer', *Analysis*, volume 32, number 4, 1972, referring to p. 26 above, says I am in error and confusion because I say that sometimes people use (1) *He deserves the penalty* to mean (2) *It's right that he get the penalty*, and hence that they cannot give (1) as a reason for (2). The main presumed error, although Davis is not sufficiently explicit, must be the failure to see what is presumed to be true, and discussed below, that (1) and like claims are standardly used only to mean (3) *there is intrinsic good in his suffering, he being guilty*. The second presumed error is thus supposing that (1) does not provide a reason for (2). The presumed confusion, also owed to failing to see that (1) is equivalent to (3), is running together (1) and (2). My reply is that there is no error and no confusion since it is not true, but false, that (1) and like claims are standardly used to mean only (3). Rather, there is a use of (1) which makes it equivalent to (2), commoner than its use as equivalent to (3). What I say depends only on the use of (1) as equivalent to (2).

10. Davis, op. cit., p. 139.

11. Jeffrie G. Murphy and John Finnis, discussed below.

12. Cf. P. F. Strawson, ' Ethical Intuitionism', *Philosophy*, 1949. For discussions and defences of what may seem in some respects a successor to Moral Intuitionism – Moral Realism – see Honderich (ed.), *Morality and Objectivity, A Tribute to John Mackie* (London, 1985).

13. Alan H. Goldman, 'The Paradox of Punishment', *Philosophy and Public Affairs*, 1979. Cf. pp. 152–62 above.

14. It is the burden of Goldman's essay that while his proposition about rights does indeed give one of the necessary reasons for punishment, a part of a justification, it is in conflict with the other part, concerning prevention. Hence the paradox of his title.

15. C. S. Nino, 'A Consensual Theory of Punishment', *Philosophy and Public Affairs*, 1983, Cf. pp. 45–8 above.

16. op. cit., p. 306.

17. op. cit., p. 302.

18. op. cit., pp. 302–3.

19. There is a related retributivist argument for punishment, essentially simply that an offender chose between two options open to him: keeping and breaking the law. This, distinct from Consensual Retributivism, is considered above, p. 33 et seq. Cf. Goldman, op. cit., pp. 54–6.

20. Nino, op. cit., p. 293.

21. Nino does write that following out this suggestion as to the justification of punishment ' would lead to a discussion of the extent to which the consent of the person affected can justify measures and political arrangements which may imply inequitable burdens upon him. I shall not develop this theme here; but I venture to say that the discussion of the justification of punishment could be considerably expanded and illuminated if it embraced this topic.' op. cit., p. 305.

22. This is one of several lines of thought in Jeffrie G. Murphy, ' Marxism and Retribution ', *Philosophy and Public Affairs*, 1973. For clarity, I treat it separately. Cf. John Rawls, *A Theory of Justice*, (Oxford, 1972).

23. Immanuel Kant, *The Metaphysical Elements of Justice* (1797), trans. John Ladd (Indianapolis, 1965), pp. 55 ff. Cited by Murphy, op. cit., p. 225.

24. Murphy, op. cit., p. 225.

25. ' Concerning the Common Saying: This May be True in Theory but Does

Not Apply in Practice' (1973), in *The Philosophy of Kant*, trans. Carl J. Friedrich (New York, 1949), pp. 421–2. Cited by Murphy, op. cit., p. 226.

26. 'The Use of the Basic Proposition of a Theory of Justice', *Mind*, 1975.

27. Restorative Retributivism of a kind is defended, although not clearly separated from other things, in Herbert Morris, 'Persons and Punishment', *The Monist*, 1968. The same is true of Murphy, op. cit., and also Murphy, 'Three Mistakes About Retributivism', *Analysis*, 1971. See also John Finnis, 'The Restoration of Retribution', *Analysis*, 1972, and *Natural Law and Natural Rights* (Oxford, 1980), pp. 260–66. Cf. above, pp. 33, 36, 43.

28. Finnis makes the point clearly.

29. See Finnis, 'The Restoration of Retribution', p. 134.

30. He develops his conclusion most fully in 'Marxism and Retribution'. There is also a related concession, to my mind given insufficient attention, in Morris, op. cit. Finnis touches on the question and appears to want to have it both ways: that the theory does and does not apply to other than 'an imaginary "well-ordered" society'. *Natural Law and Natural Rights*, pp. 264–5.

31. J. L. Mackie, 'Morality and the Retributive Emotions', *Criminal Justice Ethics*, 1982, pp. 3, 6. Kenny (op. cit., p. 69 f.) has the related view that retributivism is incoherent.

32. Mackie, *op. cit.*, p. 3.

33. The view was defended above, pp. 28–9, 42–4. It is evidently distinct from the view that punishment has an *expressive* function, although some things said in that theory move in my direction: e.g. that 'punishment generally expresses more than judgements of disapproval; it is also a symbolic way of getting back at the criminal, of expressing a kind of vindictive resentment', Feinberg, 'The Expressive Function of Punishment', op. cit., p. 100.

34. All of the views of the justification of punishment considered in this postscript are retributivist in the sense defined earlier. That is, they all involve desert-locutions. Further, they have a common character else in that they can be said to be directed *at* the offender, rather than *to* something else, and they do at least tacitly purport to give the justification of punishment inherent in the retributivist tradition. However, despite Mackie's view to the contrary (op. cit., p. 4 f.), not all are attempts to justify punishment without reference to its effects. Restorative Retributivism, at any rate, can in a sense be said to justify punishment by an effect: the restoration of a distribution of burdens and benefits. The view is in a sense forward-looking and consequentialist. The difference between this and the other views considered suggests an alternative categorization of views of punishment, involving a different definition of retributivism. Here, *retributivism* includes only views which do not justify punishment by any effect. It includes the two Old Retributivist views considered above, and all the New ones except for Restorative Retributivism. The other two categories of views would be those of a *Utilitarian* kind and those informed by a principle of *distributive justice*. The latter category would include Restorative Retributivism and my own view, set out below.

35. Nigel Walker, in 'Symposium: Predicting Dangerousness', *Criminal Justice Ethics*, 1983.

36. *General View of the Criminal Law of England* (London, 1863), p. 99. Cf. Henry Sidgwick, *The Methods of Ethics* (London, 1963), book three, chapter five.

37. Murphy, 'Three Mistakes About Retributivism', op. cit., p. 169.

38. Cf. Goldman, op. cit., on conflicting parts of ' mixed ' theories of punishment
39. See above, pp. 229–31. Cf. Goldman, op. cit., p. 44.
40. ' The Question of Well-being and the Principle of Equality ', *Mind*, 1981.

INDEX